AIKIDO AND THE
NEW WARRIOR

edited by
Richard Strozzi Heckler

North Atlantic Books
Berkeley, California

Aikido and the New Warrior

Published by
North Atlantic Books
2741 Eighth Street
Berkeley, California 94710

Cover and title-page photographs by Jan Watson
Cover and book design by Paula Morrison
Typeset by Classic Typography

This volume is #35 in the *Io* series

Aikido and the New Warrior is sponsored by The Society for the Study of Native Arts and Sciences, a nonprofit educational corporation whose goals are to develop an educational and crosscultural perspective linking various scientific, social and artistic fields; to nurture a holistic view of arts, sciences, humanities, and healing; and to publish and distribute literature on the relationship of mind, body and nature.

Library of Congress Cataloging-in-Publication Data

Main entry under title:

Aikido and the new warrior.

1. Aikido—Addresses, essays, lectures.
I. Heckler, Richard Strozzi.
GV1114.35.A37 1985   796.8'154   85–7196
ISBN 0–938190–56–3
ISBN 0–938190–51–2 (pbk.)

This book is dedicated to the spirit
of Master Morihei Ueshiba.

Acknowledgements

There are a few people I would like to acknowledge who have directly or indirectly helped bring this book to fruition. I would first like to thank those teachers who have most influenced my Aikido training: Mitsugi Saotome Sensei, Robert Nadeau Sensei, and Frank Doran Sensei. My appreciation to George Leonard and Wendy Palmer, my partners at Tamalpais Aikido Dojo; and again to George for his continuing support and encouragement towards this project. Robert Hall, my colleague at Lomi School, whose on-going support and sharp eye have enriched all my endeavors. Stan Pranin at *Aiki News* whose contributions have greatly enhanced this anthology. Finally, but certainly not least, Richard Grossinger and Lindy Hough at North Atlantic Books whose editorial and publishing skills have been both educational and inspiring.

Grateful acknowledgement is made to the following for permission to reprint work:

BOB AUBREY: "Aikido and The New Warrior." ©1985 by Bob Aubrey. Used by permission of the author.

JOHN STEVENS: Selection from *Aikido The Way of Harmony*, Shambhala Publications, Boulder, 1984, pp.3–13. ©1984 by John Stevens. Used by permission of the author.

GEORGE LEONARD: "On Getting A Black Belt At Age Fifty-Two," from *New Age Journal*, April 1979, p.50. ©1979 by George Leonard. Used by permission of the author. "This Isn't Richard," from *The Silent Pulse: A Search for the Perfect Rhythm That Exists in Each of Us*, copyright ©1978 by George Leonard. Reprinted by permission of the publisher, E. P. Dutton, a division of New American Library.

DONALD T. SAPOSNEK: "Aikido: A Model For Brief Strategic Therapy," from *Family Process*, Vol. 19, September 1980, pp.227–238. ©*Family Process*, 1980. Reprinted by permission of the publisher.

TERRY DOBSON: "A Kind Word Turneth Away Wrath," originally published in the *Lomi School Bulletin*, Summer 1980, pp.23–24. ©Terry Dobson. Used by permission of the author.

MORIHEI UESHIBA: "Excerpts from the Writings and Transcribed Lectures of the Founder," from *Aiki News*, No. 52, January 1983, pp.3–12. ©*Aiki News*. Used by permission of the publisher.

MORIHEI UESHIBA: "Accord with the Totality of the Universe," from *Aiki News*, No. 56, July 1983, pp. 12, 13 & 15. ©*Aiki News*. Used by permission of the publisher.

KISSHOMARU UESHIBA: "Interview with Doshu," from *Aiki News*, No. 30, August 1978, No. 31, September 1978, No. 56, July 1983, No. 57, August 1983. ©*Aiki News*. Used by permission of the publisher.

SADAHARU OH: From *Sadaharu Oh*, by Sadaharu Oh, with David Falkner. ©1984 by Sadaharu Oh and David Falkner. Reprinted by permission of Times Books, a Division of Random House, Inc.

Contents

Richard Strozzi Heckler

Introduction

Over the past twenty years an increasing number of Aikido practitioners have been creatively adapting the principles of Aikido to their professions. Such diverse fields as education, psychology, conflict resolution, health, law enforcement, management relations, business, and sports are positively being affected by Aikido's emphasis on the unification of mind, body, and spirit. How Aikido, a Japanese martial art, has had such a wide reaching effect is a tribute to its founder, Morihei Ueshiba, and the following generations of practitioners that have continued to practice and spread his budo of "loving reconciliation."

Master Ueshiba spent many years studying and mastering the martial arts of spear, sword, and Daito-ryu jujutsu; thus rooting Aikido in the ancient Bushido tradition of Japan. While the Master built Aikido on the foundations of these martial arts, and while its present Masters are some of the finest martial artists in the world, Master Ueshiba also spoke of his art in a revolutionary way — a way previously unheard of in the martial tradition. Master Ueshiba said his Aikido was a budo of love and that its purpose was to unite all the people of the world. He repeatedly told his students that Aikido was not to be used to hurt someone, but to provide loving protection for all people. When this word got out many came to challenge Ueshiba and his new budo. His adversaries included Sumo wrestlers, western boxers and wrestlers, and the legion of trained warriors that live throughout Japan. Many of these would-be opponents remained as students and have since gone on to teach Aikido throughout the world.

Testing his ideas in actual combat and armed confrontations

1

Master Ueshiba established Aikido as an effective, even awesome, self-defense form. At the same time he concluded that the emphasis on winning at any cost, and the domination of others through physical force and manipulation, was anachronistic to the spiritual needs of contemporary society. Searching for a martial art that would meet the needs of the modern age the Founder stayed true to the original vision of budo: the cultivation and perfection of the spirit. Asserting that Aikido was not a competitive sport, with the accompanying divisions of winners and losers, Master Ueshiba developed a martial form that empowered human beings from the inside out, without categories and contests to determine who is best. He said that the "opponent is within" and that we must first work with our own minds and bodies instead of trying to correct others. He established dignity and integrity as a priority to greed and the acquisition of fame and power. Through the techniques developed in Aikido he brought to the world an alternative to our current form of heavy-handed militarianism and turn-the-other-cheek pacifism. But ultimately the Aikido of Master Ueshiba is a spiritual path that teaches people to join their *ki* (or spirit energy) to the *ki* of the Universe. Encouraging this practice of unifying our personal *ki* to a Universal *ki* he envisioned the possibility of everyone participating in shaping a world of harmony, right action, and compassion. Through this ideal and his own ceaseless training, exploration, and struggle, Master Ueshiba created a prototype for the New Warrior.

This anthology represents the expression of this New Warrior. The men and women in this book have the experience of taking the principles of their Aikido training and applying them to their daily lives and to their professions as well. They know what it is to translate the knowledge acquired while training in the dojo into both the ordinary and high pressure situations of life. There are, of course, countless other Aikidoists who are also doing this, in both profound and simple ways; but it is this group of writers and non-writers who have committed to putting it on paper. So be not mistaken that everyone who begins Aikido quickly experiences the relevance of it in their daily life.

My desire in editing this anthology is two-fold—first, to show both the depth and breadth of this unusual martial art; second, to communicate the power and effectiveness of Aikido as a way of being in the world. In a time when spiritual values have all but evaporated, and where we are all poised on the edge of our mutual destruction or survival, I believe the message of Aikido is a meaningful one. After reading this book I wholeheartedly encourage you to find a teacher and a dojo and experience Aikido for yourself.

Richard Strozzi Heckler
Tamalpais Aikido Dojo
March 1985

John Stevens

The Founder, Ueshiba Morihei

Ueshiba Morihei, the founder of Aikido, was born on December 14,* 1883, to a farm family in an area of Wakayama Prefecture now known as Tanabe. He was the fourth born, and only son, among five children. From his solidly built father Yoroku, Morihei inherited a samurai's determination and interest in public affairs, and from his mother Yuki, he inherited an intense interest in religion, poetry, and art.

The boy at first was rather weak and sickly, preferring to read books indoors than play outside. Around the age of eight, Morihei began learning the Chinese classics under the direction of a Shingon priest, but was more fascinated by esoteric Buddhist rites, especially the *homa* fire service. He loved to listen to the miraculous legends associated with the wonder-working saints En no Gyoja and Kobo Daishi, who spent part of their lives in the sacred Kumano district not far from Morihei's home. Morihei even thought of becoming a Buddhist priest himself someday.

As an antidote to his son's daydreaming and high-strung behavior, Yoroku recounted the exploits of Morihei's famous great-grandfather Kichiemon, said to be one of the strongest samurai of the day, and encouraged the boy to take up *sumo* wrestling and swimming. Morihei gradually became stronger, and realized the necessity of possessing adequate power after his father was attacked one night by a gang of thugs hired by a rival politician.

Morihei left middle school after a year — the classes bored him and his nervous energy demanded a more practical outlet. Always

* November 16 according to the old lunar calendar.

5

good at mathematics, Morihei enrolled in a *soroban* (abacus) academy; less than twelve months later he was acting as an assistant instructor. Still in his teens, Morihei took a job as an assessor in the local tax office. He was an excellent worker, but during the course of his duties he was obliged to administer a new tax directed at farmers and fishermen. Convinced that the regulations were grossly unfair, he resigned in righteous indignation and became a leader of the protest movement, much to the chagrin of his councilman father. Yoroku gave him a substantial sum of money, saying, "Take this and try to find something you would really like to do."

Hoping to become a great merchant, Morihei went to Tokyo in 1901. He managed to open a small stationery supply store, but commerce suited him no better than tax accounting, and he closed down the business in a few months. During his brief stay in Tokyo, Morihei did discover that he had a definite affinity for martial arts, greatly enjoying his study of *jujutsu* at the Kito-ryu *dojo* and swordsmanship at the Shinkage-ryu training center. A severe case of beri-beri caused him to return home. Shortly thereafter, at the age of nineteen, he married Itogawa Hatsu.

Morihei quickly regained his health, but was at a loss what to do next. Storm clouds were brewing between Russia and Japan so the impetuous young man decided to enlist in the army and seek some adventure. Unfortunately, Morihei, who stood just over five feet tall, was slightly under the minimum height requirement. Extremely upset, he spent the next several months training alone in the mountains, hanging from branches with weights on his legs and performing other stretching exercises to expend his spine the necessary half-inch.

Morihei passed the physical on his next attempt and in 1903 joined the infantry. The tireless energy of the fastidious soldier caught the attention of his superiors and he was rapidly promoted. Morihei earned a reputation for his zeal for hard training and his unusual skill at bayonet fighting. He served with distinction in Manchuria during the Russo-Japanese War of 1904-5, displaying for the first time his uncanny ability to anticipate an attack — he

6

said that he could sense when a bullet was coming his way even before it was fired—and his commanding officer wanted to recommend him for admission to the National Military Academy. For various reasons, Morihei declined the position and resigned from active duty. During his four years in the military, Morihei greatly improved his physical condition, building himself up to a rock-hard one hundred eighty pounds, and earned his first *menkyo*, teaching license, for a martial art from Nakai Masakatsu of the Yagyu-ryu. (The *dojo* was located in Sakai, a suburb of Osaka where Morihei was stationed.)

Morihei returned to the farm and married life, but remained restless. Hot-tempered and irritable, almost manic-depressive, he began to act strangely—locking himself in his room for hours to pray, jumping up in the middle of the night to douse himself with cold water, fasting in the mountains for days on end. Concerned with his son's erratic behavior, Yoroku built a *dojo* on the property and invited the well-known *jujutsu* teacher Takaki Kiyoichi to teach there. Morihei threw himself into the training and his disposition improved considerably.

During this period, Morihei came under the influence of the noted scholar Minakata Kumagusu (who, incidentally, had spent many years studying in the United States and England). Kumagusu vigorously opposed the government's plan to consolidate smaller Shinto shrines under the jurisdiction of larger ones, primarily because he felt the sentiments of the local residents would be ignored. Morihei supported Kumagusu's position, actively petitioning officials, writing protest letters to newspapers, organizing demonstrations, and so on. Morihei's involvement in this affair increased his interest in national politics; when the government called for volunteers to settle in the underdeveloped land of Hokkaido, Kumagusu encouraged him to consider the possibility, especially in light of Japan's future food needs. The pioneer spirit of "creating something out of nothing" appealed to Morihei; in addition, the village now had many unemployed farmers and fishermen. A town meeting was held and more than eighty people agreed to emigrate *en masse*. In the spring of 1912, the twenty-nine-year-old Morihei, with his wife and their two-year-old daughter, led the group to the wilderness of Hokkaido.

The group settled in the frigid northeast section of the island around the village of Shirataki. Things began inauspiciously— no one knew how to grow potatoes, and early frosts, cool summers, and harsh winters wiped out the other crops three years in a row. Having to subsist on wild vegetables and fish, not a few of the pioneers regretted their move, and did not hesitate to blame Morihei for their plight. Luckily, circumstances improved as the demand for lumber soared and the village prospered. A fire that destroyed the central district was a severe blow, but due largely to Morihei's ceaseless efforts, everything was rebuilt within a year. He was elected to the village council and was respectfully known as the "King of Shirataki."

The tremendous muscular strength of Morihei's arms was said to be a result of the years of heavy logging in Shirataki; everyday he wrestled with huge 100 to 200 pound pieces of lumber. A number of anecdotes survive from this Shirataki period: once he single-handedly lifted a horse and wagon from a deep ditch; he subdued three bandits who tried to rob him; he calmed a marauding bear and shared his lunch with it. The most significant event of his stay in Hokkaido was his meeting with Takeda Sokaku, grandmaster of Daito-ryu Aiki-jutsu.

By tradition, the Daito-ryu was founded c. 1100 A.D. by Minamoto (Genji) Yoshimitsu, sixth generation descendant of the Emperor Seiwa. Yoshimitsu's son Yoshikiyo moved to Koga (present-day Yamanashi Prefecture) and established the Takeda clan; the art was secretly transmitted among family members from generation to generation. In 1574, Takeda Kunitsugu moved to Aizu (Fukushima Prefecture) where the special *"oshiki-uchi"* (also known as *o-dome*) techniques were taught exclusively to high ranking samurai of the Aizu-han for the next three hundred years.

Actually, the origin of the Daito-ryu seems less ancient and more prosaic. Takeda Soemon (1758-1853) taught a system known as *aiki-in-yo-ho*, "the *aiki* system of yin and yang," which he passed on to Saigo Tanomo, chief retainer of the Aizu lord. Saigo also had training in Misoguchi-ryu swordsmanship and Koshu-ryu military science. The Aizu samurai were diehard supporters of the old military regime and fiercely resisted the new Meiji government, being among the last to capitulate in 1868. Certain that Tanomo had been killed in the final battle with the Imperial Forces and determined to preserve the honor of the Saigo name, his mother, his wife, his five daughters, and fourteen other members of his family committed ritual suicide. Tanomo's life had been spared, however; following this tragedy, he served as a Shinto priest in various districts and adopted Shida Shiro as his disciple son. The extremely talented Shiro mastered the *oshiki-uchi* techniques, later applying them with great effect as the star of Kano Jigoro's newly founded Kokodan school of Judo. At an open tournament in 1889, assistant instructor Shiro defeated all comers with his *yama-arashi* ("mountain-storm") *oshiki-uchi* technique, thus securing the reputation of the Kokodan. (Shiro's story has been fictionalized in the popular Sugata Sanshiro series of novels and movies.) Not much later, however, Shiro — probably torn between his debt to his adoptive father Tanomo and his respect for Jigoro — abandoned the practice of both systems, moved to Nagasaki, and devoted himself to classical archery (*kyudo*) the rest of his life.

Fortunately, the aging Tanomo had another worthy heir: Takeda Sokaku (1860-1943), Soemon's grandson. (Since Sokaku's father Sokichi concentrated on *sumo* wrestling rather than *aiki-in-yo-ho*, the family tradition temporarily passed to an "outsider.")

Sokaku was no beginner; at an early age he had obtained teaching licenses in Ono-ha Ittoryu swordsmanship and Hozoin spear-fighting as well as studying with the "swordsman-saint" Sakakibara Kenkichi of the Jijishin-kage-ryu. A demon swordsman, Sokaku "stormed" *dojos* all over the country, engaging in thousands of contests. He almost never lost. He reportedly had more than one battle with a live sword; once he got involved in a fight with a group of construction workers and killed seven or eight of them.*

When Tanomo transmitted the last of his knowledge to Sokaku in 1898, he told him, "The way of the sword is over; from now on make these marvelous techniques known everywhere."

9

Sokaku modified the *oshi-uchi* techniques based on his long years of practical experience; he designated his composite system "Daito-ryu Aiki-jutsu," and should rightly be considered its founder.

Now an invincible master of Aiki, Sokaku traveled widely, attracting a large number of disciples; he was reputed to have had around thirty thousand disciples and nearly every *budoka* of note in that era was his student in one way or other. One of them was a Westerner, an American named Charles Perry.

In 1903, Perry, an English instructor at a secondary school in Sendai, was riding a train and asked the conductor to check the first-class ticket of the shabbily dressed Japanese man down the aisle. When Sokaku demanded to know why only he was requested to show his ticket, the conductor told him the American gentleman didn't think he belonged in this car. The short-tempered Sokaku jumped to his feet and went over to Perry for an explanation. Perry stood up, brandishing both fists, sure that his six-foot height would intimidate the diminutive Sokaku. Sokaku grabbed both of Perry's wrists and applied what modern Aikido students know as *"yonkyo"*; the pain brought Perry to his knees and then Sokaku threw him toward the end of the car. After making a humble apology, Perry asked permission to learn something of the art himself. The story goes that Perry later reported this encounter and details of his studies with Sokaku to the State Department in Washington; Teddy Roosevelt heard about it and asked that someone be sent to teach in the United States. Harada Shinzo of Sendai was dispatched to the U.S. for some months and it may well be that an American president was himself introduced to the mysteries of Aiki before Ueshiba Morihei.

---

* Details of this semi-legendary tale have been embellished over the years — one version has Sokaku fighting off three hundred enraged workers armed with iron rods, fire axes, and stones in the heart of Tokyo, with twelve slain and many more wounded. It appears that the incident occurred in Fukushima and that Sokaku cut his way through a crowd of fifty or so workers and escaped rather than standing his ground, meeting wave after wave of attackers.

10

Sokaku never had a permanent *dojo* of his own, preferring to attract disciples by Perry-like chance encounters, challenges to local *kendo* and *judo* instructors — the loser became the victor's pupil — and formal demonstrations. Sokaku would hold a twisted piece of paper and ask a volunteer to take one end; suddenly the person at the other end would start to rise off the floor. Then Sokaku would have his hands firmly tied behind his back and invite the participants to try and throw or pin him; regardless of what they attempted or from what direction they came, they could not get him down; on the contrary, each one hit the floor himself. For a finale, he would ask all those present to grab him at once; in a flash everyone would be sent flying. Another favorite trick of his was to be lifted on the shoulders of the five or six biggest onlookers; Sokaku somehow made them collapse in a heap with him on top and they would remain there immovable until he let them up. Needless to say, many eagerly became students after such an impressive performance.

Morihei was first introduced to Sokaku in 1915 at an inn in Engaru. Although Morihei was a pretty tough fellow himself — on occasion he was mistaken for Sokaku because they were about the same size — he was no match for the Daito-ryu master. Immediately forgetting about everything else, Morihei stayed at the inn studying with Sokaku for a month (the folks back in Shirataki thought he had perished in a blizzard), the minimum requirement for the *shoden mokuroku* certificate of 118 basic techniques.* Upon his return home, Morihei built a *dojo* on his property and invited Sokaku to live there. In 1917, Morihei began accompanying Sokaku on teaching tours, having sent his family back to Tanabe in Wakayama because of the intense cold.

In 1919, word came from Tanabe that seventy-six-year-old Yoroku was gravely ill; Morihei sold off some of his property in Shirataki, turned the remainder over to Sokaku, and left Hokkaido for good. On the way back to his hometown — a good ten-day trip in those days — Morihei impulsively stopped at Ayabe, headquarters of the new Omoto-kyo religion he had recently heard so much about, to request a prayer service for the recovery of his

11

father's health. There he met Deguchi Onisaburo, the "Master" of the religion, who told him, "Your father is better off where he is going."

The other-worldly atmosphere of the Ayabe compound enthralled Morihei and he lingered there for three days before resuming his journey. When he arrived home, he found that his father had indeed departed for "a better place" as Onisaburo had predicted. Sorely distressed and terribly confused, Morihei hardly ate or slept for the next three months; every night he would take to the mountains and swing his sword madly until daybreak. Finally, he announced his intention to sell the ancestral land, move to Ayabe, and study Omoto-kyo.

Like many of Japan's new religions, Omoto-kyo, "The Teaching of the Great Origin," was a mixture of Shinto mythology, shamanism, faith-healing, and personality cult. Then at the height of its popularity, with over two million adherents, it was founded by Deguchi Nao, a semi-literate farm woman whose early life was nothing but unrelieved misery. Poverty-stricken from birth, she was forced to work as a housemaid at age ten; her marriage to the poorest farmer in a poor village was tragic—of her eight children, three died in infancy, two ran away from home, and two went insane. After her husband died when she was thirty years old, Nao was reduced to selling rags for a living. In 1892 she had a "revelation" from Tenchi-kane-no-kami, the Great God of the Universe, that a messiah was coming to establish a Kingdom of God on earth and that she must be his prophetess.

In 1898, Nao met clever young Ueda Kisaburo, who claim-

---

* The oft-repeated story of Morihei paying 300 to 500 yen (equivalent to several hundred of today's dollars) for each technique is certainly false; according to Daito-ryu sources, the standard entrance fee in those days was 3 to 5 yen, and 10 yen was charged for ten days of study. What Morihei likely meant was that the great cost of privately studying with Sokaku in Hokkaido and later Ayabe—Sokaku's transportation, lodging, food, plus the voluntary donation of the Shirataki property—added up to that amount for each technique.

ed he had once left his body, toured every region of the spiritual world, and learned all the secrets of the cosmos. Nao recognized Kisaburo (who later changed his name to Onisaburo) as the promised savior, and after Onisaburo married Nao's daughter Sumiko, they started a religious sect together.

When Morihei announced his decision to move to Ayabe and study Omoto-kyo, all of his friends and family, including his wife, thought he was crazy. Nonetheless, he would not be deterred, and in the spring of 1920 he and his family rented a house near the Omoto-kyo head shrine. (This year was undoubtedly the most trying of Morihei's life. In addition to his father's death and the painful decision to abandon his home in Tanabe, both of his sons, three-year-old Takemori and one-year-old Kuniharu, caught a virus and died within three weeks of each other. His sole surving son, Kisshomaru, was born in 1921.)

For the next eight years Morihei served as Onisaburo's assistant, taught *budo* at the "Ueshiba Juku," headed the local fire brigade, farmed, and studied the doctrines of Omoto-kyo, especially *chinkon-kishin*, "calming the spirit and returning to the divine."

A pacifist, Onisaburo was an advocate of nonviolent resistance and universal disarmament who once said, "Armament and war are the means by which landlords and capitalists make their profit, while the poor must suffer; there is nothing in the world more harmful than war and more foolish than armament." Why did he welcome the martial artist Morihei, building a *dojo* for him and telling young Omoto followers to study there? Onisaburo realized that Morihei's purpose on earth was "to teach the real meaning of *budo:* an end to all fighting and contention."

Onisaburo was in constant trouble with the authorities because of his pacifist stance and his serious belief that since he was savior of the world, he should be declared emperor and allowed to run the government. In 1921, he was arrested on the charge of *lèse majesté*, but released a few months later during the general amnesty issued at the death of Emperor Taisho.

In 1924, Onisaburo hatched a bizarre scheme to set up a "Heavenly Kingdom on Earth" in Mongolia, site of the "New

Jerusalem," with the aid of several Chinese and Korean syncretic religious groups. Once the great spiritual traditions of Asia were united, he believed, the rest of the world could be organized into an association of love and brotherhood under his own direction. Since Onisaburo was under continual police surveillance, the five-man party, including Morihei acting as bodyguard, set out in utmost secrecy. Arriving in China in February, Onisaburo announced himself as the Dalai Lama incarnation of Maitreya Buddha for whom everyone was waiting. His Chinese hosts were not impressed, and only after great difficulty and many adventures (in which Morihei's ability to dodge bullets came in most handy), did they near their destination. However, the group had somehow alarmed the local warlords, who had them promptly arrested, placed in leg-irons, and taken to an execution ground to be shot. Fortunately, the Japanese consul intervened and the savior and his party were saved at the last second. The members of this fanciful expedition returned to a hero's welcome in July of the same year.

(Onisaburo, his wife, and fifty of his closest followers were arrested in 1935 and sentenced to life imprisonment; all the Omoto buildings were dynamited and the entire movement suppressed. Onisaburo was released on bail in 1942, and spent the remaining six years of his life studying, composing poetry, and making pottery. Omoto-kyo was revived following the war, but has never recovered from the death of the charismatic Onisaburo; present membership is perhaps two hundred thousand.)

The study of Omoto-kyo and his association with Onisaburo profoundly affected Morihei's life. Even his relationship with Sokaku was influenced. In 1922, Morihei invited Sokaku to Ayabe for a six-month stay, and Sokaku gave him permission to act as an instructor (*shihandai*) of Daito-ryu Aiki-jutsu. (The relationship between Daito-ryu Aiki-jutsu and Aikido is difficult to clearly assess. There were at least twenty others who were given teaching licenses by Sokaku and Morihei never formally received the "complete transmission" [*soden*] of Daito-ryu techniques.) Morihei stated that while Sokaku opened his eyes to the essence of *budo*,

14

his enlightenment came through his Omoto-kyo experiences Reportedly, Onisaburo advised Morihei to start his own tradition since Daito-ryu methods were too combat-oriented and could not serve as a means to unite man with god and promote harmony among all people. Right from the start, the two systems differed greatly in both their approach and execution. Nonetheless, Sokaku continued to visit Morihei almost every year until his death in 1943, even after Morihei had his own training center in Tokyo. Morihei always footed the bill, treating Sokaku with all the respect due one's master, albeit without enthusiasm.

His close calls in China with Onisaburo also had a great effect on Morihei. Upon his return to Ayabe, he trained more intently than ever, arming his disciples with live swords and commanding them to try to cut him in half. Something was up in the spiritual world, too; every morning at eleven o'clock, the living room of Morihei's house would shake violently as an unearthly sound emitted from the household shrine, and every evening at nine o'clock a tremendous "whoosh" was heard as if some huge object was passing by.

One spring day in 1925, a *kendo* instructor wishing to test Morihei's reputation paid a visit to the Ayabe *dojo*. Relying on his sixth sense — "a flash of light indicated the direction of the attack" — Morihei easily avoided the cuts and thrusts of the instructor's wooden sword. After he left, Morihei went out into his garden to rest. Suddenly he felt bathed in a heavenly light; the ground quaked as a golden cloud welled up from the earth and entered his body. Morihei imagined that he was transformed into a golden being that filled space; the barrier between the spiritual and material worlds had crumbled — "I am the universe." He realized that the true purpose of *budo* was love, love that cherishes and nourishes all beings. Morihei was then forty-two years old.

The Ueshiba Juku in Ayabe was originally intended for Omoto-kyo devotees, but as Morihei's fame spread many nonbelievers, mostly military men, applied for admission. The case of Tomiki Kenji, *judoka* and later founder of the Tomiki system of Aikido, was typical. When a couple of his friends, students of

Morihei, urged him to meet their master, Tomiki scoffed and said, "I've heard about Ueshiba and his fake demonstrations; if I take on an over-the-hill forty-year-old all my colleagues will laugh at me." They promised not to reveal the meeting to anyone so Tomiki agreed. Tomiki was introduced and moved confidently toward Morihei, but instantly found himself pinned to the floor. He requested another chance, this time vowing to give it his all. He ended up on the other side of the *dojo*, sprang up and rushed again; after hitting the deck for a second time, he bowed and said, "I hope to become your disciple."

Morihei spent much of 1925-26 in Tokyo teaching at the request of Admiral Takeshita and other influential people. The strain of so much travel and training took its toll; Morihei passed out after a practice session and the doctor prescribed complete rest. (Even though Morihei was occasionally physically ill, he still was able to freely perform his *aiki* techniques. *Aiki* is perhaps the ultimate example of mind over matter. *Ki*-power is never diminished, and does not depend on one's physical condition. For example, near the end of his life, Sokaku insisted on conducting his regular training sessions despite the fact that his right side was paralyzed from a stroke, and it is said that while on his deathbed he threw a six-degree *judoka*.)

After a six-month stay in Ayabe, Morihei's health returned. Onisaburo encouraged Morihei to separate himself from the Omoto-kyo organization, move to Tokyo, and found his own unique "Way." In 1927, Morihei and his family rented a house in Sarumachi in Tokyo's Shiba Shirogane district, and Morihei held classes in the remodeled billiard room of Prince Shimazu, one of his early supporters. In 1928, Morihei moved to larger quarters in Mita, and then in the following year to a still larger place in Kuruma-machi. Because the number of applicants continued to increase, land was acquired for a formal *dojo* and residence in Ushigome (present site of the headquarters *dojo*).

While the new *dojo* was being constructed, Kano Jigoro paid a visit to Morihei's temporary training hall in Mejiro. After witnessing Morihei's *aiki* techniques Jigoro declared, "This is my ideal *budo* — true *judo.*" He dispatched several of his top Kokodan pupils to study with Morihei; one of them, Mochizuki Minoru, later developed his own Aikido-style system.

In 1931, the *dojo* in Ushigome, called the "Kobukan," was finished. A "Budo Enhancement Society" was founded in 1932 with Morihei as chief instructor. Shioda Gozo, present head of Yoshikan Aikido, became a disciple around the same time. There has always been a close relationship between Aikido and swordsmanship — Sokaku and Morihei were likely the two best swordsmen of the day — and for a time there was a *kendo* division at the Kobukan. Morihei, evidently concerned that his bookworm son Kisshomaru would not be up to succeeding him, adopted a young swordsman named Tanaka Kiyoshi into the Ueshiba family, but he left a few years later for unspecified reasons.

Up to the outbreak of World War II, Morihei was extremely busy teaching at the Kobukan as well as holding special classes at the major military and police academies (he also gave lessons to actors, dancers, and *sumo* wrestlers). Here are a few of the many interesting stories handed down from that period:

The famous general Miura, a hero of the Russo-Japanese War, used to be a student of Daito-ryu and heard about Morihei from Sokaku. One day he noticed the "Ueshiba Dojo" signboard and went in to see what his "fellow-disciple" had to offer. Although Miura was cynical at first, he was impressed by the different emphasis in Ueshiba Aiki-jutsu and decided to study with Morihei. However, still not completely convinced of Morihei's ability, Miura arranged a training session at Toyama Military Academy. The students of *jukendo* (bayonet fighting) there were noted for their ferocity, size, and strength. They urged Morihei to wear protective armor because things might get a little rough; Morihei declined, saying, "You are using wooden bayonets, so don't worry. Will you attack one-by-one?"

"Of course," was the reply.

"In my *budo*, we always expect attacks from all sides. Please come in a group." Disbelieving, only one student stepped forward. When the others saw him land on his rear end, they lost their reserve and moved in together. No one came close to touching Morihei.

A similar incident occurred at the Military Police Academy. The trainees there were particularly ruthless, and one day thought of surprising their instructor. Usually, twenty to thirty students attended the sessions, but this time only one person showed up. Morihei gave a short lesson, and walked out into the open court-yard to return home. All at once, the members of the class, armed with wooden swords, sticks, and bayonets swarmed out to "greet" Morihei. In his customary unruffled manner, he deftly avoided their attacks and passed through the gate as if nothing had happened.

At the central police headquarters in Osaka, Morihei was giving a class, and asked five of the biggest officers to pin him on the floor — one on top with a choke hold, and one on each limb. Although Morihei's entire body was under the weight of the policemen, in an instant they were thrown off. Observers noticed hardly any movement, and when they questioned the men holding Morihei down, they were told, "His body was as soft as silk when we first held it; as he emitted a short *kiai* he became like a piece of iron and we flew off." The man with the choke hold mentioned that he felt his hands being wrenched off Morihei's neck. Morihei laughed as he chided them, "You'd better learn more effective arrest techniques if you are going to deal with dangerous criminals."

Morihei told his *uchi-deshi* that if they ever caught him off guard even for a moment, he would treat them all to a grand feast. Day and night, the disciples tried to sneak up on him to no avail; even when he was sleeping, as soon as they got near Morihei he stirred. Actually, they thought he was not sleeping at all and was perhaps suffering from some neurotic disorder so they summoned a doctor to examine him. "I feel fine," said Morihei. "Why did you call a doctor?" They related the details of their nightly missions; since he did not seem to be resting well they presumed he was ill. "I was sound asleep," Morihei assured them. "Invisible rays emanate from my body and whenever anyone comes within ten or fifteen feet of me I can immediately sense his presence even in my sleep." In a similar vein, Shirata Sensei recalls that he and the other young *uchi-deshi* occasionally slipped out to enjoy a modest "night on the town." Even though Morihei's room was quite far from the *dojo* gate and the disciples took every precaution not to make any noise, invariably the next morning the Founder would ask, "Where did you fellows go last night?"

One day Morihei was riding on a crowded train with several of his disciples. The man next to him suddenly froze with a strange expression on his face; Morihei apparently knew the man, his disciples thought, since he was smiling. At the next stop, Morihei said, "Scram!" and the man ran off the train. "Who was that?" his students asked. "A pickpocket," Morihei told them.

Speaking of trains, Morihei was probably the most demanding traveler in the country. He insisted on being at the station at least an hour before the train was scheduled to depart, which was not so bad; much worse was his disconcerting habit of boarding the train with his luggage and several attendants only to leap up just before the train left the station and declare, "Get off this train! I'm not going anywhere!" The disciples had no choice but to obey his orders. A few minutes after the last train pulled away, he would say, "I feel better now. Let's go." Hypersensitive to the slightest change in mood, Morihei frequently, and capriciously, altered his plans. His disciples never knew what to expect — Morihei's method of keeping them alert? — and he would not stand for inattentive or halfhearted behavior on their part.

One of Morihei's earliest disciples was Futaki Kenzo, "Doctor Brown Rice," an advocate of health food. Although Morihei did not care much for brown rice — he had trouble digesting it — he did prefer plain and simple food: vegetables and fish. His secret weapon was chicken soup; whenever he felt out-of-sorts he drank a bowl. Unlike the majority of *budoka*, Morihei almost never drank sake.

His disciples once asked Morihei if the feats attributed to *ninja* — e.g., becoming invisible, walking on water — were actually done. "You have been watching too many movies," Morihei said. "Grab your swords and sticks and I'll give you a real demonstration of *ninjutsu*." Ten or so of them surrounded Morihei in the center of the *dojo*, and as soon as they attacked, they felt a stream of air and Morihei disappeared. "Over here, over here!" they heard Morihei calling from half way up the second story stairs twenty feet away. Later, however, Morihei got quite upset when they asked him to do some more *ninja* "tricks." "Are you trying to kill me just to entertain yourselves? Each time one performs such techniques, his life span is reduced five to ten years."

Yet even Morihei lost his footing. Kisshomaru, his son, remembers well an incident that occurred when he was a primary school student. He got into a fight with an American boy who lived nearby; the boy started throwing stones, and Morihei, who sensed something wrong, ran out into the street, but slipped in a puddle, allowing the boy to escape. To this day, Kisshomaru is unsure whether Morihei was furious at the American boy for hurling rocks or at his son — then a rather weak and spiritless child — for shrinking from the challenge.

If Morihei's *budo* stood for love and peace, what was his attitude toward the "Great East Asian War"? Unlike Onisaburo, who never abandoned his pacifist principles and went to prison for his beliefs, Morihei appeared to be an ardent supporter of the Imperial cause. He taught at the major military academies, many of his disciples were among those directing the war, he went to Manchuria as a guest of the puppet government there, and so on. Yet Kisshomaru has written that both prior to and during the war, he heard his father complain bitterly, "The military is dominated by reckless fools ignorant of statesmanship and religious ideals who slaughter innocent citizens indiscriminately and destroy everything in their path. They act in total contradiction to God's will, and will surely come to a sorry end. True *budo* is to nourish life and foster peace, love, and respect, not to blast the world to pieces with weapons." Morihei hinted that his move to the Iwama outdoor *dojo* in 1942 was prompted by a "divine command"; he foresaw that the war would not end well for Japan and hoped that Aikido would become the creed of a new era.

The war had emptied the Kobukan *dojo* and Morihei, tired

20

of city life and the burdens of administering a large center, longed to return to the land where he could ideally combine *budo* and farming, two things that created life and purified the heart. He often said that "*Budo* and farming are one." Morihei placed the city *dojo* in the hands of his son, resigned his official positions, and left Tokyo with his wife to settle on their property, purchased some years previously, in the village of Iwama in Ibaragi Prefecture. Morihei lived there quietly for the remainder of the war, practicing, studying, farming, and supervising the construction of the Aiki Shrine and Shuren Dojo. Iwama may be considered the birthplace of Aiki-do, "The Way of Harmony." Prior to Morihei's move there, his system was called Aiki-jutsu, then Aiki-budo, still primarily arts rather than spiritual paths. During the years from 1942—when the name Aikido was first formally used—to 1952, Morihei consolidated the techniques and perfected the religious philosophy of Aikido.

In the aftermath of Japan's surrender in 1945, his disciples believed that Aikido would cease to exist, but Morihei was confident that, on the contrary, Aikido would flourish and its true value become known all over the world. In 1948, the "Aikikai" (Aiki Association) was formed to promote Aikido in Japan and abroad. Morihei left the organizing to his son and top disciples, preferring to pursue further training in Iwama. He rose every morning at 5 o'clock (3 o'clock on feast days), prayed and meditated for several hours, and then either farmed or studied depending on the weather. Every evening he led the training sessions. Saito Morihiro, present head of the Iwama Dojo, recalls: "When the Founder meditated the air was permeated by an intense, grave spirituality, but when he finished we felt the warmth of his love and compassion." Farming and Aikido were his life and the entire world his *dojo*.

The rapid spread of Aikido after the war under the direction of the Hombu Dojo, now headquartered in a three-story building in Tokyo, is a well-known story. Morihei became world-famous as "O-Sensei," the master of Aikido, and received a number of decorations from the Japanese government.

Right to the end of his life, Morihei refined and improved his techniques, never losing his dedication to hard training. In the early spring of 1969, Morihei fell ill, and told Kisshomaru that "God is calling me . . . " Hospitalized, Morihei's condition was diagnosed as cancer of the liver. (All through his life Morihei had had frequent liver and stomach trouble. He blamed it on a salt-water drinking contest he had with a Japanese practitioner who was pestering Onisaburo or one of the Omoto-kyo believers to take the challenge. A more likely cause was excessively hard training.) He was returned home at his request to be near his *dojo*. Even though he was no longer able to physically conduct the practice, he could tell exactly what was going on by listening to the sounds in the *dojo*. Those with him said he was never stronger — his body had wasted away to almost nothing, but he was so heavy ten of his most powerful disciples were unable to lift him.

On April 15, Morihei's condition became critical; as his many disciples and friends made their final calls, he gave his last instructions: "Aikido is for the entire world. Train not for selfish reasons, but for all people everywhere." Early on the morning of April 26, the eighty-six-year-old Morihei took his son's hand, smiled, said "Take care of things," and died. Two months later to the day, Hatsu, his wife of sixty-seven years, followed him.

Morihei's ashes were buried in the family temple in Tanabe, and parts of his hair were enshrined in Ayabe, in the Aiki Shrine, and in the Kumano Juki Dojo (headed by Hikitsuchi Michio). Every year a memorial service is held on April 29 at the Aiki Shrine in Iwama.

Morihei Ueshiba

Excerpts from the Writings and Transcribed Lectures of the Founder, Morihei Ueshiba

Aiki is the activity of being taught by God about the echoes of the soul (*tamashii*) of the Universal Design (*shikumi*). Putting Aiki into action by means of the echoes of the totality of the Universal Soul, we must constantly bring forth power that is without limits. The structure of the echo of the soul of the universe possesses a power capable of resolving all things, regardless of their nature. The echo of the soul or spirit of the Universal Design (*shikumi*) is the kotodama. "Suuu-Uuuu-Yuuu-Mu." This is the one for Honos Wake Island (which is a symbolic term for this earth). The echo of the soul of the Universal Structure learns from the entire universe and rescues all to a unity with the center of the cosmos. Nothing less than becoming one with the universe will suffice. Then you can progress in concert with the universe. In this way, you go about the job of correctly constructing this Universal Design within your own body. By means of this echoing of the soul of the Universal Structure, you absorb the many things into your individual self and blend with them. As an extension of this, you become reconciled with the spirit/mind of the people of the whole world. This is nothing less than the act of blending in harmony and unity. Of course, it goes without saying that things like wars, conflicts and arguments are wrong. Blend in harmony and unity. This is "Aiki". A person who attempts to bind the world together in peace and unity is called the True Person and Aiki is the way of cultivating such genuine people. Inasmuch as it is this, the fostering of common sense, physical health, virtue, wisdom and ki all become very important. Naturally, of its own accord, the spirit/mind of the self will be rectified and a genuine self will be constructed. In short, Aikido is a method of *misogi* (ritual purification). Through the technique of misogi you should continually forge the Great Spirit of Love and Protection toward all things while protecting the logical sequence of the multitudes of gods and all creation. Thus, you can finally accomplish your own mission. The reason or logic of all creation and the gods are laws which accurately reveal the formations of the precious workings of the beautiful, ongoing universe. All this originates from the Single-Source. Therefore, you should observe carefully the genuine images of the totality of creation and of the multitude of godly beings, and store away these observations in your abdomen. These will become your personal foundation from which there will bloom enlightenment. So, too, you must continue in your Aikido *shugyo* (austere training) ever more diligently. In doing so, you should not be negligent in devoting yourself to training and to attempting to improve. At the same time you must constantly reflect on what you have done. As a result, you will have developed and attained a balanced body that is one with your mind. At that point it becomes important for people who train in Aikido to reintegrate the logic and reason of the gods and all creation into budo. This is what I mean by observing the true images that result from the logical, sequential unfolding of creation and the gods. By observing true phenomena it is possible to construct Aikido techniques through the medium of the Principle of Aiki. This you must do while paying attention to even the most subtle changes in the universe. Without a knowledge of these true images, you will never achieve oneness with the Truth of the Universal no matter what else you may do. Lacking oneness, you will likewise be unable to fully manifest in this world the mission of your life as a human being. To attain this in actual fact it is important that you "aiki" with the Truth of the Universal. Spring, summer, autumn and winter, we see the fluctuations of the seasons in the true image of the universe. Similarly, we see in human beings the flow of emotions between happiness, sadness, anger and pleasure. Despite such ups and downs you must minute by minute seek oneness with the volition of the universe. For people who discipline themselves through Aikido, it is all important to delve deeply into the workings of the Single-Origin and to respectfully measure up to the truth of the Universal. All this means that one must be able to deal with any and all situations in the Great Spirit of Loving Protection toward all things. To be able to do so is to complete one of the tasks of the Aikido practitioner, the result of which is the building of a world where the lives of all are a pleasure. As I have so often said, 'The beautiful form of the Heavens and the Earth which the Lord has made has become as a single family.' We must construct a truly beautiful, truly splendid world. We learn of an infinite power when the gods reveal the echo of the soul of the Universal Design, a power which possesses the strength to bind together and unify this world in peace and harmony.

Aiki is the training and perfecting of the *Yamato damashii* (Japanese Spirit) in this world. In saying this I am speaking to you all as a member of the Japanese family and as a member of the world human family as well. From now on the whole world must proceed in unified accord. Here today, we see the nation of Japan waver and hesitate in this task. The country is greatly upset. We must extricate ourselves from this situation as soon as possible and in a friendly manner, like a single family, proceed toward harmony and unity based on a spiritual bond (*musubi*). As Japanese, we must start afresh in this task here, from Japan. First one must cultivate this thing we call the self, next we must put our own homes and families in order. Then comes our own nation and finally we must reach an accord with the Universe. Reality, Images and the Gods — we must reconcile all the Three Worlds, and protect them. This is the mission of Aikido.

In our country, the so-called Three Imperial Regalia (*Sanshu no Jingi*) appear in our old mythology where we hear of the Sacred Sword, Mirror and Curved Jewel. But the stories are not speaking of a physical sword or mirror. Rather these symbols are a hidden way of speaking about the jewels of the spirit which are indispensable for every person — wisdom, benevolent virtue and courage. Aikido teaches that we must sequester the forms of the ancient regalia (godly objects) inside our abdomens and then perform austere training. By looking closely at history, from the Age of the Gods onwards, one must come to a realization of this Path by one's own efforts. This act of realization is an internal thing. You scrutinize thoroughly your inner abdomen asking from where this thing called the Self arose, and just how you should deal with things and events. To know yourself well is each person's heaven-sent mission in life. Then, should we some time look back over our lives, at our pasts, I can imagine no happier sight than to see that all of us have trained joyfully.

The bright world of this life is the apparition of the total virtue of the operations of the God of the Single-Origin. We, too, are part of all this. We are part of this functioning in the world. This history and this thread of life are continuous and without gaps. It has been made from the ancient past straight through to the ultimate future. All these things you must contemplate. "To know thyself" well is of utmost importance.

The Aikido which I am now doing is a Path that builds people, a Way of forging and tempering the body and spirit. It is not a way that injures others, nor is it one that wields against them the evil sword of death. I humbly ask that you, too, give deep thought to these considerations.

The training in Aiki concerns itself most with the practicing of *ki-gata* (ki "forms") and the method of perfecting them. The most important element in true *ki-gata* is the quality called *shinken-shobu* (lit: 'a fight to the finish with real swords' and implies a certain seriousness of attitude in training). In budo there is no so-called *"shiai"* or competitive matches of the type seen in sports. If we were to have matches they would become life and death situations. Nonetheless, the vain striving after victory and defeat is a big problem since in point of fact, destruction, injury, and murder are major crimes against human life. Balancing the budo which has come down to us from the ancient days of our country there has stood the Buddhist commandments of 'Thou shall not kill' and

26

'Thou shall not destroy.' The true budo of our country is a road of great reconciliation and pacification. It is *misogi*, ritual purification, of the spirit/mind and the body. In instituting on earth the rules of heaven and the purport of humanity, the first commandment of *bu* (martial concerns) is to put the self in proper order and to protect all things. On the contrary, though, in these times we often find that those responsible for teaching *bu* have often descended to passing on not the true budo of ancient Japan but a later, militaristic budo of the medieval period. This is deplorable and causes me sadness.

Aikido is a budo of harmony and accord. That is to say it is a form which manifests the Single-Soul, the Four Spirits, the Three Origins and the Eight Powers, it is the life of Universal Governance. That rule is here in the palm of this hand. In the body and soul of each of you, in your families, as well, there is a *Takaamahara* (capital or center of command of the universe). This reason or principle is inside each of us. We have the responsibility to see it put into effect and defend it across the Three Worlds of Reality, Appearances and the Gods.

The true Japanese budo must be the spirit of harmony and loving protection of all creation. The meaning of this accord is that you help each and every person complete and fulfill their personal heaven-sent mission in life and thus you reach your own perfection.

The *'michi'* or Path means to become one with the great and holy spirit of god and never to separate from it, exactly like the blood that circulates within the body. It means to put this great and honored spirit into action. Should it digress from the great and honored spirit of God even slightly, it is not the 'michi', not the 'Way'.

Do not look at your opponent's eyes. Your spirit/mind will be drawn in. Do not look at his sword. You will be distracted ("Your *ki* will be grabbed away"). Do not look at your opponent. You will be taken in by his *ki*. True *bu* is the training of a kind of gravitation (lit.: pulling power) that is able to absorb the opponent's whole being. Thus, I simply stand here like this and I am ready.

In Ueshiba's Aikido, there are no enemies. The mistake is to begin to think that budo means to have an opponent or enemy; someone you want to be stronger than, someone you want to throw down. In true budo there is no enemy or opponent. True Budo is to become one with the universe. It is to reduce everything to unity with the center of the universe or, it is to return to the unity of the self with the universe. In Aikido we do not train to become powerful or to throw down some opponent. Rather we train in hopes of being of some use, however small our role may be, in the task of bringing peace to mankind around the world. In this hope we become one with the Universal. It is necessary to have a heart that strives to achieve this unification of the self and the universe. Although some may ask if the Aiki of my budo comes from religion, it is not so. The True Budo shines forth and illuminates religion. It is a guide which leads incomplete religion to perfection.

In my own case whatever may happen, no matter what becomes of me, it matters not. There is no attachment, neither to life nor to death. I just leave it all in the hands of God. This applies not only when one takes up the sword and stands ready, but in all situations and at all times, abstain from attachments to life or to death. One must have a spirit of entrusting all to God.

In True Budo there is no enemy. True Budo is the work of love. It is not fighting and killing. Rather it gives life and fosters all things; it is the task of generation and perfection. In love, the protection of all is uppermost, and without love nothing can be. Indeed the "Way" of Aiki is a manifestation of love.

All the works of man are the subtle functions of the *kotodama* (spirit-of-the-word). If a person really looks deeply into the self he will understand by means of auditory echoes. More than anything else, Aikido comes to life in the echo of auditory sensations. Though on this earth, ceaselessly reach for the heavens; aim for the sky! One must progress in concert with the echo. The echo, and everything else are wholly contained in the self.

In a certain sense Aiki means to replace the sword with one's own living or breathing sincerity, and grasping it, to banish all evils. In the end, it is to change the world of physical soul into the world of the spiritual soul. This is the task before Aikido. The physical soul is below, while the spiritual soul is above and it becomes the surface or exterior. What is more, Aikido makes a fine flower of the soul bloom in this life and world, and brings forth the fruits or truth essence, or the sincerity of the spirit. Aikido becomes the main force of governance, and an art which offers up service to the Supreme Sincerity which is the Ultimate Good and the Ultimate Love of this world.

Without *Bu*, a nation perishes. Indeed *Bu* is the life, the soul, that protects love. It is the root of science.

For people who are resolved to do austere training through Aikido the task before them is to open the eyes of the spirit. By means of Aiki, they must listen to the Supreme Sincerity of God and cause it to become an active reality. They must master the feeling of the *misogi* of this great Aiki, put it into practice and move along with the Great Universe in a way that does not disrupt its course. They must joyfully engage in the tempering of the soul. Therefore, I would like to see people with heart listen to the voice of Aiki. It is not to correct others but to rectify one's self. This is Aiki. This is the mission of Aiki. And this must become the individual mission for each of us as well.

Morihei Ueshiba

"Accord with the Totality of the Universe"

The road to reconstruction for the physically weak people of today lies in Aikido. This is a great truth handed down from the (Universe of) Heaven and Earth. Aikido is the *budo* (martial art) which opens the road to harmony; it is that which is at the root of the great spirit of reunification of all manifest creation.

The Great Universe embodies all the forces and powers (lit., "the one soul, the 4 spirits, the 3 origins and the 8 powers") and from them have come the origins of the human life force. The universe and mankind are as a single body. However, while mankind has the ability to unify with the universe, the fact that man is unable to accomplish this union is his unhappy condition. When a person stands before a shrine and prays his silent prayers it is for no other purpose than to unify himself with the godhead.

> *The beautiful form of the Universe of*
> *Heaven and Earth*
> *Has become one family made by the Lord.*

This world and all of Mother Nature's greatness are but one. In this unity there is nothing that defines an enemy, nor does it distinguish a friend. We must hope for peaceful and pleasant surroundings where fighting has been forgotten.

The universe itself, all that is manifested in Mother Nature, can be called "a Crystalization of the Wisdom" or the "United Body of Love".

Mankind's role is to fulfill his heaven-sent purpose through a sincere heart that is in harmony with all creation and loves all things. By so doing he fills his days with happiness, and such a life would help those who are weak of body.

30 years ago I was extremely weak of body. At that time I secretly harbored a dream. In this dream I wanted to be the strongest man in all of Japan — no, more than that, in the entire world! I decided I would become the possessor of a martial power unequaled by anyone. With this dream before me I trained severely. One day a navy man confronted me, a person said to be a 7th-dan-holder in Kendo. Strangely, as I faced him I felt as if my body were surrounded by a shining brightness and I easily secured victory.

After that, however, a conceited feeling was born inside of me, and while walking through a garden I thought that innumerable golden threads came down to me from the universe. Then, a golden light whelmed up from the earth and engulfed me. Eventually I attained a feeling that my body was turned into a body of gold that expanded to universal proportions. Here I felt that the God(s) were chastising me for my ever-growing conceit and I cried tears of gratitude.

In the past, there have been a number of superlative masters of martial arts but we should never forget the great number of them who disappeared on the battlefield of this martial world simply for lack of enough training in the true spirit of *budo*, in sincere love, and in the battle against the self.

Thus, by imbibing the principle of the Universal, and receiving the *ki* of the Heaven and Earth, when I unified this entire human body, I realized the subtle depth of Aikido that manifests such great power, and attained the principle of oneness with the Universe.

Even so, as I travelled down this path I found human interaction had become more and more of a hindrance so I moved up to Tokyo and now I have retreated to (a farm in) Iwama, in Ibaraki Prefecture. It seems that by lessening my interaction with human beings I am much more able to acutely intuit the principle of oneness with the Universe.

To put it briefly, the problem with the weak-bodied people of today is that they are unable to survive in a world of absolute accord and absolute non-desire. So here I would like to introduce my daily regime because I think it can be a great help to the physically weak.

In the early morning hours, before dawn, at 4:00 I am out of bed, and immediately perform a *misogi* (purification ritual) by wiping off my entire body with icy water. Then I go outside barefoot, and pray to the eastern sky. Tying my *ki* together with that of the universe, I greet and commune with all creation. This is when I become one with the Universe and imbibe and inhale the holy teachings of Heaven and Earth. My form, standing in front of the shrine (of the Universe) is in a state of harmony with the Heavens and the Earth.

Next I pray to the 4 directions and lift my eyes to the shrine of the eight gods in the Imperial Palace wishing His Imperial Majesty, the Emperor, long life *(banzai)*. So doing we placate all the gods and pray for their pacification.

There is also the method of vocalization known as *Aikido Kotodama*. The intoning of the 75 sounds forms words of purification for the universe.

> *Heavenly Father, by creating the 75 utterances*
> *You deign to teach the Way of Aiki.*

In this state a person becomes one with the plants and trees and there is no discrimination of any sort. Here lies the opportunity for feeling the greatest happiness possible in life. A joy to which nothing can be compared.

Next I stand before the household shrine. After a short time I perform prayers before the nearby Aiki Shrine which honors *Hayatakenushi No O Mikoto, Sarutahiko No O kami* and various others of the gods. Recently the number of those coming to pay their respects at this shrine has grown ever larger. I'm sure that many readers may be interested in joining their numbers. (The shrine is located in Iwama town, Ibaraki Prefecture, and can be reached by taking the Joban Line from Tokyo to Iwama. It is only a 7 or 8 minute walk from the station.)

In summary, weak people are the result of not knowing the truth of the unity of mankind with the Heavens and the Earth. By realizing the principle of unification with the Universal (*ten-chi*) and making it active in your daily life, human beings become capable of sending forth the "holy technique of the gods".

(From "Ningen no Shinri", September 1958, courtesy of Sadateru Arikawa Sensei)

Kisshomaru Ueshiba

Interview with Doshu

The following is an interview of Mr. Kisshomaru Ueshiba, Aikido Doshu in Hombu Dojo. Present were Aiki staff members Stanley Pranin, Ikuko Kimura and Mayumi Kudo, with Stan Pranin editor, presiding.

Editor: Why is it important for those who aspire to learn Aikido to study O-Sensei's biography, or to put in another way, the path the Founder walked?

Doshu: I think it is a fine thing to study Aikido, or make the decision to study Aikido and continue to practice whether it's because you find Aikido a wonderful thing or because you consider it exactly suited to your needs. And I think it's proper and necessary to practice keeping firmly in mind the origin of Aikido. However, today you often find people who will start off running after having tasted only a little. They have no idea what Aikido is about. If people think that Aikido is merely moving the arms and legs and if it begins to develop into a form which bears little resemblance to original Aikido, it would be most unfortunate. That would injure Aikido. So, it's important to realize the hardships that Morihei Ueshiba endured to create his art. It goes without saying that the physical aspect of Aikido is important. However, the main thing is not only moving your arms and legs. It's a matter of the spirit, a matter of the heart. If this spiritual training isn't expressed in the body's movements, then it isn't the true thing. It is wrong to think you are doing Aikido because you can throw your opponent or knock down your opponent or because you are strong. For example, in Judo and Karate there are strong people.

34

There are also strong people in Sumo. In Aikido, too, there are strong people. However, true Aiki is not merely having a strong body, it is not simply muscular strength. It is the unification of the mind and body. If a spirit which remains unperturbed whatever the crisis, whatever the circumstances is not cultivated, then a person cannot be called strong as a man. So if one practices understanding how O-Sensei created this path, from what viewpoint of humanity, of life itself he departed, then one won't misunderstand the true Aikido path as it should be. That's why I'd like everyone to actively read things like this biography. There's one more thing I'd especially like to say. There are many people who idolize Morihei Ueshiba as "almighty" or as a kami (a divine being). I think it's a fine thing as long as it inspires hard training. However, as long as he's a human being, he cannot be almighty. So I think the most important thing in Aikido is to cultivate your own individuality, or rather, better individual characteristics through one's own Aiki training having an understanding of the efforts made by the Founder to construct the Aiki path.

Editor: In the first chapter of your biography you also mentioned the fact that it's dangerous to regard O-Sensei as a kami and his techniques as divine.

Doshu: Well, to some extent, his technique was "divine technique." It was truly incredible. In Japan, generally speaking, it is believed that kami dwell in everything. Japanese Shinto is not monotheistic. So, in that sense, naturally O-Sensei is a martial arts' kami, an Aiki kami. That's fine, that's one way of looking at it. But I think it's extremely dangerous to regard anyone as "almighty." It can be carried to an extreme just like it was during the "Greater East Asia War" (World War II) when Japan regarded herself as a "divine nation." What is important is not that kind of attitude but to realize the true nature of Aikido keeping in mind the hardships the Founder, Morihei Ueshiba Sensei, endured to forge his path and how he paved the way for us.

Editor: During O-Sensei's long martial arts experience he underwent a number of changes. In the initial period he especially emphasized power and technique; later, I understand he attached

greater importance to spiritual matters. How did O-Sensei's teaching method change as changes occurred in his martial art?
Doshu: During his later years, rather than teach, my father demonstrated movements which were in accord with the flow of the universe and unified with nature. Thus, it was a matter of students watching his movements, learning them by themselves, in that way understanding his technique. He wasn't deeply concerned about teaching students . . . his movements were so spontaneous and natural. I think we should attain that point in the end. But since we have dojos, we tend to think in worldly terms, how to get people to come, how to develop a lot of strong students . . . and we get these egotistical, selfish things as a matter of course. But this was not the case with the Founder. He was innocence itself in his later years expressing his movements spontaneously and having the attitude that those who wanted to learn would come to him and follow him . . . that's what his techniques were like. I think that's something to be respected. The world we live in today is a selfish one, a "give-and-take" world. It's a world of calculation . . . where people think how much profit they can gain by this or that. But it's not conducive to spiritual training as a human being. . . . It's becoming more and more animalistic. Under such circumstances we are strongly attracted to this kind of movement which originated from within the Founder. My father was a very powerful man in his youth even though he was short . . . I mean in his thirties, forties and fifties. He was wider in breadth than the ordinary person so his technique used to be awesome and powerful. But as he grew older his power and strength came to be hidden and his techniques grew to be soft and round. I think that is true technique. Aikido should be like that. It should be strong at the core rather than on the surface. Within this core tremendous energy is always burning but on the surface there is soft movement which embraces all people. Otherwise it's not true Aiki. With his great efforts in training and spiritual discipline the Founder's Aiki developed into soft, pleasant movements which hid his inner severity. I think that's the reason Aikido attracts so many people. If it is only violence people won't

follow. That's what I think.

Editor: You mentioned earlier that O-Sensei in his later years would demonstrate his technique in front of his students and that the students learned Aikido by watching and being attracted to his movements rather than O-Sensei teaching them. Was O-Sensei's teaching method like that from the beginning?

Doshu: No. At first he taught techniques point by point although it didn't seem that he was attached to a specific teaching goal. But he emphasized that you have to do things exactly, one by one, so you won't make mistakes. Recently, there has been a tendency for Aikido training to become too soft and flowing and some beginners lightly bypass hard training. That's not the way it should be. If you are going to practice you must practice basics earnestly. This he told me frequently even in his later years . . . exactly, not changing anything . . . if you don't reach the level of softness beyond technique by getting the basics down perfectly, you won't develop true strength. If, from the beginning, you practice a "tofu-like" (bean-curd) soft style, you will be vulnerable to an attack. So it's necessary to do solid training in the beginning. Over time, through this kind of solid training your technique will become effective. A soft effectiveness will emerge.

Editor: Would you tell us about when you first began your study of Aikido prior to the war?

Doshu: It would be more appropriate to say that I had already started studying Aikido by the time I was born than before the war. There is a Japanese proverb which says, "A shop boy near a temple will chant a sutra untaught." In just the same way, I had already begun my practice when I was a boy without even realizing it. You could even say that I started while my mother was carrying me. It was 1921 that my father started using the term "Aiki". This is very clear in the records. In 1919, he moved to Ayabe and the following year I was born. In the same year, 1919, my father built a small 18-mat dojo which went by the name of "Ueshiba Juku" in Ayabe. There, with students who were mainly Omoto followers, they began to do some training. This was nothing but a "**shugyo**" (ascetic training) dojo mainly for the Founder's personal training. There around 1921, Sokaku Takeda Sensei appeared. He stayed with us for three or four months. Then he talked to my father and they decided to add "Aiki" to the name of his school *(ryuha)*, that is, it became *"Daito-Ryu Aiki Jujutsu."* Up until that time there were some "Aiki" techniques here and there, but they didn't exist as schools. At that point in time *Daito-Ryu* was called *"Daito-Ryu Jujutsu"*. It doesn't seem that there were any *Daito-Ryu Jujustu* schools before Sokaku Takeda Sensei. People talk about the origin and history of *Daito-Ryu*, but it seems those names mentioned are wrong.

To continue, we moved to Tokyo in 1927. At that time, "Daito-Ryu" had already disappeared from the name of my father's budo. Starting in 1926 through the beginning of the Showa period (end of 1926-   ), people had already started calling the art by such names as *"Ueshiba-Ryu Aiki Jujutsu"*, *"Aiki Jujutsu"* and *"Aiki Budo"*. The reason we had occasion to come to Tokyo was that we had a connection with a number of naval officers when my father was with Omoto. A person who made tremendous efforts to insure my father's success after coming to Tokyo was Admiral Isamu Takeshita. Without him, we cannot talk about the development of the art at that time. Isamu Takeshita was always with Morihei Ueshiba. During that period, Japanese admirals or Commanders-in-Chief of the Combined Fleet of Japan had great power, more so than the present Prime Ministers. Also, Admiral Takeshita was from the Satsuma Clan. People used to say that the Satsuma Clan produced naval officers while the Choshu Clan produced army material. That trend still continued up through that time. Admiral Takeshita introduced my father to Admiral Gombei Yamamoto. One can't speak of Japanese naval history without mentioning his name. Admiral Yamamoto was greatly impressed by my father's demonstration and brought him to the Aoyama Imperial Palace. There, my father taught those close to the Emperor. But this was for a very short period.

When my father came to Tokyo in 1927, he taught various people. At that time, there were only a few students.

Although I was born in 1920, it was in 1927 that my father

called my mother and me to Tokyo. There was Admiral Yamamoto's son, Kiyoshi Yamamoto in Shirogane Saru-machi in Shiba. My father rented a house on his introduction. They trained in the morning on the first floor of the rented house where the doors to adjoining 8- and 10-mat rooms were removed. A number of different people trained at that time but, there were only two rooms so only about three and five persons could train in the two rooms, respectively. Also, they trained in a remodelled billiard parlor formerly owned by Mr. Shimazu. There were many young ladies such as university students who trained. Among them was Miss Makiko Yamamoto whose name became very famous in relation to Cuba. At one time in Cuba people used to say that there could be no link between Japan and Cuba without her. She was the grand-daughter of Admiral Gombei Yamamoto. Anyway, such unusual people trained at that time.

Although, I didn't train much at that time I had already done techniques like *ikkyo* and *nikyo*. It was at the end of 1930 that this dojo was built. We used to live in a corner where there were only pillars and no rooms. Then, in 1931, the dojo was completed and we held the opening ceremony. An eighty-mat dojo in those times was an extraordinary thing. Our residence was even larger, more than 80 tsubo of floor space. Those who were present at the opening ceremony and are still living are Hajime Iwata, a present shihan, Mr. Hisao Kamata and Mr. Hoken Inoue. Mr. Inoue is my cousin and an old-timer. I understand that he came to live with our family at the age of thirteen and was brought up by my mother. I think that he was an *uchideshi* until he was 45 or 46. Then, he left. Now he runs the *"Shinwa Taido"* School. I think it's all very well that he is head of his own art under another name. I, myself, little by little, began to practice. I mainly took *ukemi* for sword techniques rather than *taijutsu* (body techniques). By around 1936 it had become my duty to take sword *ukemi* for my father when he went places to give demonstrations. I had practiced a little kendo. I practiced old style *Kahima Shinto-ryu*. These various *ken* styles are the parents of the present Aiki sword. I don't take too much to the sword. The Founder seemed to prefer that beginners not practice sword movements. It is better to master basics first, then, if you learn to swing the sword with the body, it becomes good practice. But I grew up with a sword. I have many old acquaintances in the kendo world, so perhaps in that sense, I am the only one who has consistently linked kendo and Aikido together. I received most of my instruction in the sword from my father.

The dojo was entrusted to me around 1942. That is because my father left for Ibaraki with the rest of the family. My advisor was the present chief instructor of the dojo, Osawa Sensei in his younger years. I don't think anyone other than myself knows the circumstances of those years including both the pre- and post-war periods. There are others who are familiar only with certain times. No one has been more involved than me. My father left details to other people and taught Aikido only to a few people rather than the general public. Of course, the few I mentioned are of high caliber. I don't think there is anyone other than myself who knows the sequence of events up through 1938. After the war, I began to practice seriously because I thought it was my duty. In my opinion, if Aikido is publicized and many people are afforded the opportunity of practicing, there will always be a certain number of persons who are very good at the art. Yet, at the same time, we must spread Aikido. Although it might be a good idea to develop only a few expert practitioners, if they disappear then the art will cease to exist. That would be a problem. So we must seek ways to publicize Aikido. I have come to hold the belief that the most important task for Aikido since the war has been to conform our way of thinking, teaching and philosophy to the trends of the time. It was around 1937 or 1938 that I began to practice Aikido seriously. I had already learned techniques by then. One can learn techniques in two or three years. In 1940 I began to suffer from ill health. This lasted for one or two years and I had to recuperate for a while. Then the war ended.

It is all well that Aikido has reached this stage. I think that the fact that, although Aikido sprang from the old jujutsu tradition and has become quite different from other surviving *kobudo*

40

(traditional martial arts), it was greatly influenced by circumstances and attitudes after the war. If we try to raise Aikido to the level of a modern budo we must deal with various problems. It is through changes in ways of thinking that Aikido is now considered one of the modern budo along with Judo, Kendo, Karate, Kyudo and Shorenji.

Editor: There is a story we heard regarding the war period. We understand that you had to make an extraordinary effort to save the dojo from fires caused by air raids during the war. Would you tell us about that incident?

Doshu: Yes, if I wasn't here, the entire dojo would have burned down. Buildings surrounding the dojo on three sides were destroyed by fire. In all of Wakamatsu-cho there were only 30 or 40 houses left. The houses next door and in the entire area behind us were burned down. All the area in that direction there was reduced to black fields. The section from here to Shinjuku was burned. At that time, I was a student at Waseda University. There were a female receptionist and Mr. Hirai other than me. He was a shrewd fellow. (Laughter) I think he must be eighty years old by now. On March 10th that year there was an air raid, but there was no damage in this area. In those days I was a student and full of energy so I slept calmly indifferent to the bombings. But the following day many people came walking almost naked including women who were beyond any sense of shame. I thought it was really awful. So I began to sleep wearing a helmet the next night. I really think human beings are simple. (Laughter) I think it was during an air attack in April when this area was destroyed. When I came back to Nippori station from Iwama there was an attack. Through Kanda and the burned down areas I came to a road block. I said: "I'm going back home!" I walked back here to find that the dojo was unburned. After that, the fire began to spread. Then, I ran around carrying water in the middle of the night. There were only old people and women at that time. But when I shouted commands: "Go there! Come here!, etc.", they moved about frantically. Then the dojo was safe and I was relieved. But then, someone shouted to me: "Mr. Ueshiba!". I answered: "What?" The

41

answer came: "There's smoke coming out of your roof!" Sparks were igniting all over the roof. It was terrible. There was a well in the back of the house. When I tried to fetch water, fortunately, it was not dry. So I told everybody to gather around the well. I told them to hand up buckets of water to the roof. I was standing up there and poured water on the fire. I broke open the roof and poured water inside and was able to put out the fire. Otherwise, the dojo would have been completely burned down and Aikido after the war would have been different. After that, an unexploded shell fell on a stone storeroom in the back of our house which wasn't burned. This destroyed the roof we had saved at no small pains. Then, the leak in the roof became worse. When we went to the bathroom we needed an umbrella. Around the end of the war people were only concerned with eating. So I didn't think of repairing the roof at all. Everybody lost their house. Until the war ended the dojo was closed. After the war I re-opened it and about 100 people came to live in it but unfortunately they had no sense of propriety. They brought in a portable cooking stove and cooked there as if it was a special right for them. The dojo became black from all the cooking. We had a wooden fence and they broke it and used it for cooking. That was too much. I thought I had better kick them out but they refused to leave. I was at my wit's end. It took until about 1955 to get them all to leave. I had a really terrible time. Then I remodelled the dojo but it eventually proved to be too small so we built the new building.

I usually write in my books about the occasion of a public demonstration in Takashimaya about 1956. That occasion marked an important change in our usual demonstration format. Before then, there was a very strict rule that no one other than my father should demonstrate. I high-handedly asked my father to let all of the other *deshi* demonstrate first with my father appearing at the end. And so we proceeded on that basis. After that, anybody and everybody started giving demonstrations. That demonstration set the standard for our typical Aikido exhibitions. After the Takashimaya demonstration, the fact that an Aikido teacher named Morihei Ueshiba was still on the active list became widely known. Thus, the course of Aikido was set. Everything developed naturally and Hombu Dojo became active.

Editor: While families were still staying in Hombu Dojo after the war, did you start training?

Doshu: Yes, I did. I started practicing seriously in 1949. In 1948, Mr. Otake from Kamishi came. He was really powerful. He used to belong to the Kendo Club of Waseda University. When participating in a *gasshuku* as an alumnus he struck the wrists of two juniors and ended up cracking their bones. He was once told that he was not welcome to train. After he had practiced Aikido for one or two years, Mr. Tada began training in 1949. Mr. Arikawa started in 1948. I think Mr. Yamaguchi began in 1951. You can check the dates. Mr. Okumura started in 1940 at Manchuria Kenkoku University. Mr. Osawa came in 1941. He started the same year as Mr. Tohei. Mr. Saito in Iwama started in 1946.

Editor: After the war, you took the lead in developing a large organization. Would you tell us about the difficulties you encountered while the number of students was gradually building up?

Doshu: Difficulties are not obstacles after they've been overcome. I have only reached this stage step by step without doing anything out of the ordinary. I used to work in a company for a living until 1955. At the same time I managed the dojo. There was a time I had to borrow money from the company in order to repair the dojo roof. Those were hard times. Around 1950 or 1951 one earned a seven- or eight-thousand yen monthly salary. Our four-member family had to live on that amount. On top of that, there were several *uchideshi* for us to feed. Can you imagine what it was like? This is why those people who were dependent on us still cannot raise their heads before my wife.

Editor: Did the demonstration you mentioned just now gradually lead to the spread of Aikido?

Doshu: That demonstration was just one of our activities. Just after the war on February 9, 1948, the "Kobukai Foundation" was approved by the Ministry of Education as the "Aikikai Foundation". In other words, it became acceptable to practice Aikido. Beginning in 1949, I settled here in Tokyo and had those who

43

stayed after the war leave and we started the dojo as the headquarters. At that time there were no branch dojos. In 1954 and
1955, a branch dojo was finally established in Tokyo. That was
the Kuwamori Dojo in Sakuradai which is the oldest one in Tokyo.
After a time, the next branch dojo was established in Kawasaki.
Next was the dojo in Asamamachi in Yokohama headed by Mr.
Nishio. That was the dojo I had Mr. Nishio take charge of. He
started the dojo one year after the Sugino dojo was opened. Those
dojos are very old. I started many branches and clubs in Univer-
sities but there were many people who practiced in the dojo as
if it were their own. I wish they would give full recognition to
how the branch dojos were established and how they reached this
stage. If one only thinks of the here and now, there will be differences of general viewpoints.

Editor: Would you describe the first international activities of
Hombu Dojo?

Doshu: For one reason or another, people with varying viewpoints
regarding Aikido were the first to go abroad . . . The first thing
I thought of was the fact that just after the war Japanese students
who went to foreign countries were very miserable. This was
because Japan lost the war. They walked timidly. When Americans
approached them they avoided their path with hunched shoulders.
That was a problem. I thought we should encourage young people so as to avoid Japan going downhill in the future. I felt we
should send students abroad to study while feeling proud to be
Japanese. I thought Japan would deteriorate if people were only
good in terms of knowledge but not in humanity. That's why I
encouraged people who came to this dojo to go abroad. Japan has
this fine *budo* as one of its traditions. If one learned Aikido well
and went abroad one could tell that although foreign nations might
have some aspects superior to Japan, we had this fine *budo* we
could be proud of. If foreigners wished to study it, we could teach
them. I felt that if we proceeded in this manner our youth would
feel confident of its humanity. Also, I set my mind to training
students for the benefit of the Japanese people. At the beginning
I didn't think of becoming a martial artist or anything of the sort.

Just after the war I reflected upon how I should live my life. The idea closest to my heart was to spread the Aikido developed by my father throughout the world. It would benefit not only Japan but also people abroad. Also, it would be a positive factor in the development of human beings. In the old days, it was said that Japan was the most ethically advanced monarchy of the East. I thought our future task would be to raise Japan to the level where there would be no other country as advanced spiritually. I encouraged young people to take the initiative in travelling abroad. I felt that although there was no free cultural exchange between Japan and foreign countries, if we actively approached countries abroad some would send inquiries. As a result, some Aikidoists went abroad. I think Aikido is highly regarded as a Japanese *budo* in the sense that, although Aikido is very new historically in comparison to Judo, Kendo and Karate, it is relatively unified and widespread. Around 1952 or 1953, Mr. Mochizuki went to Europe in connection with Nyoichi Sakurazawa (George Oshawa of the Macrobiotic Diet system). At about that time, we sent Mr. Tohei to Hawaii around 1953 through the introduction of Mr. Fujioka who was a professor at the University of Hawaii for Aikido and western cultural studies. He was the first one Hombo sent as an official *shihan*. Then, we sent Mr. Murashige and Mr. Kuroishi from Kyushu to Burma around 1950's . . . I took Mr. Kuroishi at his word that he would come back with a tiger skin. (Laughter) At that time I believe he could really have brought one back.

Editor: What about your own trips abroad?

Doshu: In the beginning I didn't travel abroad very much. I left everything to Mr. Tohei. It was around 1963 when I first travelled abroad. I went to Hawaii, Los Angeles and San Francisco in California and stayed for about three months. After that I travelled abroad many times. I forget exactly where.

Editor: I remember it well. There was a small YMCA south of Los Angeles where I saw you for the first time.

Doshu: Mr. Akira Tohei was along too, wasn't he?

Editor: There was also Mariye Yano (Takahashi) and Isao Takahashi from Los Angeles.

Doshu: Yes, Yes. Mr. Takahashi . . . At that time there were many other people including Mr. Hirata and Mr. Sekishiro. He was from San Diego, wasn't he? Had you already started?

Editor: I have been practicing for twenty-one years.

Doshu: That's great! Well done! That's history. (Laughter)

Editor: Since this year is the 100th anniversary of the birth of the Founder I am sure that everyone expects that Aikido will continue to develop. Would you describe your views about the future of the art?

Doshu: I think that the main feature of Aikido is that there is no victory and no defeat. The day before yesterday when the demonstration was held in the *Budokan*, Minoru Genda Sensei was present. He said: "Aikido created a monistic philosophy where you are one with your opponent and where victory and defeat are determined in an instant. I think this is splendid!" Aikido is not training to fight with your opponent. By harmonizing with him, you can unify the mind and body transforming them into one entity and create a monistic world by becoming one with nature. Thus, there are no *shiai* (matches) in this *budo*. In this respect, there might be some aspects which are lacking in interest for young people, but the more you try it, the more you come to like it (lit., "like dried cuttle-fish, the more you chew it, the tastier it becomes"). In this respect, there are some people who call it moving "*zen*". It really has religious and artistic aspects. It possesses beauty of harmony or nature — a natural beauty which is exuded from the body as a result of being in harmony with the flow of nature. People like Kiku Goro or Enosuke, Kabuki actors or Sumi Hanayagi, a Japanese dancer, understood their professions in an artistic sense. At present, frontier technology or scientific technology have been greatly developed, but our spiritual selves have been detriorating. In this respect, I am sure that the way of Aikido will be accepted by the public in the 21st century. Aikido is not something where you speak of strength or weakness. People who studied old *budo* always talk about strength and weakness, about who is stronger or who is weaker. Honestly speaking, the attitudes of these people present a problem. I suppose that's okay, but if you don't appreciate the higher levels of this art, Aikido won't develop. Things are progressing, you see. Spiritual techniques of human beings must develop, too. Like the "Warring States" (*Sengoku*) period, if there is someone who says: "I am strong! I am the best Aikidoist in Japan!" That's not right. He is a vulgar type. How we raise the hearts of humanity to higher level is the most important thing. We really must think about how to create and run an organization which suits this higher level. The movements of Aikido are in perfect accord with the movements of the spirit. If one talks about spiritual matters after having struck and kicked his partner, it's not convincing. In the case of Aikido, we strengthen the body and mind through soft movements which are in harmony with nature. If we proceed in this manner, it will still continue to develop. In order to continue to progress we cannot avoid contradictions in terms of administrative matters. Always keeping this in mind, if we think about progressing, there will be future development. Aikido has its own way of thinking and an advanced philosophy which are different from those of other budo—I don't mean that other budo don't have advanced philosophies—Aikido has its own unique philosophy. Thus, I think it will assume an extremely valuable role in the coming new generation.

Editor: Sensei, I have been wanting to ask you this question for a long time. Do you think one can apply the Aikido we learn on the mat to the social or political realms?

Doshu: Training on the mat is related to the way of thinking of becoming one with your opponent, not fighting with the partner in business. Just after the war people always talked about revolution and so forth. However, little by little that type of thinking is disappearing and changing into an amicable atmosphere. I think it's because Japan has become really well off. In that respect, the spiritual structure of Aikido is in conformity with the surroundings and I think that is a good thing. The other day, Genda Sensei said: "I learned *irimi* and *tenkan* from O-Sensei at the Naval University. *Irimi* and *tenkan* are the techniqiues where we lead the opponent to the position we formerly occupied by moving in rapidly without hurting him. If we had recognized this, we wouldn't have had such a stupid war as the Greater East Asia War (World War II). We could have acted in consonance with the opponent. We made a mistake, didn't we? If you have an attitude of fighting and winning over your opponent, he won't follow you. Of course, we have to be strong. We have to have strong arms and minds. Everything must be strong, but if you focus solely on these aspects, the human aspect will be neglected. One can be said to be strong if he hides away in the mountains and develops his fists. Then, if he unleashes a blow anyone would be knocked down. But that is meaningless from the social point of view. In that respect, I think the Aikido is something completely different and useful for people in the political and economic world and anyone who plays the part of a leader.

Editor: At the present Aikido is very popular abroad and there are many students who come to Japan from foreign countries. Some are very earnest practitioners and speak fluent Japanese. Does the possibility exist for foreigners to be trained at Hombu Dojo and sent abroad?

Doshu: Does that mean that foreigners can become expert practitioners? Yes, I think so.

Editor: Take the example of Mr. (Christian) Tissier who is a very serious Aikidoist and speaks fluent Japanese. If a foreigner like him were to live the life of an *uchideshi* and understood Japanese culture well, and then returned home, I think this would serve to improve the relationship between Japan and foreign nations.

Doshu: Although Mr. Tissier was not an *uchideshi* he trained diligently at the dojo. Some foreigners train diligently and some return to teach in their countries while others stop when they go home. There are many people who train for the purpose of teaching or for their own training. If not only Japanese, but American, French and African understood the true way of Aiki and trained earnestly, it's fine for them to teach anywhere. As long as they don't misunderstand the vertical structure. Aikido as I mentioned before is a path which originated in the East. If one deviates from this path it's no longer Aikido. It's difficult to use it efficiently for the structure of the organization. Since there are no matches, I don't think Aikido can exist other than as a vertical structure where the Path is emphasized. We're not running an organization to decide what to do with strong people or weak people but rather for development of the path of moral training. One's view of the organization varies depending on how he understands it.

Editor: What are your views on the education of the *shihan* sent abroad from Hombu Dojo?

Doshu: I have been thinking about this subject, but it's difficult. It's something easier said than done. We have to educate not only the *shihan* we send abroad but also those in Japan. There are many tasks.

Editor: My final question concerns the future of Aikido. I'd like to ask your perspective on the future of Aikido internationally. I understand the current goal of the International Aikido Federation is to spread a standardized teaching method to serve as a basis for what may be called true Aikido. There are many splendid teachers at Hombu Dojo each of whom, however, has his own individual technique. Under these conditions, how do you think true Aikido can be spread throughout the world together with a teaching method?

Doshu: Well, I think that to spread a teaching method or something of the sort is secondary. The first thing is to achieve friendship through Aikido. To attack someone saying, "What you're doing is wrong!" or "You shouldn't do that because it's not true Aikido!" or to criticize saying, "Your way is wrong!" is something we shouldn't do. The Founder underwent hardships to develop the Aiki Path and it turns out that we are all practicing Aikido. If people are practicing what is called Aikido they are conscious of some link with here (HQ's). If that's the case, I hope above all that everyone will join hands around this center through Aiki despite differences in technique and nationality and practice the art and train daily. In order to improve techniques we have to change the teaching method little by little, but I don't think we will do something unreasonable like fixing a framework and forcing everything into it. I think we shouldn't do that. The way

Aikido should be is spontaneous and naturalness itself. Aikido exists as the ordered movement of the divine principle which is nature herself. Aiki techniques are varied and multi-faceted. They seem to be separate from one another, however, there is a unity and single order about them. This is where the exquisiteness of Aikido lies, I think. Therefore, we have no intention of fixing a framework whether it be political, ideological or economic, that is, to form an organizational structure and force everything into it. So, the Aikido Federation should grow to achieve friendship above all else.

(Sincere thanks go to Mrs. Ikeda of the Hombu Dojo office staff for her kind cooperation in the editing of the transcript of this interview.)

Bob Aubrey

Aikido and The New Warrior

In taking up a concept so provocative as the "new warrior" let me begin by pointing out that the young adults living in America, Europe and Japan who constitute the bulk of the million or so people practicing Aikido in the world today are living in a rare period of peace. For thirty years our civilizations, having been built as much upon war as upon industry and culture, have had little taste for war. The American exception of Viet Nam only proves the rule. As a result, the *battlefield warrior*, when he is not the figure of some romantic past, is someone we have had equally little taste for.

Nevertheless he exists.

Today there are over 25 million soldiers in the world. For each fighting man or woman 3 people are employed to support him in preparation for battle. The world spends more than $600 billion a year in readiness for war, yet leaves five hundred million human beings malnourished.

Is it this state of affairs that gives us a bad conscience about the warrior? Or is it rather thirty years of anxiety over ULTIMATE war, one where in a single day we can destroy not only ourselves but all life on the planet?

The answer is that nonsense has been made of the warrior by the nature of modern war itself. The 80/20 ratio, where 20% of the population enjoy 80% of the world's wealth has been around for a long time. It is not for moral reasons that the warrior has been condemned. He has become quixotic: worse than attacking windmills with a lance, he would have to attack satellites in space. As any military man since Clausewitz will tell you, nuclear war is not war at all; it is not a continuation of politics by other means. As a means it is devoid of meaning.

Does the bomb mean the end of the warrior? Or is it the birth of a new warrior, no longer defined by war?

In the period spanning the time when the warrior first became cannon fodder to the time he pushes the button of holocaust, the history of war has been one of using ever more lethal arms in an ever more deadly atmosphere. The battlefield offers no hiding, no respite, no difference between the warrior and the bystander. It is no longer the stage for acting out the warrior virtues of strength, courage and audacity. Today's wars, because of the terrible effectiveness of new weapons, kill more civilians than soldiers.

In founding Aikido, Master Morehei Ueshiba announced to the world that he was teaching a new way for the warrior, a way out of the dead end of war:

> As *ai* (harmony) is common with *ai* (love), I decided to name my unique budo "Aikido", although the word "aiki" is an old one. The word which was used by the warriors in the past is fundamentally different from mine. *Aiki* is not a technique to fight with or defeat the enemy. It is the way to reconcile the world and make human beings one family.[1]

World War II was the last suicidal lunge of the Japanese samurai in modern warfare. Morehei Ueshiba, instead of supporting the war, quietly retreated to a small farm in Iwama and waited out the folly. Ueshiba had not come to his position by analyzing history or by philosophizing; he was a man of Budo, a warrior, who had come to realize that there was no place left for him in war. By the time that Hiroshima and Nagasaki had been bombed, this truth was evident to all Japanese warriors.

But what is a warrior to do when he can no longer relate to war?

Japan was perhaps the first to face this question as a nation, and it was all the more dramatic as the warrior ethic pervaded all things Japanese. Japan's answer has been a lesson to us all. The winner of the war, who had made as its proud boast: "The business of America is business" — came to see what happens when the

Japanese samurai carries out "war by other means."

This transformation of the Japanese warrior ethic is a fascinating story in itself, but I refer to it here as a backdrop to the warrior's dilemma universally, and to Aikido's promise of a new way.

Morihei Ueshiba was offering more than just a way out. The new way of Aikido is the possibility of becoming a *nonviolent warrior*.

But what does this concept mean?

Nothing, I think, shows more the difference between Eastern and Western thought than the question of what being a warrior is all about.

The Oriental tradition of the martial arts has always taught that the warrior must make nonviolence his inner virtue in keeping the peace— with others but especially within himself. Is not the very meaning of the way of the warrior "Bushido" which is written as: "the way of stopping the use of arms"?

In the West, on the other hand, the English word "warrior" and the French "guerrier" are deeply rooted in war, coming from Old North French "were" meaning strife and confusion. The West, with all its history of ethical thought, never developed a major tradition of educating the nonviolent warrior. The warrior competes, defends, punishes, suffers stoically, crusades, revolutionizes — or if he is nonviolent he turns the other cheek, no longer a warrior but a martyr.

Ueshiba carried the Oriental tradition a step further in introducing an art of bodily combat using nonviolent techniques steeped in an attitude of "goodness" or "generosity", what the Japanese call "Jin". In Aikido this means that when faced with someone who has the intention of doing you harm, you must be able to "surround him with your heart" and attain the "victory of peace".

This nonviolence is something different from Christian meekness and Gandhi's ahimsa.

Ueshiba's ideal of "love for all things" is the ultimate state of awareness for a warrior. It is not a digression, I think, to point out here that Ueshiba rejoins a broken line of Oriental warrior philosophy going back over two thousand years to Mo Tzu.

This philosopher-general lived during the period of Warring States in China (he died around 381 B.C., a contemporary of Socrates) and taught:

> Righteousness consists in having one's mind set upon loving the world and being able skillfully to benefit it.[2]

Although Mo Tzu's school had three hundred warrior disciples and constituted during Mo's lifetime the major alternative to Confucianism, no Moist philosopher appears after his death. Historians can only speculate as to why. Wing-Tsit Chan writes:

> . . . the centuries of war in which Moism thrived was no time for hair-splitting and sophistry, and their condemnation of war did not endear them to the rulers. Their asceticism and utilitarianism was too extreme to be practicable. But why did their lofty doctrine of universal love fail to continue? Was it too idealistic for the Chinese? Or was it inherently weak because it is largely motivated by the benefits it would bring? The question is open to speculation.[3]

The time we are living in is clearly no "period of warring states"; it is a period when we are becoming aware of the implications of war for the planet. In such a context Mo Tsu's philosophy appears neither a "lofty doctrine" nor "inherently weak" because it is utilitarian. It seems rather to define the ideal of the new warrior while keeping the traditional Oriental warrior meaning of "stopping the use of arms".

Morihei Ueshiba understood well that his new way of the warrior should be more than a philosophy. On the other hand as a martial art it should not lose the ideal inscribed in the very meaning of Aikido and become a sport with competition, a method of self-defense or a fitness program. It must fulfill Mo Tzu's double purpose of "loving the world and being able skillfully to benefit it."

A characteristic that plagues most nonviolent ways is a tendency of their followers to become passive idealists rather than warriors. Ueshiba, in developing Aikido, carefully planted the seeds of nonviolence in the Aikido techniques and concentrated on making warriors of his disciples — which he did, for today's Aikido masters are among the best martial artists in the world. The Aikido spiral is a symbol of harmony just as it is an effective movement in harmonizing opposing forces. The attitude of "go-no-sen", where one foregoes the option of attack in favor of taking a "defensive initiative" in extending ki is likewise both symbol and strategy. In Aikido the superior awareness of the warrior is something that matures through the regular practice of ritualized combat. Harmony and universal love are the ideals, but Aikido also maintains the warrior's edge by cultivating attentiveness, energy, adaptability and willingness to act in conflict.

Although rooted in the Oriental tradition of martial arts, Aikido marks a step forward not because of the ingeniousness of its technique but because it clearly affirms that war is no longer the essence of the way of the warrior; the goal of the new way is to realize universal love while being skillful in benefiting the world.

The philosophy of Aikido thus contains a transcendental or spiritual element as well as an ethical element. Let us examine these two dimensions more closely and ask ourselves how well today's Aikido lives up to its ideals.

A story that a beginner in Aikido inevitably comes to hear is about the enlightenment of Master Ueshiba which led him to create Aikido. This story is found at the end of Kisshomaru Ueshiba's classic book, *Aikido* and has become the most identifiable statement of transcendence in Aikido. The story is repeated over and over again in dojos throughout the world, in more or less the same words as the original narrative, so let me set it forth here:

> In the spring of 1925 a navy officer, a professor of fencing, visited the Master and asked to become his student. Then during a conversation, they happened to disagree over a trifle matter. Tempers rose. They agreed to have a fight. The officer dashed forward to strike him, swinging his wooden sword. But as the Master dodged his sword very easily each time, the officer finally sat down without having once touched him. The Master says he

felt the opponent's movements before they were actually executed in the same way as during the time in Mongolia.

He took a rest after this game and went over to a nearby garden in which there was a persimmon tree. As he was wiping off the perspiration from his face, he was greatly overcome with a feeling which he had never experienced previously. He could neither walk nor sit. He was just rooted on the ground in great astonishment.

The Master recalls his experience:

I set my mind on budo when I was about 15 and visited teachers of fencing and jujitsu of various provinces. I mastered the secrets of the early sects, each within a few months. But there was no one to instruct me in the essence of *budo* which could satisfy my mind. So I knocked on the gates of various religions but I couldn't get any concrete answers.

Then in the spring of 1925, if I remember correctly, when I was taking a walk in the garden by myself, I felt that the universe suddenly quaked, and that a golden spirit sprang up from the ground, veiled my body, and changed my body into a golden one.

At the same time my mind and body became light. I was able to understand the whispering of the birds, and was clearly aware of the mind of God, the Creator of this universe.

At that moment I was enlightened: the source of *budo* is God's love — the spirit of loving protection for all beings. Endless tears of joy streamed down my cheeks.[4]

The experience of Ueshiba is typical of Oriental satori as it is of mystical experiences everywhere, described by William James in the 19th century in *The Varieties of Religious Experience*. Since the 1960s the development of transpersonal psychology has allowed thousands of people to explore such experiences through both traditional techniques and new ones: mystical experiences, birth experiences, out-of-the-body experiences, telepathy, dreams, hallucinations, trances, etc.

The value of such an experience depends on why one has had it and what one is willing to do with it more than on having the experience itself, as obviously Ueshiba's inventing Aikido is in no way a cause-effect result of his enlightenment.

What Ueshiba did in creating Aikido is not possible for anyone who does not combine learning, training, and spiritual seeking.

Unfortunately, Ueshiba's enlightenment has become an Aikido "myth of the Creation" rather than an experience which his followers see as a necessary dimension in the making of the new warrior. I do not know why this is so unless it is more convenient for the Japanese mind to let Aikido do one thing and leave it up to religions like Zen to do the other. Both are obviously part of the warrior's path and it is my opinion that the transpersonal dimension should be integrated into Aikido teaching.

That this is possible is supported best by the books of Carlos Castaneda which describe his initiation as a warrior-sorcerer by a Yaqui Indian, Don Juan. (In Ueshiba's case, a most profound influence on him was Reverend Deguchi of the Omotokyo sect, in which many shamanic elements are to be found.) Castaneda's narrative is a fascinating report of experience in a tradition that was believed primitive or lost, but it has opened the door to real treasures of wisdom to be found in warrior paths of all American Indian tribes. Castaneda describes how he is taught to dream, seek allies, cultivate personal power, and overcome the warrior's enemies of fear, clarity, power, old age. He introduces us to the *nagual*, a separate reality of transpersonal experience, irrational and unexplainable, where the warrior must learn to cope and be as at home as in the ordinary world of action, the *tonal*.

> Our eyes are the eyes of the *tonal*, or perhaps it would be more accurate to say that our eyes have been trained by the *tonal*, therefore the *tonal* claims them. One of the sources of your bafflement and discomfort is that your *tonal* doesn't let go of your eyes. The day it does, your *nagual* will have won a great battle. Your obsession or, better yet, everyone's obsession is to arrange the world according to the *tonal's* rules; so every time we are confronted with the *nagual*, we go out of our way to make our eyes stiff and intransigent. I must appeal to the part of your *tonal* which understands this dilemma and you must make an effort to free your eyes. The point is to convince the *tonal* that there are other worlds that can pass in front of the same windows. The *nagual* showed you that this morning. So, let your eyes be free;

57

let them be true windows. The eyes can be the windows to peer into boredom or to peek into that infinity.

Don Juan made a sweeping arc with his left arm to point all around us. There was a glint in his eyes, and his smile was at once frightening and disarming.

How can I do that? I asked.

I say that it is a very simple matter. Perhaps it is simple because I've been doing it for so long. All you have to do is to set up your intent as a customs house. Whenever you are in the world of the *tonal*, you should be an impeccable *tonal*; no time for irrational crap. But whenever you are in the world of the *nagual*, you should also be impeccable; no time for rational crap. For the warrior, intent is the gate in between. It closes completely behind him when he goes either way.[5]

Perhaps more than anyone else, perhaps even more than the Oriental martial arts, Carlos Castaneda has influenced the meaning of the word warrior, giving it a rich dimension of spiritual self-development. Today's Aikido teachers would do well to think long and hard about the possibility of "nagual training" as it is only too obvious that Master Ueshiba himself was a master of it. Moreover, he taught it to his advanced disciples. Master Gozo Shioda recounts how O Sensei Ueshiba would take a group of four or five disciples to a mountaintop and give them special training. This consisted, among other things, of night training where O Sensei would put on a blindfold and ask his students to attack him with wooden swords. Ueshiba however had a live blade. Shioda remembers that each time he raised his sword to strike he would be stopped by the point of Ueshiba's sword in front of his eyes, a terrifying experience: "The whistle of that blade sounded like death itself and my blood froze in my veins during the exercise."[6]

The second dimension of Aikido philosophy is practical ethics and the question of how best to live one's life. This is a traditional concern for all warrior paths and is clearly present in Japanese Bushido. But once again we are confronted with a major shift in what being a warrior means. For the traditional warrior, war was a way of life. The new warrior, on the contrary, sees his way of life as his war.

Teachers often talk of the importance of Aikido in daily life with phrases like "practice is just as important off the mat." Aikido has this in common with the other modern martial arts; indeed the "do" (way) of Judo, Karate-do, Kendo, and Aikido replaced the word "jutsu" (technique) in the late 19th and 20th centuries to emphasize that their primary purpose was no longer combat but ethical training. Unfortunately the complexity and changing values of modern life have discouraged martial arts teachers from taking on the burden of students outside the dojo, leaving it up to therapists to give advice.

Another warrior path outside the martial arts that has recently been revealed is Shambhala, the Tibetan warrior path taught by Chögyam Trungpa. Though the Tibetan way is mystical to the point of being arcane, Trungpa shows well that the starting point of the transcendental awareness of the warrior begins at home.

> Abstractly caring about others is not enough. The most practical and immediate way to begin sharing with others and working for their benefit is to work with your own domestic situation and to expand from there. So an important step in becoming a warrior is to become a family person, someone who respects his or her everyday domestic life and is committed to uplifting that situation.[7]

Trungpa has not limited himself to suggestions in books; the Shambhala training program based on meditation has five levels of warrior training and is offered in several countries. There is no doubt that as the new warrior theme continues to interest people concerned with the practical application of the warrior way to their lives, other paths will develop training programs, Yoga and Sufism to name two of the most obvious. Nor are the sources for new warrior training limited to non-Western traditions. More and more seminars are now being taught which mix traditional practices and humanistic psychology techniques, with titles like "Spiritual Warrior Training", "The Way of the Warrior", "Warrior Awareness" as well as more psychological titles like "Self-Affirmation", "Creativity Out of Conflict", "Fear Into Power"; these are now extended to business-seminars and workshops to teach one how to "manage with power", etc.

A major consequence of our changing lifestyles is increased stress: individuals are more isolated, familiar values are called into question, role identities are changing, and the pressures for performance are high. Statistics show that two out of every three visits to the general practioner are for symptoms related to stress. Heart disease has become the number one killer in modern industrialized countries with cancer running second: both are directly related to stress. The type of person most likely to fall victim to stress is the warrior personality, called Type A by stress specialists. In reading the following characterizations of Type A behavior, one becomes immediately aware of how Aikido could contribute to stress mastery seminars since it is a form of physical training in nonviolent action. In this case the violence that the stressed warrior personality perpetrates is on himself.

> Type A Behavior Pattern is an action-emotion complex that can be observed in any person who is *aggressively* involved in a *chronic, incessant* struggle to achieve more and more in less and less time, and if required to do so, against the opposing efforts of other things or other persons. It is not psychosis, or a complex of worries, or fears, or phobias, or obsessions, but a socially acceptable—indeed often praised—form of conflict.[8]

The point I want to make is that there is a growing area of teaching for what could be called "new warriors" which Aikido teachers have been slow to integrate.

On the contrary, we have been only too happy to let students work it out on the mat or else on their own. We have been content to sign up a new student, no questions asked; we would do well to accompany him or her in reflecting on why one wants to be a warrior and what type of warrior to be. We teach Aikido as if everybody wanted to become like us, whereas it is possible to leave the pyramidal teacher-student relationship to the mat and develop other warrior training off the mat with relationships in a more circular pattern. In any case the modern Aikido class is far from the traditional Japanese dojo. And as I have tried to show, a great deal of material for new warrior training is readily available.

On the other hand, I believe that the "new warrior" programs now being offered are going to be short-lived if they do not integrate the Oriental martial arts. The long-term discipline of mastering conflict through body work in a skilled technique is a firm grounding for warrior awareness.

In encouraging Aikido teachers to go beyond the martial arts in their warrior training I hark back to a basic tenet of Japanese Bushido, "bun - bushi", study and martial arts, which go hand in hand. I would like to add that the transpersonal dimension should be included also in training of the new warrior.

Up to now I have referred to the "new warrior" as if the concept were self-explanatory, yet I realize that this is far from the case.

The new warrior is new only insofar as we consider our context today in which the word itself is undergoing redefinition. Self-awareness in the realm of action is certainly not new, even in Western tradition, as the late French historian, Michel Foucault, has shown. Concern for the self has its own history going back to the Greeks, reaching a pinnacle in the Roman stoics, becoming transformed into Christian morality, and suffusing the modern conceptions of mind and body. Foucault distinguishes three forms of individualism, of which concern for the self is one, which will enable us to understand the relationship of the new warrior to Aikido.

> . . . the *individualistic attitude*, characterized by the absolute value that is attributed to the individual in his singularity and by the degree of independence granted him in relation to the group he belongs to or the institutions he is a part of; *the value of private life*, that is the importance recognized in family relations, in forms of activity in the home and in the domain of inheritance; and finally the intensity of *the relationship to the self*, that is the forms in which one is called to take oneself as an object of knowledge and the domain of action, in order to transform, to correct, to purify, and to find salvation.[9]

In the context in which Morihei Ueshiba was offering a new way of the warrior one can see that much was already present in the traditional Japanese Bushido relating to the third form of individualism, namely the relationship to the self. However, neither the individualistic attitude nor the value of private life are addressed in Aikido. It is well known that Japan is a society where the individual does not exist outside the tissue of social structure unless he pays the price of severe alienation; Japan is the best example in the world of how a modern industrial nation can build social relationships on the model of the family. By contrast, the new warrior mentality is an individualism encompassing all three forms described by Foucault. Current interest in "creative lifestyles" shows both the prevalence and the interaction of the first two forms, which with the new warrior has become an ethic.

It may therefore be useful as a conclusion to summarize the main features of what I think the new warrior ethic to be.

The new warrior is a man or woman who seeks self-realization through action. In the Bhagavad Gita, Krishna admonishes the warrior Arjuna to remain *in* action but not be attached to its results.

> To action alone hast thou a right and never at all to its fruit;
> let not the fruits of action be thy motive; neither let there be in
> thee any attachment to inaction.[10]

Aggression for the warrior is an energy that he seeks to integrate and to master rather than avoid: he is able to become angry or to remain calm, to hold his ground or go with the flow, doing so spontaneously and without stress.

In the polarization of conflict the warrior may take sides but exercises freedom in choosing. This distinguishes him from the soldier whose situation is polarized and who follows orders without understanding. In striving for right action the warrior trains his mind to penetrate the complexity of human affairs and to glean from them the moral action, whether this be in the details of his daily life or in the important issues facing humanity as a whole.

In the test of conflict the warrior is able to act because he has been trained in courage and has attained the level where he has the courage to be himself. In his training for action the warrior has learned strategy and is not afraid to assume the consequences of success. In the words of Miyamoto Musashi:

> The warrior is not like others because studying the Way of strategy is based on the fact of defeating men.[11]

In losing — for losing is inevitable — the warrior takes death as a friend who lets him see his own ultimate loss, so that rather than become discouraged the warrior seeks to improve himself by his mistakes. He has an open mind because he knows he is never invulnerable. He does not see himself as a victim nor does he seek a scapegoat. Thus he does not spread violence to the innocent.

The new warrior is a man or woman who seeks and carries his vision as his emblem. He has gone beyond strategic thinking to the realm of the unconscious and thus dances to the beat of invisible drums. His claim to truth is his sincerity in action, "truth to" as distinct from "truth about".

The new warrior is autonomous, that is, creator of his own rules of conduct. Knowing discipline and the traditional virtues, he takes it as his duty to develop his talents with a constant eye to balancing himself.

The new warrior can thus say with Nietzsche's Zarathustra: That is my way, and you, where is yours?

NOTES

1. Kisshomaru Ueshiba, *Aikido* appendix
2. Fung Yu-Lan, *History of Chinese Philosophy* (Princeton University Press) vol. 1 page 250
3. Wing-Tsit Chan, *A Source Book in Chinese Philosophy*, (Princeton University Press) page 212
4. Kisshomaru Ueshiba, op. Cit. appendix
5. Carlos Castaneda, *Tales of Power*, Penguin edition pages 169-170
6. Interview with Gozo Shioda, Bushido magazine, May 1984
7. Chögyam Trungpa, *Shambhala, The Sacred Path of the Warrior* (Shambhala) page 92

8. Friedman and Rosenman, *Type A Behavior and Your Heart,* (Fawcett Columbine) page 68
9. Michel Foucault, *Le Souci de Soi* (Gallimard, France) page 56. My translation and underlines. This book is the third volume in his study of the history of sexuality. Michel Foucault died the year of its publication, 1984.
10. Radhakrishnan and Moore, *A Sourcebook in Indian Philosophy,* (Princeton University Press) page 110
11. Miyamoto Mushashi, *A Book of Five Rings* (Allison & Busby)

Terry Dobson

A Kind Word Turneth Away Wrath

A turning point in my life came one day on a train in the suburbs of Tokyo. It was the middle of a languid spring afternoon, and the car was comparatively empty — a few housewives out shopping with their kids in tow, some old folks, a couple of bartenders on their day off poring over the racing form. The rickety old car clacked monotonously over the rails as I gazed absently out at the drab houses and dusty hedgerows. At one sleepy little station, the doors opened and the drowsy afternoon was shattered by a man yelling at the top of his lungs. A string of loud, shocking, violent oaths filled the air. Just as the doors closed, the man, still yelling, stumbled into our car. He was a big man, a drunk and exceedingly dirty Japanese laborer. His clothes were stiff with dried vomit, his hair matted and crusted with filth. His eyes were a bloodshot, neon red, and his face was apoplectic with hatred and rage. Screaming unintelligibly, he swung at the first person he saw — a woman holding a baby. The blow glanced off her shoulder, but sent her spinning across the car into the laps of an elderly couple. It was a miracle that the baby was unharmed. The couple jumped up and scampered towards the other end of the car. The laborer aimed a kick at the retreating back of the aged grandmother. "YOU FUCKING OLD WHORE," he bellowed, "I'LL KICK YOUR ASS!" He missed, and the old lady scuttled safely beyond his reach. Beside himself with rage, the drunk grabbed the metal pole in the center of the car and tried to wrench it out of its stanchion. I could see one of his hands was cut and bleeding. The train rattled on, the passengers frozen with fear. I stood up.

I was still young, back then, and in pretty good shape. I stood six feet, weighed 225, and had been putting in a solid eight hours of Aikido training every day for the past three years. I was totally absorbed in Aikido. I couldn't practice enough. I particularly enjoyed the harder workouts, the ones with the badass college jocks where teeth pattered on the floor like hailstones. I thought I was tough. Trouble was, my skill was yet untried in actual combat. We were strictly enjoined from using Aikido techniques in public, unless absolute necessity demanded the protection of other people. My teacher, the Founder of Aikido, taught us every morning that Aikido was *non*-violent. "Aikido," he would say over and over, "is the art of reconciliation. To use it to enhance one's ego, to dominate other people, is to betray totally the purpose for which it is practiced. Our mission is to *resolve* conflict, not to generate it." I listened to his words, of course, and even went so far as to cross the street a few times to avoid groups of lounging street punks who might have provided a jolly brawl in which I might test my proficiency. In my daydreams, however, I longed for a legitimate situation where I could defend the innocent by wasting the guilty. Such a scene had now arisen. I was overjoyed. "My prayers have been answered," I thought to myself as I got to my feet. "This . . . this . . . slob is drunk and mean and violent. He's a threat to the public order, and he'll hurt somebody if I don't take him out. The need is real. My ethical light is green."

Seeing me stand up, the drunk shot me a look of bleary inspection. "AHA!" he roared, "A HAIRY FOREIGN TWERP NEEDS A LESSON IN JAPANESE MANNERS!" I held onto the commuter strap overhead, feigning nonchalance, seemingly off-balance. I gave him a slow, insolent look of contemptuous dismissal. It burned into his sodden brain like an ember in wet sand. I'd take this turkey apart. He was big and mean, but he was drunk. I was big, but I was trained and cold sober. "YOU WANT A LESSON, *ASSHOLE?*" he bellowed. Saying nothing, I looked cooly back at him, then slowly pursed my lips and blew him a faggotty little kiss across the car. He gathered himself for his big rush at me. He'd never know what hit him.

A split-second before he moved, somebody else shouted,

"HEY!" It was loud, ear-splitting almost, but I remember it had a strangely joyous, lilting quality to it — as though you and a friend had been searching diligently for something, and he had suddenly stumbled upon it. I wheeled to my left, the drunk spun to his right. We both stared down at this little old man. He must have been well into his seventies, this tiny gentleman, immaculate in his *kimono* and *hakama.* He took no notice of me, but beamed delightedly at the laborer, as though he had a most important, most welcome secret to share.

"C'mere," the old man said in an easy vernacular, beckoning to the drunk, "C'mere and talk with me." He waved his hand lightly, and the big man followed as if on a string. The drunk was confused, but still belligerent. He planted his feet in front of the little old man, and towered threateningly over him. "WHAT THE FUCK DO *YOU* WANT, YOU OLD FART-SNIFFER?" he roared above the clacking wheels. The drunk now had his back to me. I watched his elbows, half-cocked as though ready to punch. If they moved so much as a millimeter, I'd drop him in his tracks. The old man continued to beam at the laborer. There was not a trace of fear or resentment about him. "What you been drinkin'?" he asked lightly, his eyes sparkling with interest.

"I BEEN DRINKING *SAKE*, GOD DAMN YOUR SCUMMY OLD EYES," the laborer declared loudly, "AND WHAT BUSINESS IS IT OF YOURS?" "Oh, that's wonderful," the old man said with delight, "absolutely wonderful! You see, I just love *sake.* Every night me and my wife (she's 76, you know) we warm up a little bottle of *sake* and we take it out into the garden and we sit on the old bench that my grandfather's student made for him. We watch the evening fade, and we look to see how our persimmon is doing. My great-grandfather planted that tree, you know, and we worry about whether it will recover from those icestorms we had last winter. Persimmons do not do well after icestorms, although I must say ours has done rather better than I expected, especially when you consider the poor quality of the soil. But, anyway, we take our little jug of *sake* and go out and enjoy the evening by our tree. Even when it *rains!*" He beamed up at the laborer, his eyes twinkling, happy to share the wonderful information.

As he struggled to follow the intricacies of the old man's conversation, the drunk's face began to soften. His fists slowly unclenched. "Yeah," he said when the old man finished, "I love *sake* too . . ." His voice trailed off.

"Yes," said the old man, smiling, "and I'm sure you have a wonderful wife."

"No," replied the laborer, shaking his head sadly. "I don't got no wife." He hung his head, and swayed silently with the motion of the train. And then, with surprising gentleness, the big man began to sob. "I don't got no *wife*," he moaned rhythmically, "I don't got no *home*, I don't got no *clothes*, I don't got no *tools*, I don't got no *money*, and now I don't got no place to sleep. I'm so *ashamed* of myself." Tears rolled down the big man's cheeks, a spasm of pure despair rippled through his body. Up above the baggage rack, a 4-color ad trumpeted the virtues of suburban luxury living. The irony was almost too much to bear. And all of a sudden *I* felt ashamed. I felt more dirty in my clean clothes and my make-this-world-safe-for-democracy righteousness than that laborer would ever be.

"My, my," the old man clucked sympathetically, although his general delight appeared undiminished, "that is a very difficult predicament, indeed. Why don't you sit down here and tell me about it?"

Just then, the train arrived at my stop. The platform was packed, and the crowd surged into the car as soon as the doors opened. Maneuvering my way out, I turned my head for one last look. The laborer sprawled like a sack on the seat, his head in the old man's lap. The old gentleman was looking down at him kindly, a beatific mixture of delight and compassion beaming from his eyes, one hand softly stroking the filthy, matted head.

As the train pulled away from the station, I sat on a bench and tried to re-live the experience. I saw that what I had been prepared to accomplish with bone and muscle had been accomplished with a smile and a few kind words. I recognized that I *had* seen Aikido used in action, and that the essence of it *was* reconciliation, as the Founder had said. I felt dumb and brutal and gross. I knew I would have to practice with an entirely different spirit. And I knew it would be a long time before I could speak with knowledge about Aikido or the resolution of conflict.

Susan Stone

Blending With Death

I've heard it said there's a window that opens
from one mind to another,
but if there's no wall, there's no need
for fitting the window, or the latch.

—Jelaluddin Rumi
from Quatrain 511

For me, it all started with a dream—a night vision. However, the message didn't reveal its gift until some time later . . .

We, my dad and I, are sitting in his aluminum fishing boat, quietly adrift, following the currents of the Sacramento River. There is nothing unusual about this, for fishing is a favored pastime of his. But on special occasions, I get to go along. (Special to me because at age seven an invitation to be with my dad is a treasured event. I don't think he has ever realized what a tomboy I am; that my idea of life is to play hard and work hard. I don't like dolls. His constant admonitions to "be a lady" fall on cringing ears, not because I don't behave like one, but because I feel misunderstood. How can I be a lady and climb trees?)

This particular afternoon on the river is noteworthy in many ways. The outboard motor, a little six horsepower, is gone, and in its place are two oars. I am at the helm, but the oars are still. We have two lines in the water, but the fish aren't biting.

The surface of the Sacramento River is deceptively calm. Her passengers are wise to take caution. Many a traveler, caught unaware, has been swiftly carried downstream, or pulled beneath her surface in one of the many eddies or cross-currents. The shoreline in many spots is choked with roots and branches of fallen trees and overgrown bushes. There is little beach along the many winding valley miles. Maybe that's why it is so good for fishing.

Serious fishermen have a steadfast rule — no talking in the boat, lest you scare the fish away. So, our exchanges are in hushed whispers. Otherwise, we are enveloped by complete silence. It is so still. No movement in the air, no movement in the water, no time.

And then, without warning, without moving, my father is in the water holding onto the rim of the boat, calmly looking ahead as we continue to drift downstream. There is no panic, no alarm on his face. He is searching, scanning the shore for something he knows is there.

And then again, as if a few picture frames are missing from the movie, he is no longer holding onto the boat. He is gone. He has let go. I peer around all sides of me, my eyes and mind penetrating the depths of the water without finding him. He has vanished.

I begin to row. Up and down that stretch of river I row. Forward and back, stretch, pull, quietly gliding, cutting through the water without a ripple. I strain my eyes, extend my muscles, stretch my mind. I am searching, rowing back and forth, again and again. Rowing, rowing. The oars numb my hands, the rhythm numbs my mind. Finally, I pull into the landing, gliding to a stop at the old wooden dock that reaches out into the shallows. Several familiar faces await me. His body has been found, they say. He is gone, they tell me. The service will be tomorrow.

I slowly open my eyes, allowing for the delicate transition between dream and contact. Moving from weightlessness to gravity, I am back in my dark, cool room knowing that I have traveled a previously untested distance. I have no foreboding. I have resolution. I feel more rested than I have in a long time.

For Dad, I suspect, it started much earlier. But time-lines

are funny, and they can be painfully separate within families. Finally, his and mine began to line up with each other. Within a few days of my dream, he called. Yes, there was a lump; it was to be biopsied. It didn't look good.

Dad's cancer eventually killed him, but it brought unexpected blessings along its way. His was a disease with great pain. (He had also suffered from multiple sclerosis for ten years.) The task ahead was to work with that pain and face his death. Morphine eased the body. The path to acceptance eased the mind. His, mine, my mother's, my brother's. Death, that which is present daily throughout our lives, that which we look at furtively, that which we give sidelong glances as it mirrors us in constant activity and avoidance, is that which meets us squarely in the eye as we turn the corner. It is the sensation of coming face to face with something only flirted with before, that now takes us by the hand as if it were an old friend. It is recognizable. It is even a relief to face it. A door opens and we enter the unknown. The fear may still be there — in fact it may intensify — but a lifelong shadow becomes a guiding light. A passageway to "the other side" appears.

That door can most easily be entered through surrender and acceptance, and perhaps by understanding that death is not just a concluding chapter to a life lived out in a rational, sequential way. We experience death every day of our lives when we deny our losses, bury our grief, or angrily push away someone who has hurt us. This creates fear and confusion, which deadens our mind to the possibility of change and joy. However, by responding to our emotions, we become involved in and shape the energy and flow of our lives. We move from resistance to acceptance. We drop hopelessness and resignation, and instead, enter into and blend with our experiences so we can participate fully in our lives. We become enlivened. A meeting with one's death brings with it the privilege of knowing one's life.

These principles of entering and blending are beautifully embodied in the Japanese martial art of Aikido. They form the basis of all movement and are the precursor to all technique. They also serve as powerful metaphors for daily life. Entering and blending can only be done from a strong center with positive movement. "*Irimi*," or entering, is that critical moment of surrender and decisive action when a student must face and move directly into the heart of an oncoming attack. Entering is done not aggressively or with the intention of striking back, but rather with the purpose of moving next to and blending with the direction and force of the attacker. Blending is the simple, yet sometimes difficult, transition of body and mind that allows a student to see the world from her attacker's point of view. From the vantage point of a new perspective, which can bring compassion, the energy can then be redirected into a non-violent resolution.

In daily life, the attacker can be a physical threat, a verbal assault, or an emotional crisis. It is said that the solution lies at the heart of the problem, so the point is to find that center, blend with it, and move from there.

Here is a simple Aikido exercise to illustrate these principles: On a cushioned mat, two partners (called *uke* and *nage*) face each other. *Uke* grabs *nage's* wrist. *Nage's* practice is to find the opening, the point of non-resistance, that will allow her to enter and step through to *uke's* side. From there she sees and experiences the momentum of the attack, which allows her to shape and redirect its force. It no longer has power over her.

Picture one of those large revolving doors leading into busy hotel lobbies. As the door slowly spins, you wait until you can safely proceed. You enter on one side, walking and blending with the speed and circular direction of the moving door, and emerge from the other side. The trick is to time your movements with the rhythm of the door. Closed, open, closed, open, closed, open, NOW. Enter, blend, move, exit. Otherwise, you get bumped by the door.

It is the same in Aikido. *Uke* approaches *nage* with a strong strike, punch, or grab. *Nage* enters and accepts the attack. She blends with *uke's* incoming energy, moving in such a way that propels both of them into a spiral, circular direction. Both exit the other side. If *nage* does not enter completely, or if the blend is not achieved, the encounter can result in distrust, mutual antagonism, or physical injury. If there is a true blend, no one is hurt and for a moment the two of them become one. Through the commitment to the union there is an elegance and a grace that touches and empowers both partners.

And so it is with life and relationships of every kind. For Dad and me, *irimi* was a given. He was dying and I was committed to accompanying him to the "door." It never occurred to me not to. The whole family was in this together. There were moments, entire days, when I was terrified, bewildered, and angry. There were times when I temporarily had to leave the situation, leave the house for a few hours so I could return refreshed and continue to be with him. On one occasion I left for two days to return to my home 190 miles away. Driving, I made the trip in two hours, twenty minutes. Normally it takes four hours. I was driven by fear. But I had to return. It wasn't from a sense of obligation, but from an inner drive to face this unknown, to face my father, to face myself.

The greater struggle for us was in finding the blend with the situation and with each other. We passed the summer in long visits, wrapping up business, wrapping up a father-daughter relationship. We both wanted a "clean" ending. Could we have it? We talked about his death and my life. We discussed work, values, relationships, other people, photography, reincarnation, and the spirit. Sometimes we agreed, sometimes we didn't. We reminisced about our lives. We covered a lot of ground. We hadn't done this before, this waiting for death. We were in uncharted territory. We wandered together, using the time to explain ourselves, trying to find some common thread other than blood that tied us together.

Although five months from diagnosis to death is a short time, we both believed it would be shorter. There was even a pervading sense of restlessness as we entered the last month. His affairs were in order, he had said his goodbyes, he no longer had anything to "do." His pain and the TV were our constant companions. Even the hospice nurses didn't understand why he hung on. As his pain and fear increased, so did my impatience. He wanted to die and wouldn't. I wanted to live and couldn't. I was becoming numb and indifferent. We were locked in a death grip, neither of us knowing how to move, neither of us knowing how to let go.

Then one day we came face to face. I finally, truly saw who my father was. From the inside. It was my first internal experience of the "blend."

The scenario was this: The Pulmonary Home Care truck had just delivered a special oxygen machine. It was a simple device to be used in home convalescent care. All one need do was plug it in, flip a switch, and it worked. I was all-around support person, so I immediately set about this new task. It would take approximately one minute to wheel it into place and plug it in. I had it all figured out.

To appreciate what happened next, one must know who this dying man was. He was a weakened body, a broken heart, and a grasping mind. All of his life he had been in control—of himself, his family, his surroundings. Life was according to Father. Through the process of his disease, he slowly lost that control. He depended now on his family and others to take care of him. Much of his fear of dying came from seeing that control slip from his grip. As a result, he became angry, bitter, and demanding. We who were closest to him couldn't do anything right.

Dad's world had shrunk to the size of one small room. The family room had been transformed into a hospice, complete with electric bed, recliner chair, oxygen tanks, and trays full of pills, vials of morphine and dozens of hypodermics. It was all that he had left. It was his life-support system. Enter a new piece of equipment and he wanted, he needed, to direct its placement.

It was the straw that broke both of us. He said plug it into the wall; I said I knew where to plug it in and to quit telling me what to do. There, I spit it out. And the devastation it wrought opened my eyes and my heart. In a slow, controlled but teary voice he said, "If it helps me to tell you where to plug it in, then please let me do it." And I saw him for the first time. I saw his pain, his suffering, his grief, the inner sword that had severed his life cord. For one pure moment I was him. I was stunned. Tears filled my eyes. So this was the Aikido blend I had practiced for so long on the mat.

The next moment my impatience and anxiety fell away. My confusion disappeared. I came into sync with Dad and myself. I changed. He changed. The situation changed. My days took on a single purpose—to be with my father and to help ease his pain. It became my meditation, my Aikido practice. I relaxed. I felt an inner aliveness. We developed a rhythm with each other that had a spirit and presence not there before. Shots every four hours, 'round the clock. My mother and I were the nurses from dawn until bedtime. A hospice nurse came in at night. Friends and neighbors delivered meals daily. We did nothing else. We just kept moving with it and with him. Row, row, stretch, glide. He set the pace. His dignity returned. My love returned. Even humor returned. It became effortless to clean up after meals, prepare the trays of medication, bathe him, massage his back and legs, watch TV with him or just sit on the patio in the warm summer evening breeze. We were *uke* and *nage*, father and daughter. In spite of my own sense of impending loss and sadness, the days now had an air of peace that almost touched on joy.

The last week he slipped into a coma. For brief moments he would pull out of it and talk sleepily about the good times. The hunting trips to Montana, the marlin he caught off Baja, the one that got away. They were the pleasant memories. The pain and bitterness of the years had faded away.

But one afternoon, as memories surfaced from the depths of his mind, his tone of voice changed and my blood ran cold. With eyes closed, face drawn in fear, he cried, "Get me back in the boat, help me get into the boat! I'm afraid the fish will bite my toes." For a moment I was startled, but then I felt my body fill with a powerful energy and a memory—my dream! Why had I been given a vision of his death? Where was that window now? Why was he frightened? His breathing quickened, with short, shallow, breaths. I held his hand and told him I was there, that the fish weren't biting that day, to hold on a little longer, that he was almost there. I found myself transported to the river and to the memory of sitting in the boat while he clung on. I watched his face, I protected him with my heart. But I couldn't pull him back into the boat. This was his path, his passing. I could not change that, but I could help calm his fear and be witness to his mortality. That we had in common. It was a long moment, but soon his expression softened and his breathing became relaxed and flowing again. I held his hand until he slipped back into his sleep.

He died two days later, briefly moving in and out of his coma a few more times. His last breaths were soft sighs, with no more effort, no more fear. My mother, brother, and I were with him as he exhaled for the last time. It was so gentle. He just stopped breathing and became still as his spirit floated away. He finally made it to the other side.

I, too, finally made it to "the other" side. Not to death, but to a deeper level of life. Living through my father's dying was a significant experience for me. It showed me the strength and ability of the heart to continually open. My training in Aikido prepared me for the journey and was my companion throughout.

In Aikido it is taught that we have an energetic body that can actually be developed like an organ. It is the mechanism through which we touch and embellish our aliveness. It is through this that we make contact with others, our environment, and events in our lives.

On the mat in our daily practice, if we forget or do not understand a technique, we can still form ourselves with this energetic body and maintain a relationship with our partners and with ourselves. Off the mat in our daily lives, life is full of change and technique is unpredictable. However, whether we are working, caught in traffic, doing the dishes or facing a crisis, we can do it with aliveness and awareness.

I now believe that in times of great emotional stress or shock, this developed "sixth sense" can take on a life of its own and guide us. It is an exercise of the spirit. Through it we can tap into our inner resources, discovering our innate wisdom, trust of self, and harmony with the Universe. It empowers us to heal ourselves and others, and to love deeply.

George Leonard

On Getting a Black Belt
at Age Fifty-two

It was the longest, darkest night of the year, and the cold night air was pouring into the *dojo* through windows opened wide behind me. I was sitting in one of the chairs provided for visitors, but on this holiday evening none of the usual crowd of onlookers was there, and very few students—only the hard core—were on the mat. Anybody with good sense would be home in a warm room with an open fire and a Christmas tree and good food and drink, but I was up for my black belt exam in just seven weeks. Sweat clouded my eyes and dropped off the end of my nose. Though my face was burning, my body was cold and clammy. I pulled my quilted *gi* jacket closer around me, but it was soaked through and felt as if it were turning to ice. Anyway, what difference did it make? What really concerned me—and though I was gasping for breath, I could examine the matter with a certain detachment—was whether I was going to die in the next two minutes.

According to what I had read, the pulse rate of a man in his fifties rarely exceeds 175. My heart must have been beating at least 200 times a minute. Even more alarming was a periodic shiver that seemed to rise up from somewhere inside me. Was this the beginning of cardiac fibrillation? And just what the hell *was* fibrillation?

I squirmed in my chair, panting for air. The lights in the dojo seemed simultaneously too bright and too dim. Why wouldn't my heart slow down? Or was it speeding up? At this point, I remembered *centering:* that's what Aikido is all about, isn't it? If I was going to die, I might as well die centered. I put my attention on a point about an inch beneath my navel and rested my left hand over that point. There was no sudden deliverance, but somehow I felt better. My heartbeat slowed. My breath came easier. The lighting began to look normal again.

When the class ended, I followed my follow students into the dressing room. Two of those who had been attacking me in the final set-to had some suggestions: My *atemi*, or defensive strikes, had been too rigid and aggressive, while my throwing power, which rises up from the hips, had been uncertain. This disproportion had had the effect of creating aggression and determination in the attackers, making it harder for me to throw them. I was grateful for their help and concern, yet felt somewhat put down. I was the highest-ranking among those in the dressing room. I was also, in effect, the rawest recruit in Marine boot camp, fair game for hazing by my teacher and by any fellow student who might be called upon to attack me.

This hazing, this three-month-long period of intensive preparation, was my teacher's gift to every black belt candidate. After five years' training in Aikido, my opportunity for the ordeal had come around. I had arranged, at some financial sacrifice, to cancel all lectures, workshops, and other distractions so that I could train five or six days a week from November 1 to February 8, the day of the exam.

Having witnessed the preparation of fellow students, I knew what to expect. The candidate would be separated from the other students. While they were going through their regular training, he and an experienced *uke* (attacker) would retire to the back mat and concentrate on the techniques that would most likely be required during the exam. Fifteen minutes before the end of class, the candidate would be summoned to the center mat. The other students would kneel around the edges and my teacher would call out various attacks. The evening would end with multiple attacks on the candidate. The attacks would continue until the candidate was driven beyond the limits of his or her stamina.

When I went home that night, and for the next two days, I felt truly wasted, as if something at the very center of my body had come unsprung. On the scales I saw I was down from 184 to 177, weight I could ill afford to lose at 6′4″. "You don't have to do this, you know," I told myself, considering the spectacle of one of my age and body build working out so intensely with men and women mostly young enough to be my children. Yes, it was quite mad. But even on that darkest of nights, I really had no intention of quitting, fibrillation or not. A black belt would be a nice thing to have for my workshops, both as an ego-booster and as a credential — a sort of Ph.D. in movement.

But it was more than that. It was not the belt or the credential or even the exam itself that brought me to the dojo night after night, but rather a more primitive longing. It was the ordeal itself that held me enthralled, the chance to confront difficulties and dangers within an ordered setting. At age fifty-two — at last! — a rite of passage.

My involvement had been unlikely from the very beginning. In October 1970 I had just resigned from *Look* magazine, a publisher's advance in hand, to write a rather difficult book. After seventeen years of hectic travel, tough deadlines, two-martini lunches, and other journalistic joys, I had finally realized that I would have to stay in shape in order to do my best intellectual work. Facing perhaps two years of concentrated research and writing, I had rejoined a nearby tennis club and signed up for lessons. I had, in fact, just mailed off the check for my initiation fee when I received a phone call from my close friend, Michael Murphy of Esalen Institute.

Before I realized exactly what was going on, Mike was well into a discussion of a Japanese martial art called "Aikido." I had never heard of it. In fact, I had never given more than a passing thought to judo, karate, kung fu, or any other "martial art." But now Mike was telling me of the sophisticated and esoteric nature of this art. Its mysterious power, he said, lies in a practice of blending or merging with the force of any attack. Then there is an even more mysterious quality called *ki:* through control of this putative force, comparable to the *élan vital* or life spirit, the Aikido master can apparently "create" an unbendable arm, become rooted to the earth, sense attacks from behind and, in effect, change shape and size.

I listened casually; Mike is an encyclopedia of eastern lore. Then he got to his point. He had discovered an Aikido teacher who had an Aikido dojo, or school, in a community south of San Francisco. He was having this teacher come up to the city twice a week to lead an experimental Aikido class for the Esalen San Francisco office staff. Classes would be on Tuesday and Thursday afternoons from four to six.

"What I'm really calling for," Murphy said, "is to invite you to join the class. Let's do it together, George. Let's go all the way to black belt. Let's do it."

Without giving it much thought, I agreed to join the class. As it turned out, I never made it to the tennis club. Not even once. I just kept sending in my dues for several months, until I finally had to admit that my new pursuit had won me entirely.

Our Aikido class started off inauspiciously. Traditionalists would have gnashed their teeth at our lack of discipline, our informal, talky, indeed disreputable demeanor. People wandered in late, gossiped during practice, drifted in and out of the room. There were no gi (practice uniforms). There was no bowing.

Our teacher seemed perversely reluctant to demonstrate advanced Aikido for our group of klutzes, but on certain rare occasions, to make a point, he might motion one of his disciples to attack. The most constant of these was a twenty-three-year-old woman, who had a fine-boned, long-legged body and the face of an angel. She would come at him with, say, a flashing strike to the belly. Faster than the eye could follow, he would be at her side, somehow embracing her. Then there would be two indescribable whirling motions that had the feeling of *sswwish* and *whooossh*, with the two bodies exchanging positions, yet remaining perfectly linked — and suddenly this young woman would be flying through the air.

At such times, there would be a moment of stunned silence, after which someone would say, "Would you do that again?" But our teacher would merely smile and go on with his instruction.

Only when I visited a working dojo, some six months later, did I understand my teacher's reluctance. He invited me, after class one night, to accompany him and a group of his disciples to an Aikido class across the Bay. We drove up to a storefront halfway between Berkeley and Oakland, got out of the car, entered, and there it was: a brightly lit, fully matted space with forty students in their white gi kneeling in the Japanese meditation position. By then I had my own gi and I wore my white belt (the mark of the brand-new beginner) proudly. I kneeled stiffly with the others at the edge of the mat, and for an hour that night I tried to train with those far-more-advanced white belts, those masterful blue belts and brown belts, taking my lumps as they came. I was dazzled by the strenuous training, the discipline, the complex techniques, and, most terrifying of all, the spectacular falls.

If I had been presented with such "advanced" Aikido at the very beginning, I probably would have turned my back and run all the way to the tennis club. But now, after six months, I was hooked. So I nursed my sore muscles and bruises, and continued training with the fast-dwindling group of raw beginners organized by my friend Murphy. Any fantasies I might have had about ever making black belt were long gone. I was training because it was fascinating and deeply satisfying. My book was moving along very well. Aikido was beginning to be my thing, my practice, my discipline.

Our teacher taught us to think of ourselves and our fellow students as fields of "energy" — or, better, since that word has questionable power connotations, as fields of "awareness." We practiced sensing the approach of fellow students from behind, feeling the quality of the approach as well as its direction. We imagined our arms linked with beams of energy or awareness that reached to the ends of the universe, thus making the arms supple yet strong, virtually unbendable. We made ourselves feel lighter or heavier. One day we spent a half-hour imbuing our "energy bodies" with the quality of slabs of granite. One student succeeded in making the upper half of his body into granite but failed with the bottom half; this top-heaviness caused him to collapse to his knees.

82

Sometimes our teacher would give us individual balancing sessions. I remember sitting in a chair facing him; we both had our eyes closed, and he held my hands in his. While he spent a couple of minutes tuning in, I tried to relax a knot of tension in my right shoulder blade.

"There's a tightness in your right shoulder blade," he said. "Send your awareness into that spot. Let it flow."

How could he possibly know that?

"There's excess energy in your head, especially in the eyes," he said a moment later. "You're like one of those balloon figures with all the air in the head. Let it flow downward."

I sat in silence, eyes closed, becoming aware of my head, which did indeed seem more alive than the rest of me. After five minutes or so, I felt a sort of tingling and aliveness rush down about as far as my heart.

At which, my teacher said, "Good. Now it's down as far as your heart."

The process continued, with me receiving feedback and encouragement, until I glowed with a balanced sense of aliveness from head to toe. I had no idea how my teacher could tell exactly what was going on inside me. In fact, I would have been more comfortable if I could have denied the message of my senses. Nevertheless, the experience was quite undeniable, so I did not deny it.

Nobody ever *said* they were going to quit, but after about a month the class started getting smaller. Without exception, we remained enthusiastic. We demonstrated our crude applications of Aikido wristlocks on anyone who would offer a wrist. (Aikido neophytes can be a menace to the community: upon their approach, friends and relatives soon learn to cry out, "Come not a step closer!")

Still, my classmates began attending class less regularly. Instead of twice a week, they would come once a week, then once every two weeks, then once a month. All of them assured me (me, the most faithful student) that they loved the training and had every intention of starting to train regularly next week. Even months after they quit, they would tell me of their plans to resume training. After eight months, our group of fourteen had dwindled to three. Even Mike Murphy was gone. I wondered what the hell was going on. Some people were simply too heavy or uncoordinated to take the falls. Others had competing sports; Murphy, for example, was to become a disciplined Masters-class athlete, running everything from the 100-yard dash to the marathon. But there was something else happening. The dropout ratio in this class, I learned later, was typical of Aikido classes all around the country.

The problem is, there is simply no tradition in American culture for a longterm, strenuous practice that offers no specific payoff, no guaranteed progress. Our best minds conspire to make everything painless, quick, and easy — "Enlightenment in Ten Easy Lessons." Rewards are constantly dangled before our eyes: If you do *this*, you'll get *that*. Even educational television programs strive desperately to be entertaining, diverting. If the audience is bored for as long as four seconds, for God's sake, *do something*. After doing everything in our power to create short attention spans in children, we test them and conclude that, yes, children have short attention spans.

The notion of an attention span as long as a lifetime is foreign to us. In fact, to practice diligently while making no obvious progress for weeks on end seems downright un-American. Later, you learn the rewards have been there all along, primarily in the practice itself. But there is no guarantee and, wherever you look, no Ten Easy Lessons. Small wonder so many people quit.

At the end of the year, in fact, only two of the original group were left. I and my friend Leo, who is my age and a writer and former philosophy teacher. We gloried in our training. We discussed Aikido tirelessly (ad nauseam, according to our friends) — Aikido as philosophy, as literature, as self-defense. At my wife's urging, I converted our dining room into a miniature dojo, complete with bright blue gym mat. Leo and I upped our practice time. We never missed a class.

But our situation was too good to last. Esalen finally got around to closing down a class attended only by two non-Esaloids. The last session was festive. Many of the original students came back for a final shot on the mat. Mike Murphy took some harrowing falls. Our teacher put me and Leo through our paces. At the end of the class, with conspicuous lack of ceremony, he handed us blue belts. It was an ending and a beginning.

Seeing our afternoon class dwindle, our teacher had opened an evening class for the public. Leo and I, somewhat despondent on having lost our privileged status, joined in.

The classes were held at the Unitarian Center near downtown San Francisco, a place buzzing with activity. Drunks and bums, stoned hippies, urban radicals, and other street types would drift in and have a go at the class. Recently divorced men and women would arrive with their hungry eyes. Ferocious jocks would take to the mat as if it were a football field, and strive mightily to win it all in a single night. One young Japanese, sinister in tinted aviator glasses, showed up with a putative brown belt from Tokyo. For several weeks, he crunched people to the mat, then disappeared into the night. Sometimes I felt I was playing a bit part in a Fellini movie.

This period of my training turned out to be invaluable. After a few months, I began to feel that nothing could surprise me. I silently repeated a favorite chant: *Expect nothing. Be ready for anything.* There was a kaleidoscopic quality about those nights on the mat, with so many faces, bodies, egos, spirits passing in and out of my life. But sometimes, in this dreamlike procession, a face and form would reappear over the weeks and months; gradually a hard core of devoted Aikidoists coalesced.

Most of my fellow students were young enough to be my children. The youngest could have been grandchildren. As it turned out, however, age was not a major consideration. Competition is forbidden in Aikido; insidious comparisons are avoided. The older student can practice the same techniques as everyone else, but somewhat more slowly, more carefully. Ultimately, a rather high degree of physical fitness is required. Every student spends half the time playing the part of the attacker, who always takes a fall; just getting off the mat hundreds of times in an evening makes you aware of every extra pound. The older student can keep up by staying in excellent shape. As my training progressed, I got into the habit of running two to five miles on most of my days off from Aikido — recently even farther — and taking an extra fifteen minutes to stretch and warm up before class.

The results shatter some cultural stereotypes. Older people are supposed to be stiffer, less resilient than younger people, but as my years of Aikido have passed, I've become steadily more supple and flexible. Older people are supposed to heal less readily, but my injuries have healed just as fast as, and sometimes faster than, anyone else's in the dojo. Older people are supposed to be resistant to learning, set in their ways, but I feel I'm a much faster learner now than in my youth. The fact of the matter is, I can do everything now that I could do in my twenties and a lot that I wouldn't have dreamed of doing.

We do grow old, wither, and die. But I'm convinced that most of the ill effects of aging are psychological and social and the consequence of our truly dreadful modern lifestyle. We are so sedentary, so addicted to sweets and fats and nicotine and alcohol that what appears as "normal" on the medical charts is actually quite sick. In this richest, most powerful nation in history, we have turned our energy toward comfort, convenience and goodies, and have managed to settle for a pathetically low definition of human potential — at any age.

Our classes thrived. The hard core grew to around forty students, and our teacher opened a large San Francisco dojo in addition to his operation in Mountain View, 40 miles south of the city. Two more teachers were brought in to share the increasing student load, and our training became somewhat more structured and formal.

A few months before the new dojo was to open, Leo and I attended a weekend *gasshuku* (extended period of practice) at Mountain View. Students bring sleeping bags to such events and spend the night on the mat. There is strenuous practice, morning meditation, meals together, a delicious sense of community, and deliciously aching muscles on Monday morning. After the session ended on Sunday afternoon, our teacher called me and Leo into his office and presented us with certificates of our promotion to second *kyu* (first-degree brown belt) and brand-new belts to go along with the rank.

It was June 1973, a gentle, golden afternoon. The promotions came as a surprise. Driving home, we settled back and let the satisfactions of the moment wash over us; the sensual ache of our muscles, the warmth of long-time friendship, the pleasure of sharing a strong, beautiful discipline. We arrived in the city at sunset and decided to go to a bar to celebrate. We ordered tall, foamy cocktails and drank them down as if we were teenagers who had just graduated from high school.

Karate has a fierce and powerful look to it — cries and shouts, bricks and boards shattered. Aikido seems gentle, almost dreamlike. I hardly know what to say when my friend, George, a karate teacher, teases me about the perils of my "nonviolent, nonfighting" art: "In twelve years of teaching karate," he says, "I've had fewer injuries at my school than you have in any one year."

This seeming paradox is solved by looking closely at the nature of the two arts. In karate, punches and kicks generally are pulled — that is, stopped short of their mark. There are not many falls; in fact, some karate students consider falling a disgrace. Aikido, on the other hand, requires that attack, response, and recovery run their full course. *Ukemi*, the art of falling, is developed in Aikido as in perhaps no other martial art. The accomplished Aikidoist has mastered a full complement of falls, from the silent, circular roll to the spectacular *sutemi* ("sacrifice of the body"), with its noisy, open-palm slap on the mat.

Once ukemi has been mastered, the fear of falling is transformed into the joy of flying. There's nothing quite like sailing through the air towards what seems certain disaster, then landing without a bruise or pang. However, flying is not without its risks. Some rough landings are probably inevitable. And should you come unhinged while in flight, there might be a serious crash.

Most injuries, in my experience, are incurred at the brown belt level, where you deal with advanced techniques without mastery of those techniques. Here, too, you are tempted to disregard the basic teaching of Aikido, which is simply to flow with daily practice rather than strive for some sort of linear "progress." Aikido is a lifelong discipline; it cannot be pushed. When you *try*, the feedback is swift and sure. During one three-week period, in fact, the four most advanced brown belts in our dojo all suffered serious injuries — a broken toe, torn ligaments in the elbow, a dislocated shoulder (mine), and an arm broken in three places. After the fact, we agreed that we had somehow sniffed the possibility of making black belt, and had become inflamed with ambition. The injuries were effective teachers. After recovering, we settled back into steady, goal-less practice. A year and a half more was to pass before all four of us made black belt.

From this and other experiences, I've become convinced that every student is responsible for his or her own safety on the mat, and that when injuries do occur, there are important lessons to be learned from them.

While serious injuries probably are avoidable, minor strains, muscle pulls, and miscellaneous aches and pains probably are not. The advanced Aikido student, like any dedicated athlete, often "plays hurt." Ace bandages and elastic knee and elbow supporters are a familiar part of the dojo scene. So when my friend Leo came up with a bothersome and persistent pain in his left knee, I considered it nothing out of the ordinary. Leo went on practicing, but less regularly than usual. By the autumn that followed our promotion to brown belt, I came to the alarming realization that my friend was displaying the by-now-familiar symptoms that often precede the end of an Aikido career. The times were not auspicious for him. Not only was the knee a bother, Leo was also having trouble with the early stages of a new novel. As he pulled away from practice, our relationship became strained. I found myself becoming increasingly demanding. The more he resisted coming to class with me, the more I urged. The more I urged, the more he resisted. Over lunch one day, we discussed this vicious cycle.

"I don't like myself in this role," I told him. "I'm getting to be a nag. I don't want to do it anymore."

"But George," he said, "I want you to push me. I *count* on

you to push me."

I told him I was going to stop. "I really want you to come to Aikido, but I'm not going to push you anymore. It's up to you."

My secret hope was that, once I stopped pushing, Leo would push himself. Surely he wouldn't stop entirely. But I was wrong. By January 1974, I knew that Leo was not coming back. Of our original class, I was the only one left. I kept practicing, but for a while the joy was gone.

Our dojo now had well over a hundred students, and the teachers could no longer give out promotions through intimate observation of each student. A notice appeared on the bulletin board: There would be formal examinations every four months.

"There's no competition in Aikido," one of our teachers told us. "Taking an exam gives you the opportunity to perform under pressure, with all your fellow students watching. Think of it as a gift."

My very first exam would be for first kyu (first degree brown belt), the most comprehensive exam prior to black belt. Three months before it was to take place, I agreed to serve as uke for the fouth kyu (blue belt) exam of my friend Arthur. A trim, fit man in his early forties, Arthur is a psychiatrist trained in both Freudian and Jungian analysis, a graduate of Harvard Medical School, an author and public speaker. The fourth kyu exam is relatively short and simple. Surely we would have no problems. We practiced a few times over a three-week period, until Arthur had all the required techniques down pat.

We were called out to the center of the mat before the eyes of our teachers and a long line of fellow students dressed in their gi and sitting in the formal Japanese meditation position. The teacher/examiner asked for the first technique. I attacked with a strike to the head, and Arthur brought me down to the mat. As I lay there for a moment, I became aware of the rather terrifying silence, and the unduly loud sound of our breathing. As we continued, our breathing became even louder. I tried to breathe more softly, but that only made things worse. Arthur's hands, I noticed, were beginning to shake. Were mine also shaking in response?

The exam was mercifully short, and there was no question but that Arthur had passed. "You know," he said, "I've been under all sorts of pressure—for example, my oral exams at medical school—but I must say I've never been this nervous."

A friend of mine, a scientist in a controversial field, a master of the cool comeback in public debate, once told me of going completely blank during his brown belt exam: "When my teacher called out the first technique, I simply didn't know what he was talking about. I heard words in a foreign language that didn't make any sense at all. So I just stood there, and when my uke came in with an attack—a strike to the top of the head—I just grabbed his hand and started grappling with him. It wasn't Aikido. It was survival. My teacher suggested I try the technique again, and it was even worse. Then he called out the next technique. By this time, I didn't know who I was or where I was. I had never heard of Aikido. I looked around and wondered. Who are these strange people dressed in white suits? Why are they sitting in this weird way?"

Forewarned, I decided I'd better be *over*prepared for my first kyu exam. For three months I practiced diligently, creating pressure situations for myself, working until every muscle ached, every tendon burned. The day of the exam, as cool as ice, I gave what I considered a lackluster performance, and was promoted to first kyu.

At this point, I had to face the fact that I might eventually be put up for black belt. I was fifty-one, but it wasn't unheard-of for people of my age to take the exam. The best thing, I decided, would be to go on practicing without thought of what might or might not come. But a few months after my first kyu exam, my teacher called me in to his office and suggested I drive to another city and witness a black belt exam, since I might someday face that challenge.

Spectators ringed the mat. Students in their gi knelt along the edges. An examining board of five ranking black belts from various dojos sat in judgment at one end. I joined a crowd clustered along the railing of a balcony overlooking the scene. The event had not yet begun. There were hushed voices, smiles of greeting for latecomers. It was like being at a wedding just before the music begins.

The host sensei clapped his hands and led all the Aikidoists in a deep bow to begin the exams. The first candidate flowed through his techniques without a false move. During the climactic three-person attack (*randori*), he easily eluded his attackers and sent them flying, as the spectators gasped and applauded. I had always wondered if the attackers in a black belt exam would come in with real intent. My doubts were put to rest; I was impressed by the speed and abandon of the attacks.

After a short intermission, the second candidate, a stocky, tough-looking man in his early thirties, came to the center of the mat with his uke. Right away I could tell something was wrong. The man's movements were rough and uncertain. My God, I thought, *he's not blending!* Things went from bad to worse; the exam was endless, one of those nightmares in which you seem to be struggling through mud. Time came for the randori, and the attackers roared in, hard and clean and true. Again and again the failing candidate was nailed. He took a hard blow to the belly, a chop to the neck. Twice he went down.

I was awestruck. Driving home, I tried to sort out my feelings about this art, which now seemed somehow darker and more mysterious. No, I wouldn't have it any other way. At the heart of the mystery lay the possibility of failure. Without that, without failure or even tragedy, neither the art nor the world would be so rich, so full of joy.

Months passed with no break in the steady rhythm of my practice. The endless succession of classes was rewarding precisely because it was, in the Zen sense, "nothing special." Sometimes, when the time came to go to class, I would be feeling particularly sluggish; on those occasions I would be tempted to do almost anything, even sit and watch television, rather than face myself once again on the mat. And sometimes I would give in to that inevitable human resistance against any change for the better. I knew full well, however, that when I did overcome my lethargy, I would be rewarded with a little miracle: I knew that, no matter how I felt on climbing the dojo stairs, two hours later — after hundreds of throws and falls—I would walk out into the night tingling and fully alive, feeling so radiant, in fact, that the night itself would seem to sparkle and gleam.

By this time, my closest companions at the dojo were the three other high-ranking brown belts, two handsome, athletic young men and Wendy, a woman in her early twenties who had wandered into the dojo one day, her aspect frail, humble; in four years that "waif" had persevered to become probably the most gifted Aikidoist among us. The four of us worked out together, kidded around, and served as *sempai* (assistant instructors) for beginning students.

More and more, Aikido was influencing other areas of my life. My experience as a lecturer was transformed. Instead of striking back at hostile questioners with hurtful repartee, I simply blended verbally, looking at things from the attacker's viewpoint. After a few months of this, another miracle: I no longer received hostile questions—not even one!

My book *The Ultimate Athlete* was inspired and informed throughout by the art of Aikido. I began giving workshop sessions, accompanied by Wendy whenever possible, that brought the essence of Aikido, without the strenuous throws and falls, to groups ranging in size from 20 to 600.

There were a few milestones. Wendy was given the chance to teach Aikido at a large public high school. To establish her credentials (she didn't yet have her black belt), she presented a demonstration before the student body. Four male fellow students, myself included, served as uke. With perfect composure, Wendy went through the equivalent of a black belt exam for an audience that was primed to hoot at the first false move. She showed her basic techniques against unarmed attack, her defense against *tanto* (dagger) and *bokken* (wooden sword). We ended, as usual, with a spirited randori.

As the four of us attacked her repeatedly, I had a sample of that quality of Aikido that so often is called "magical" or "occult": *I simply could not get to her.* It was as if she were surrounded by the kind of force field you see in *Star Trek*. Twice, just as I attacked, Wendy threw one of the other attackers into me, right into my belly, so that both of us went down. Dancing, whirling, ducking, she was constantly in motion—motion that to the untrained eye might seem aimless, anarchic, daring. Actually, every startling move was an attempt, at levels deeper than thought, to remain in the moving center of action, a place of calm and safety, "the still point of the turning world." Finally, I found a clear path for an attack. I rushed in with a whistling roundhouse chop to the side of her head. At the last instant, Wendy disappeared— that's exactly the way it seemed—and I tumbled head over heels to the mat. When we finished, our audience stood and cheered and whistled and stomped their feet.

Practice itself is the reward. The magical moments are something else again. I, too, have had a few of those moments by now, yet I'm at a loss for words to bring meaning from that moving center, that still point, back into this world. Maybe an exercise physiologist could videotape such a randori, submit it to minute scientific analysis, and publish a paper with explanatory diagrams and vectors. But that also would beg the question.

Let me try to say it another way: To be at the calm center of violent action is—"literally" and "by definition"—to be in harmony with the universe. But isn't this true of every art? Surely, everyone who pursues a discipline—painting, music, writing, dancing, skiing, weight lifting—eventually comes in contact with the underlying structure of the universe, "the way things are." At such moments, there is the possibility of surrender and grace. But the ancient paradox prevails: To pursue the moment of grace directly is to lose it. The moment is offered only after years of practice, and then it requires some sort of renunciation—of old habit patterns, of ego, even of personality.

> In order to arrive at what you do not know
> You must go by the way which is the way of ignorance.

On the mat, the words of T. S. Eliot took on new meaning for me—in my experience, in my muscles. There is no "answer." There is no "solution." There is practice.

I was up for black belt. My three-month-long ordeal had

begun. And it was true that my teacher was laying it on pretty thick. He himself would attack me, then resist being thrown until my ki was moving in just the direction he preferred — which might take several agonizing minutes. His instructions were elliptical, enigmatic. He wanted something of me — I couldn't tell exactly what. The nights got longer, the dojo colder. Somehow, with all that, I trusted him. I knew he would move with all the certainty of his intuition to my weakest point, just as he did with everyone up for the exam. There was one candidate who had a burning desire to make a name for himself. During the last two weeks of that young man's ordeal, our teacher never once looked at him or addressed him by name. "Tell what's-his-name to get out on that mat," he would say to no one in particular. These bizarre tactics were obviously effective: what's-his-name's exam was selfless and thus especially transcendent.

So he was taking me down a notch. Well, maybe I needed taking down a notch. Even without a black belt, I led workshops all over the country using insights and methods from the art. I did articles and books on the subject. Once, as a lowly blue belt, I had been on the cover of a national magazine — disgraceful, if you stop to think about it, what with so many Aikidoists who have devoted their whole lives to the art.

In a few weeks I would be up on the mat before friends, fellow students, strangers, and a board of examiners. The books and articles would do me no good in that setting. Under the pressure of the exam, a sloppy technique could not be disguised. A poor randori would lead to disaster no matter how well I'd written about it.

Though I trusted my teacher in the depths of my heart, my mind started playing tricks. What was going on between us? Was there a touch of mutual envy in our interactions? In any case, I found myself turning to another teacher at our dojo for additional training. Like my teacher, he was a fourth-degree black belt, but that was just about the only similarity between the two men. This teacher had studied in Japan under a master noted for his "firm" style. He was a fine technician, a stickler for the basics. An engineer by training, he often taught by breaking each technique down into detailed segments. Where my teacher talked of waterfalls and whirlpools and clouds of energy, this other teacher talked of fulcrums and lever-arms. I began going to his classes. I took several private lessons from him. The attention to detail was reassuring. I saw several of my techniques improving.

Still, I followed my teacher's classes faithfully, through that pre-Christmas night when I thought my heart might fail, through the very last moment of 1975. We were led in a special New Year's Eve training, from 11:00 P.M. to 1:00 A.M. When the horns blew and the bells rang, we simply continued our training. It was a good way to begin the year.

Three weeks before my exam, it was clear my techniques were solid. But something was lacking. One night, after I ran through an adequate randori, my teacher had an idea.

"Your techniques are okay," he said. "The only problem is in your *air*. It's the way you step on the mat. The key to your exam is going to be the way you get on the mat. The techniques will take care of themselves."

He mused a moment, then stepped off the mat.

"Why don't you try this? When you step on the mat, say to yourself, 'This is *my* mat.' Be expansive, generous. Look around at the other people on the mat. Be glad they're here. Welcome them. Welcome them to your mat."

He showed me what he meant, then gestured for me to give it a try. I stepped on the mat several times, saying silently "This is my mat." It felt good.

He continued, "Are you willing to take responsibility for this mat, to *own* it? That doesn't mean it isn't everybody else's mat, too. If you're big enough to own the mat as yours, you're big enough to let it be theirs, too."

Again and again, I stepped on and off the mat, feeling better each time.

"You can even be a little cocky, George. That's not too bad in this situation. I think this will be your most important practice from now until your exam — not your techniques, but how you get on the mat."

The next night when I was called to the mat, I wasn't there just "to take anything he can dish out," but to *own* the mat, to make it mine. This new *air,* and it alone, made a huge difference in my randori. I stepped on the mat expansively, looking around graciously at my attackers. When they came in, I welcomed them, moving swiftly to greet each one as he or she dashed toward me, and throwing them easily to the mat.

My teacher nodded thoughtfully. No way was he going to say anything faintly resembling a compliment. For the next randori, he motioned to three of the more rough-and-tumble students along the edge of the mat. "Come in crazy," he said. "Unorthodox attacks."

The three of them rushed in with jerky, off-center grabs and strikes, something more like street attacks. But it was *my* mat, so I was pleased to welcome these eccentric attackers. The only difference was, they went down quicker and faster.

The next few nights were even better. My sessions under attack at the center of the mat were transformed from ordeal to joy. I couldn't get enough randori. But my teacher wasn't going to give me a break. In the last few days before the exam, he chose to ignore me. Instead of setting up a randori for me, he let me sit on the edge of the mat and meditate.

Sunday, February 8, 1976, was a rainy day. I made the hour's drive south to Stanford University alone; I had to be there, at the Encina Gymnasium, in time to get dressed and warmed up. My God, practically everyone I knew would be coming down — my wife, children, mother, sister, friends, acquaintances, relatives, and relatives of relatives. Mike Murphy would be there, as would Leo who had put his gi back on and practiced privately with me during my three months' preparation.

The day was chill and damp, but the air inside the gym was suffused with a warmth and radiance I'd never before experienced. Eight candidates were up for their exams, and 150 Aikidoists from all over northern California were coming in to witness the exams and then to participate in an Aikido workshop led by a visiting sensei, a Japanese sixth-degree black belt. Spectators were arriving in increasing numbers.

My uke for the exam would be a tall, graceful twenty-three-year-old Stanford student named David. A fairly new black belt himself, David intended to dedicate his life to the art. Insofar as is possible in this culture, he was already living the life of a *samurai.* When I asked him to be my uke, he had responded almost in a formal manner: "I'd be honored to be your uke. I'd like to do what I can to make the exam a truly spiritual experience." David was an elegant uke, and I knew he would give me strong, flowing attacks. A half-hearted, off-target attack is no favor to the Aikidoist. For a spiritual experience to occur, clean, true strikes are required.

As the time for the exams came closer, the atmosphere in the gym, as at all such gatherings, became increasingly expectant, and I became aware that the Aikidoists of northern California and their friends and families were truly a community. I could feel that this whole community wanted each of the candidates to do well. It was as if I were circled about with love and support. Warming up, we candidates shook hands with our ukes and embraced, smiled at friends and relatives gathered around the mat, and exchanged best wishes for the exam.

The visiting sensei clapped his hands and led us in formal bows. There was a chant, an introductory talk, and the exams began. I was first on the mat, *my* mat. As is traditional, David and I began on our knees, samurai style, going through a series of eight attacks and pins as subtle and precise as a Japanese tea ceremony. The exam took us on to *hanmi handachi* (uke standing, nage kneeling), then techniques with both standing, then attacks from behind, knife attacks, body throws, free style, and finally randori — a half-hour of intense physical, mental, and spiritual experience. Everything flowed. Sometimes David and I, attacker and defender, smiled at each other. His care and respect for me were expressed in hard, true blows and graceful falls.

Ten minutes after the exams were finished, word was out that everyone had passed. The candidates moved from one happy group to another, accepting congratulations. I noticed the other teacher I had studied with standing to one side. He motioned me to come over, out of earshot of all the others.

"It's an old custom," he said, smiling and beginning to untie his own belt, "to pass on your belt. So if you'll just give me your brown belt to hold my jacket together . . . "

He handed me his belt—long, snaky, well used. The gesture was totally unexpected. Taking the belt, I realized I had never felt so much a beginner.

It happened that a few months after my promotion to black belt Wendy and I were giving an Aikido demonstration before a group of around one hundred people who hadn't witnessed the art. After playing the part of the attacker and being thrown around for ten minutes or so, I gave Wendy a knife and asked that she attack. She rushed at me (just as the young woman had rushed at my teacher the first time I saw Aikido), thrusting the knife at my belly. I stepped aside, spinning around and grasping her hand from the bottom. There were two whirling motions that had the feeling of *sswwish* and *whooossh*, with our bodies changing position, and I stepped beneath her arm and threw her in the direction in which she was already going. As I threw, I gave a twist of her wrist that opened her hand and let me take the knife. Wendy sailed through the air and landed with a loud slap 15 feet away, while I swept the knife back in a wide arc (as I had been taught) and held it aloft.

As I stood there, I realized that all eyes were on Wendy. *No one knew I had the knife.* It was one of those moments in which perceptions do a flip-flop.

Oh, my God, I said to myself, all in a period of maybe two or three seconds: they didn't see me take the knife away. In about half a second they're going to look over here at me and see the knife and they're going to believe I'm some sort of master and that Aikido is magical, and their eyes are going to bug out and they're going to gasp and cheer. It was just a regular Aikido technique that any Aikidoist could do, and isn't this awful and embarrassing?

Sure enough, they looked from Wendy to me and saw the knife, and their eyes bugged out and they gasped and cheered. It was awful. It was embarrassing. I loved it.

Sadaharu Oh with David Falkner

A Zen Way of Baseball (Excerpts)

One day — or rather, late one night — Arakawa-san confronted me as I was about to retire. "A discovery!" he said. He was waving a book in his hand. It was by yet another actor, the well-known Kikugoro. The celebrated performer had disclosed in his book that he had tried to incorporate Aikido into his own training. Specifically, what he had sought from Aikido was the idea of *ma*, the space and/or time "in between."

"This," Arakawa-san said, was the "essence of what we are looking for. All that remains is to apply it. Now you may wonder how this is to be done? Here we have a chance, because we have a living example to learn from."

He had me read a chapter of the book. This excerpt told of Kikugoro's visit to the great Aikido Master Ueshiba Morihei Sensei. Kikugoro waited around and waited around until the Sensei would speak to him. He asked, "Sir, what is *ma* ?"

To this, the great teacher coolly replied, "If that's all you've got to ask me, you must be a lousy actor."

I was puzzled. I handed the book back to Arakawa-san, with no idea as to what I was supposed to have drawn from it. He could barely contain himself.

"Can you imagine a guy saying something like that to Kikugoro!"

I nodded, still uncomprehending. "So?"

"So, the Sensei is a living master. He is there for us as well as for Kikugoro. We will go to him."

When we got back to Tokyo, we took our first trip to the *dojo* together, seeking the widsom of Ueshiba Sensei. Twenty years have passed since that day, and I know now what I did not know then. Ueshiba Sensei was not only a great master of Aikido, he was its founder. Through his own study of all the ancient martial arts, principally in the uses of the sword, he had distilled those old forms, their essential movements, into this new art, Aikido, weaponless self-defense. People all over the world traveled to see him. Among those who knew, he was a living connection to the legends of our history.

His *dojo* in Shinjuku was an unpretentious wooden structure attached to his living quarters. Beyond the opened sliding panels of his windows, trees were visible, their spring branches delicately touching an old-style gabled roof. The *dojo* was rather small, perhaps twenty tatami, its simple wooden walls decorated sparsely with a paper calendar and some sayings written in brushwork by the Master. With all that I didn't know about Ueshiba Sensei that first day, it was very much like walking into yet another new world.

Arakawa-san and I, as any other students, sat at the far edges of the room, on our heels in the proper position, toe touching toe. All of the fledgling warriors wore combinations of white or white and black blouses with *hakama.* Ueshiba Sensei alone was dressed in a full-flowing black kimono. The time I first saw him, he was approaching eighty. His appearance and manner, though, were vigorous. He had a long, wispy, snow-white beard and moustache along with bushy white eyebrows. Severity and kindliness both seemed etched into his features. He looked more like a fifteenth-century village elder than a master of the martial arts — that is, until he began to perform the movements he had perfected over a lifetime. The beauty and power of these movements were astonishing. Trained athletes or dancers could not easily have duplicated them. They were the fruits of unparalleled accomplishment. When he finished his session, we spoke to him. It was Arakawa-san's turn to play the straight man.

"What is *ma*?" he asked, deliberately echoing Kikugoro. But the Sensei answered him differently.

"*Ma* exists because there is an opponent."

100

"I understand," Arakawa-san said. This seemed to jibe with something he was thinking. He took me by the elbow.

"You see," he said to me, "in the case of baseball it would be the pitcher and the batter. The one exists for the other; they are caught, both, in the *ma* of the moment. The pitcher tries in that instant of time and space to throw off a batter's timing; the batter tries to outwit the pitcher. The two are struggling to take advantage of the *ma* that exists between them. That's what makes baseball so extraordinarily difficult."

The Sensei looked at us both as if we were crazy men. His eyes seemed to darken as he turned them on Arakawa-san. He remained silent for a moment, then said:

"I will tell you something, you're a lousy teacher!"

I tried not to smile as I saw Arakawa-san lower his head, bowed with almost the same words that had been heaped on Kikugoro. And yet — I couldn't put my finger on it exactly — there was something a little too predictable in all this.

"You see, you're no good when you're thinking of *ma*," Ueshiba Sensei continued. "*Ma* is there *because* the opponent is there. If you don't like that situation, all you have to do is eliminate the *ma* between you and the opponent. That is the real task. To eliminate the *ma*. Make the opponent yours. Absorb and incorporate his thinking into your own. Become one with him so you know him perfectly and can be one step ahead of his every movement. . . ."

This was the fundamental idea of Aikido itself, within which *ma* was only one of a number of important concepts. Arakawa-san bowed respectfully to the Sensei, and we were soon on our way.

And thus began the first really intensive phase of my training with Arakawa-san. Although I did not understand exactly what he was leading me to, I trusted him. I believed that Aikido, as Arakawa-san promised, would help me, although I did not actually practice it. This I was forbidden to do because, I was told, "injuries and martial arts are one and the same."

"How can I learn then?" I asked.

But Arakawa-san would not even consider it. "I can't afford

101

to let you get hurt," he said. "I'll go through it myself and learn what is necessary, and you'll have all the information you need passed on to you. Perhaps you should go to the *dojo* and observe. You may learn things for yourself."

I then went to the *dojo* whenever I could, sometimes with Arakawa-san, sometimes without. I learned rather quickly that he had been a regular there for some time, that none of this was really new to him. He had, apparently, begun taking lessons there around 1960 with both Ueshiba Sensei and one of his assistants. He was absolutely scrupulous in his attendance, never missing a class whenever he was in Tokyo — and he was absolutely devoted to his Master. This became painfully apparent to me when I was a spectator. I watched Arakawa-san suffer manhandlings that would have left a weaker person gathering the remains of his own carcass. And this he always did in the best of spirits — and with the deepest sense of respect for what he was being taught. There is an atmosphere in the *dojo* that is very hard to convey to anyone not familiar with the setting — but it involves a sense of courtesy and respectfulness that is too often not duplicated elsewhere in life. We Japanese make much of fidelity to form, but in the *dojo*, respect and veneration for your teacher live in your spirit. For, after all, you are there in ignorance as one seeking enlightenment. You may, as I was, be there following your own First Mind (the first and strongest longing you have for a life path). Even as I watched him get battered, my sense of belief and trust in Arakawa-san grew.

"I've come to think that there is something more important than *ma* between yourself and the opponent," he told me one day. "How shall I put it? It is really more a question of how you coordinate your five senses. Put differently, it's about fully controlling the movements of your own body. Winning over yourself rather than the opponent."

I tried to understand everything Arakawa-san said to me. It was hard. There are things, after all, that words can never explain. But he was always patient with me. Many of our talks took place in his car as we went back and forth from *dojo* to home or from home to stadium — and whenever he saw me grow confused, he would invariably stop the car and begin gesturing out whatever concept he was trying to explain. Once, we got out of the car entirely and, in the middle of the street, enacted the *ma* of the batter alone, incorporating the doubts and desires he inevitably had to contend with in facing a pitcher.

"So you see," he said to me, with traffic whizzing by us, "even if you've got your timing right, it's no use if your body doesn't fully respond. You've got to coordinate your mind, your body, and your batting skill."

These theories were quite interesting, but the problem, of course, was how to apply them. Try as I might, the fog that had plagued me through three years of pro ball would not lift. While I coordinated things in my mind, my muscles just would not go along. I wondered whether Aikido would really do any good. Our first league games in April came and went, and I had little to show for it. At the end of the month, I had managed to hit only two home runs.

One day I went to the *dojo* early to watch the trainees practice. Arakawa-san was to join me later. When he arrived, I was absorbed in watching what can only fairly be described as a spectacle. On the floor for the better part of half an hour was Ueshiba Sensei — a man who stood barely five feet tall — throwing off big, hefty trainees one after the other, as though they were bags of feathers. They came at him in twos and threes and seemed to go flying in sixes and sevens. It was incredible! Or it was all prearranged.

Arakawa-san insisted it was absolutely genuine, that Ueshiba Sensei was demonstrating a basic technique to escape from multiple attackers called *Yamabiko no michi,* or the path of an echo. Even though Arakawa-san had seen this before, he was just as impressed as I was when we took our leave that day.

"Can you believe it, Oh?" he said. "How can it be that there can be so much strength in a man?"

I obviously had no answer.

"Of course it was not strength we were witnessing today, but the extension of power. Today," he explained, "we have had the most amazing demonstration of the use of *ki*. We saw what the spirit-power in a man extended beyond himself can accomplish."

But the word *ki*, as I understood it then, had both a good and a bad connotation. I suggested that to Arakawa-san.

"Of course," he said. "There is an old saying, 'Sickness comes from *ki*.' That means that you will get sick if you think you are sick. Likewise, you will be strong if you discipline your mind to think you are. Don't you see? Make use of an opponent's strength and yours will be doubled. What Ueshiba Sensei did was in the words of his oral instruction:

> *Many enemies*
> *Surrounded me*
> *In attack.*
> *Thinking of them as one,*
> *I do battle.*

That is what we have just witnessed. The moment you are able to draw another's *ki* to that which you extend from yourself, you have more power than you could ever have imagined yourself to have."

What was Aikido anyway, I wondered? Was it a mental activity or a form of the martial arts? By this demonstration there seemed to be no doubt what it could effect, but theory and practice when it came to baseball were almost impossible to reconcile. How could I begin to do in a batter's box what Ueshiba Sensei did in the middle of the *dojo* floor? Rather than feeling elated at what I had just seen, I felt even more confused than I had in the past.

*   *   *

I do worry that people might mistake Arakawa-san for some strange practitioner of the occult. He is much too down to earth, very conservative and modest in his lifestyle, one for whom spiritual philosophy leads inevitably to life practice. When he told me that I was to understand what it meant to bat on one foot, he did not mean that I should go off somewhere and comtemplate my navel. His meaning was hard, hard work. The difference was that now that I had come to this gamble of last resort, I also had reached a point where Aikido had become absolutely necessary rather than merely complementary to what I did. Without Aikido, I would not learn to stand on one foot, I would not "understand" it.

The problem, both of us knew, was gaining balance. This is what our work focused on for the remainder of the season. If this sounds like a technical problem, it is. But if it is thought of in technical terms alone, it will be misunderstood. The most obvious thing to say about standing on one foot in order to hit a baseball coming at you at ninety miles an hour is that it requires as much belief as technique. In Aikido, though, belief and technique are one.

One of the first things a student of Aikido learns is to become conscious of his "one point." This is an energy or spirit-center in the body located about two fingers below the navel. While many martial and spiritual arts make use of this center, it is essential in the practice of Aikido. Aikido, which means the Way of Spirit Harmony, requires tremendous balance and agility, neither of which are possible unless you are perfectly centered. So much of our early work was getting me to pose simply with the one point in mind. I would get up on my one foot and cock my bat, all the while remaining conscious of this energy center in my lower abdomen. I discovered that if I located my energy in this part of my body I was better balanced than if I located it elsewhere. If I located my energy in my chest, for example, I found that I was too emotional. I also learned that energy located in the upper part of the body tends to make one top-heavy. Balance and a steady mind are thus associated with the one point. In Aikido you inevitably deal with both the strategy and the psychology of combat. *Uke* and *nage* are the names given to attacker and defender. Aikido takes into account the action of both. If the attacker, for example, is mentally ahead of the defender, his tactics will probably be successful. The defender, not really being prepared, will react instinctively, bracing for assault by bringing his shoulders up in a protective manner — thus shifting his balance away from the center of his body, where strength and agility must be concentrated. So this problem of *uke* and *nage* became a basis for exploring what it was to stand one leg facing a pitcher.

Aikido is different from other martial arts in the clear distinction it makes between the directing of energy and the gathering of strength. Even Judo, which relies on expropriating the movements of an opponent, rests on a lot of pushing and tugging. There is no particular emphasis on the spirit-energy that directs the strength. Aikido, though, as its name suggests, is about the projection of spirit-energy, or *ki*. It is the most spiritual of the martial arts.

The notion that one use *ki* in action is really the simplest of ideas. But seeing it employed, as I did, in the thick of battle, with bodies flying this way and that, can be deceptive. As Arakawa-san told me, "The same *ki* that is available to a Master like Ueshiba Sensei is available to anyone. *Ki* is universal energy." One day in the *dojo* Arakawa-san and Ueshiba Sensei demonstrated something. Ueshiba Sensei took a long wooden pole and held it before him in the ready position of a swordsman. Arakawa-san took a baseball bat and hit the sword as hard as he could. The pole in Ueshiba Sensei's hands did not move at all. It was as though Arakawa-san had hit the side of a tree.

"You have seen focusing of energy," I was told. "This is what achieving balance can do."

As long as I had this fatal hitch in my swing, I could not begin to think of using *ki* in my batting. But posing on one foot, having eliminated the hitch, the goal of using *ki* did not seem so farfetched — if I could learn to steady myself enough.

Earlier in the season, when we had simply been trying to overcome my hitching habit, Arakawa-san had had yet another discussion with Ueshiba Sensei about the problem. The Sensei, not being much of a baseball fan, had cut the talk short.

"Look," he said, "the ball comes flying in whether you like it or not, doesn't it? Then all you can do is wait for it to come to you. To wait, this is the traditional Japanese style. Wait. Teach him to wait."

With this new pose that could be secured only by gaining real balance, the notion of waiting became the means to an end. Arakawa-san became intrigued then obsessed with the idea. All that he knew about baseball, all that he had ever studied and thought about, seemed to flow into this one idea.

"This will be easier said than done," he told me, "but we will learn how to wait." He had me reread *Musashi*, reminding me that it had been Musashi's great task to learn the secret of balance through waiting. Waiting. This was the key. In waiting, said Musashi, one learns the "Immovable Self-Discipline," the ultimate aim of which was to "acquire the Body of a Rock."

"The Body of a Rock!" The image entered my mind as simply as a bird alighting on a branch. If I could not take seriously the idea of pursuing Babe Ruth, the goal of perfecting what was in my own body seemed entirely natural.

We worked on exercises in concentration that would enable me to wait. All of Arakawa-san's training, all the hours we had spent talking and reading mattered now. Because so much of what we did then was geared to the mental side of the game, it is hard to describe. Concentration, like everything else in Aikido, is both a spiritual and a physical term. Its goal is the unity or harmony of all forces that are employed. Mind, body, technique are one in Aikido. This oneness is the expression of nature. And so from the start Arakawa-san enabled me to understand that our work was not to triumph over natural forces but to become one with them, to discover that what was in and outside my body were part of a single force even when they seemed to be divided in opposition.

"This business of standing on one leg," Arakawa-san purred, "we discover is a matter of life and death. Accordingly, when you step into the batter's box, you may never do it casually. Too much is at stake. The center in your lower abdomen prepares you for any contingency just as if you were a warrior awaiting the moves of a deadly opponent. Likewise, when you are good enough to have mastered *ma*, you bring your opponent into your own space; his energy is then part of yours. Together you are one. This is what concentration can bring, why it is so crucial. So you must locate it properly, in the one point, and be conscious of it at all times, even when you're walking down the street or sitting at a meal. Once your concentration is thus focused, you automatically begin to see things better. In a state of proper concentration, one is ready for anything that comes along. Even a baseball hurtling toward you at ninety miles an hour!"

I thus discovered, in standing on one leg, that concentration, maximum concentration, is something natural to *ma*. It is necessary to reacquire only because somewhere in our long history we have forgotten it.

Because I continued to hit, my confidence increased as I went along. I began to see how important it was to be united in mind and body—as the samurai were—if I was to be more than a mediocre hitter. Hitting a baseball is a matter of timing. How simple that sounds—but how difficult. All the craft of pitching goes into throwing off the batter's timing. On one foot or two, what difference does it make if a batter's mind says "fastball" but his body somehow reacts to a change of pace? If your body is not as one with your mind, you are lost. And no amount of strength you put into your swing will help. You can tell yourself anything, but it is something else to join what it is you know to the snap of your wrists and swing of your hips.

What Arakawa-san and I both knew was that my batting on one foot was meaningless as long as I felt unsteady. We were both blessed by Fortune that good results continued to come from my new pose. But it was more a gift of time than achievement. Time to practice, practice, practice. Time to learn what it "meant" to be balanced on one foot.

I practiced with a mirror. Over and over again, I stood there under Arakawa-san's watchful eye, trying to pick up things in the position of my body as I swung. I stood on my left leg with my right leg in the air. Sometimes I saw myself as a dog at a hydrant, and I laughed myself off balance. Or I would stand there and see my leg, after a minute or so, begin to quiver, and would wonder why God permitted scarecrows to hit home runs! Most often, I scrutinized myself as though I were a pitcher. I kept imagining how I would throw this one-legged fellow off balance: *He's ready for the hard one, I'll throw him a terrible forkball. He's looking for a curve. I'll throw him one that jumps over his bat.*

My objective at the time was to root myself as powerfully as I could. I did this by imagining ki power as a fat iron bar that ran straight down from my kneecap through my toes into the ground. Rooted thus, I would take my swings again and again. I don't know how many swings I would take in a single training session, but there were surely hundreds.

I would simply pose this way, too, and whenever I was in the *dojo* working along with Arakawa-san, I would have my balance checked by a slight push or tug on my arm. Some days I felt that I was improving; other days I would seem to be as un-balanced as before. If I truly were an iron bar, I would be strong enough not to be bent by anyone. I confessed this to Arakawa-san.

"Well, what kind of bar have you turned into?" he asked.

"What *kind*?" The question seemed absurd. I laughed. "I don't know."

"You must. Concentrate."

"Well . . . " I forced myself to visualize the image I had created. An iron bar is after all an iron bar. Eventually I described the bar as a straight line from the knee through the top of my shoe.

"Very good," Arakawa-san said. "Now you say this bar is fat?"

"That's right."

"You don't need to make it fat. *Ki* can be thin, too. But take your image seriously. Now, an iron bar can be bent. You know the wrestler Takamiyama?"

He was referring to a popular Hawaiian-born sumo wrestler. I nodded. Everyone knew Takamiyama.

"In his demonstrations of strength, he bends iron bars," Arakawa-san said.

"Yes?"

"Yes."

"What are you telling me?" I asked.

"I'm telling you that you must make yourself into a bar that cannot be bent."

And how was I to do that? By envisioning this bar not as a straight pole but as something like a gymnastic bar attached to supports at either end. The ground, the earth, instead of being a passive receiver, was also to be seen as an active support. Thus no amount of opposing strength would be able to bend the bar.

And so we continued, trying to incorporate this new image of a parallel bar that was my own *ki*, looking for the strengthened balance that was fundamental for my new pose. Slowly, day by day, I was able to increase the time I could stay steadily on one foot. The one foot was now an iron bar joined or fused to the iron of the earth. I could feel myself grow more secure. My confidence increased not only because I was having good results at the plate but because I saw tangible progress in my employment of *ki*.

I often get the feeling that when people ask me about the use of Aikido in baseball, they are looking for a secret source of strength. It does not matter how many times I suggest that this is a wrong-headed approach, the question keeps coming up. So I had best be as clear as possible before I go any further. *Aikido and the use of ki power have nothing to do with strength.* How to show this?

During this period, several of the Giants players who were also interested in Aikido used to make occasional visits to Ueshiba Sensei's *dojo*. These players became somewhat more involved in the actual exercises than I did. Sometimes when they were by themselves, they practiced one of the elementary throwing techniques of Aikido on the tatami floor. The movement employed is very swift, very graceful, and most effective. It is called a *tenkan* movement, which denotes pivoting (as opposed to the *irimi* movement, which involves thrusting). The use of *ki* in this movement enables *nage* to harmonize with the *ki* of his attacker, *uke*, to join his movement by this pivoting movement and, by so doing, much in the manner of a vortex, add unbelievable centrifugal force to the act of throwing. The actual throw involves nothing more than the placing of a single finger in the small of *uke*'s back, and the fall is as complete as the felling of a tree! It is a most amazing thing to see, and it has absolutely nothing to do with the employment of physical strength. A child might do it easily.

A more vivid example occurred many years later when a team of American all-stars came through Japan and some of the players expressed an interest in my one-legged batting. Among these stars were Pete Rose, Rod Carew, Mike Schmidt, and "The Bull," Greg Luzinski. Arakawa-san, wanting to explain my form to the all-stars, got Luzinski to help him illustrate. With the assistance of an interpreter, he said, "I'll show you how. Oh manages to bat on one foot. I will hold out arm horizontally; you try to bend it."

"The Bull" told us later that he thought the interpreter had not translated the request accurately. Arakawa-san is just under five and a half feet tall and had to look up to Luzinski when he talked to him.

"Are you sure? What will you do if I break your arm?" Luzinski asked.

Arakawa-san smiled and replied ever so softly, "Let's worry about that later. Try it. See what happens."

At first, Luzinski was a little tentative with his strength. The arm did not move an inch. He smiled sheepishly, looking around at the small circle of people who had gathered to watch.

"Well, all right," Luzinski said, "here I go." He now tried with all his might. He turned red from the effort. Nothing! Arakawa-san's arm remained rigid and motionless.

"Fantastic!"

"Oriental magic!"

"What strength!"

The foreign pressmen were very taken in by this seeming feat of great strength. But it was not that at all. It was the use of *ki*, in a rather elementary way. Luzinski used strength, but Arakawa-san used *ki*. If you are dubious, this is an exercise you can try for yourself. No prior knowledge of Aikido or *ki* is necessary.

To do this, get a partner, someone in the room with you, a friend, anyone, and instruct that person to hold his arm out rigidly and with all his might resist your effort to bend it at the elbow. Unless this person is very, very much stronger than you, you will succeed in bending his arm. Now instruct this partner to hold out his arm again and, instead of having him contract his muscles in a pose of strength, have him imagine that power flows from a point below his navel in a direct line to his shoulder and then through and beyond his arm, beaming outward from his fingertips through the wall of the room you are in. Make sure you instruct your partner to keep his hand open (rather than clenched in a fist) and to consciously forego all thought of using great strength to resist you. The chances are that you will now have no more luck in bending your partner's arm than Luzinski did when he tried with Arakawa-san.

*　　*　　*

And so the 1962 season came to an end. And what had been accomplished? By year's end, I had not only improved my batting form, I had achieved previously unimaginable results. Our training enabled me to hit thirty-eight home runs, twenty-eight of them coming after July 1. I raised my batting average to .272 and my RBI total to eighty-five, both career highs. Most important, I won the home-run and RBI titles for the Central League that year. I cannot begin to say what joy this brought. I cried over this. I remember the feeling of my swollen eyelids! And I remember feeling also that these titles had nothing to do with me! It might have been different if Arakawa-san had been merely a batting coach whose advice in the future I could have accepted or rejected as I chose. But he was so much more now. I could no more choose my way with him than I could with my father or brother. I received no particular praise from the Master of the Arakawa School that year. I accepted that. I knew he had his reasons.

"Think of it this way, Oh," he said to me. "Gain and loss are opposite sides of the same coin. It is best to forget them both."

It turned out that Arakawa-san had all the while been making his own plans. These had little to do with my having won a title or two. His mind was already in the future.

"You are ready now," he said, "to truly acquire the Body of a Rock."

112

I suggested that this was what I had been striving to achieve all season, but he replied that there was far more to what we were doing than simply gaining balance.

"Immovable Self-Discipline comes only when you master the use of *ki*. And this you have only just begun to do."

To that end, he said, we were now going to turn to the use of the Japanese sword.

Richard Moon

Aikido and Healing:
Does this Stuff Really Work?

I was deeply involved in yoga when I felt an attraction toward the kinds of movements that are taught in the martial arts. I began looking at the various forms and was thinking about training in one of them. However, as my study at the time was concerned with spiritual awareness, healing, and non-violence, it was difficult to find a martial art that did not conflict with my values.

Many of my friends were concerned that study of martial arts inevitably attracts violence. Clearly, history teaches that guns lead to bigger guns; that wars have never ended wars. Training martial skills did not seem as though it would resolve in me the dilemma between the desire for peace and a growing sense of responsibility for power. Yet neither did total receptivity, weakness, or avoidance of power seem like an answer.

One night I went to the local college to teach my yoga class. A man came in and asked if I was there for the Aikido class.

"No, I am here to teach yoga," I replied.

"Well, we have a scheduling conflict," he said, "because I am supposed to teach Aikido in this room tonight."

I asked him to tell me about Aikido.

"It is a non-violent martial art," he responded, "based on the loving protection of all beings, protection which extends to include the attacker. It is not based on strength since the attacker's force is not opposed; instead one blends with it."

Now, to fight with an opponent or to run from one — these are old solutions. But to neutralize his attack by blending with it, by becoming one with it, was not only creative but satisfied my most far-reaching desire for peace and an ability to handle power and energy, and potential physical violence. This Aikido practitioner said: "Do not respond by becoming a physical threat to your opponent but by blending with his attack as a flow of spiritual energy."

My first Aikido practice was to handle the scheduling conflict over the room by blending with the situation. I asked him to teach, and I took my first Aikido class that night. Halfway through the break, my yoga students came up and asked if we could have our class. We did, but it was already too late for me. From my first roll I fell in love with Aikido. I was transformed by the perceptions and understanding of power revealed through the art. It was obvious I had run into something of importance for me. How much so I couldn't even begin to guess.

As I came into more contact with the art, and especially with the memoirs of the Master, I could see O'Sensei was a man who had transcended traditional limits of perception about the dynamics of creation. He had made a quantum leap beyond the world of apparent form, beyond physical matter, mass and motion, to the subtler energy forces which shape the physical universe. He had seen beyond duality to the unity of the universal system and moved in response to energy laws which were not as yet generally recognized.

There is a universe unfolding in which change is the only constant. The power that drives this evolving universe is *ki*. *Ki* literally translated means steam, implying expanding pressure or potential, untapped or unmanifested force or power. Simply translated *ki* means life energy.

Through what O'Sensei described as the gift of the *Aiki kame* or the divine spirit of Aikido, he brought forth an art which transcends humanity's identity as isolated physical beings and invites us to the awareness of ourselves as energy beings of the universal spirit. By precise balance of the known with that which is as yet unknown, O'Sensei achieved critical mass in the moment, producing the white heat necessary to melt understanding and bring forth Aikido.

Whatever he was doing, as a martial artist he was a legend in his own lifetime. He had the reputation of being unbeatable. Though people came from all over the world to challenge him, no one could claim to have as much as laid a finger on him without his permission. He had developed a mastery unparalleled in the world, a state-of-the-art martial form. Yet achieving this pinnacle of success, O'Sensei said:

> "Victory at the expense of others is not true victory. Winning means winning over the mind of discord in yourself. Aiki is not a technique to fight with or defeat the enemy. It is a way to reconcile the world and make human beings one family."

Here was a martial art which merged the handling of power with the ability to love.

A friend had a dream in which O'Sensei showed him a sword so incredibly sharp that it cut things together. This describes the effect Aikido has had in my life. O'Sensei showed a world of infinite possibilities open to one able to unify the energetic forces of being. Something that radiated from the quality of his being changed my life.

Evolutionary force is an indication that the universe is in an ongoing process of unfoldment. Aikido is the study of total participation in this unfolding of existence. It's almost contradictory to think of Aikido as a martial art because its focus is not on destruction but on the enhancement of life energy.

In O'Sensei's words:

> "Aikido keeps all beings in constant growth and development and serves for the completion of the universe."

> "True budo is a work of love. It is a work of giving life to all beings, and not killing or struggling with each other. Love is the guardian diety of everything. Nothing can exist without it. Aikido is the realization of love."

Fifteen Years Later

It was almost light out when I woke up. I was in San Diego visiting my mother. Hearing voices I dressed and went towards her room. Her door was ajar and I could see her talking to my aunt.

"I've got bad news," she said. Her voice dropped; there was a pause. "Gene called from Minneapolis. Bil was in an accident."

Gene is my younger brother and a doctor. Bil is my older brother and a wild card.

"It's serious," she said. "Gene's afraid he's going to die."

He was at a stoplight on his scooter and a drunk hit him from behind. The guy said he never saw Bil, who was knocked off his scooter and hurt his head. He wasn't wearing a helmet. What they told me produced an image of Bil falling off the scooter and bumping his head. It wasn't until much later that I found out he had flown about 30 feet through the air, and his scooter had been completely demolished.

They'd taken Bil to Hennepin County General where my younger brother Gene had been an intern. Gene had spoken to the doctor in charge, whose prognosis had been: "The head trauma is severe. The next twenty-four hours will be critical. There is a good chance he will not make it."

He was in the ICU on life support systems, unconscious and suffering from internal hemorrhaging. They had drilled holes in the skull to relieve the pressure from the bleeding. If he held, there was a good chance his condition would stabilize. Even so, there was no telling whether Bil would wake up and if he did, who he would be.

I was numb from the rush of emotional energy accompanying my shock. I thought maybe the reports were exaggerated. At any rate, my fears didn't square with other intuitive feelings in myself Aikido had trained me to recognize. I thought maybe I was just afraid to deal with the truth, but I've since come to trust these feelings from my right brain sensory awareness.

"He'll be all right," I said assuredly, almost as if someone else were speaking. The voice seemed to come out of an inner quiet.

Through Aikido practice, the unification of mind, body, and spirit makes intuition accessible to the conscious awareness. At this point in my training I wasn't thinking about it, I was just doing it — like a good technique where the body moves without plan or understanding.

To be able to tap the realm of unknown knowledge and intuition has been a major goal of my study of Aikido. When the energies of *uke* (the person who attacks and symbolizes any life situation) and *nage* (the person who throws in response to the pressure of that situation) flow together, the intelligence of the unified energy system generates and directs the physical, or, in this case, emotional, movement. For this to happen, mind, body, and spirit must stay fused and grounded. Relaxation and centering are basic, whether in the application of Aikido techniques or the activity of daily life. When O'Sensei would ground himself no one then could move or upset him. Through this physical dimension he demonstrated this possibility in the emotional sphere.

I went home and waited, every moment expecting the phone to ring. Days passed. Nothing. It became a week. Still nothing.

My mother wanted to go to Minneapolis, but Gene discouraged her. After a week and a half she decided to go there for Bil's birthday. He turned forty in coma.

A couple of days later she called, very excited; Bil seemed to have opened his eyes. The first filament of hope streamed into our lives.

Infused with her excitement, I felt able to go on a trip to Yosemite. When I got back, however, the message was grim: there's been no further response; if anything, Bil was sinking deeper. I felt something sink inside of me. I'd been so sure that Bil was going to be all right. Now fear started to overcome me and I saw the seriousness of the situation. I began to doubt my intuitive perception, and I drifted into a fog of depression.

Aikido trains us to access intuition, but what intuition is and how it works is beyond my ken. Though I have used it many times, on the other side of my brain the voice of a skeptic is still audible. Louder than those doubts, I felt, in another way altogether, beyond the battle of faith and skepticism, that something was being asked of me.

Knowing my brother's condition was deteriorating, I started thinking about going to Minneapolis. The thought stayed with me through the night and I woke up with it the next morning. My sense of concern and responsibility was growing.

I went to teach my class that night and, as often happens in training, the details of my personal life began to fade. Driving home, the thoughts of my brother came back stronger; and the impluse that had been driving me to be with him intensified. About ten that night, still enumerating all the reasons I couldn't go, I called the airport. There was a midnight flight arriving in Minneapolis at six in the morning.

My mother was planning to return home in the morning but I called, thinking if she knew I was flying there, she might change her plans. She and Gene both felt there was no sense in my coming. They felt, as I was willing to make the trip, I probably could do more for Bil when he woke up. There was certainly nothing I could do yet. It would be futile to come just to sit by his bedside with them.

I contacted my inner self as the center of my experience. I was going to take my one shot with Bil. I phoned the airlines and booked the flight. I called my mother back and told her I was coming in at six. She was too tired to argue with me and said she'd pick me up at the airport.

What I was doing really scared me. The image of myself charging in on my ego trip, an idiot on a big white horse, and then having nothing happen, chilled my resolve. But, strangely, the hardest feeling was the opposing sense there was something within my power I could do and it was imperative I go. I feared that power more than anything. I got on the airplane and fell asleep.

I woke up as we touched down in Minneapolis. Though it was still early morning the sultry heat of the end of the summer was already permeating the city as we drove towards town. An internal anxiety and pressure were taking my attention. I recognized the symptoms of an intense energy rush.

Through a partner's attack Aikido teaches us to utilize and not resist this energy. Looking back I see this preparatory rush as an important part of the healing process. At the time I was mainly conscious of an immense amount of energy — the energy that the situation called up. I was doing my best Aikido to try to get myself there.

After seven hours of travel I finally pulled up in front of the hospital. The last time I'd been there was years ago with Bil and a mutual friend. We'd gone to see my younger brother Gene who was then an intern.

This time it was different. When I walked in I felt as though I were invisible. We moved through the lobby, and the reality of what we were facing pressed in on me. I realized Bil had been laying there unconscious for almost a month, oblivious to the bustling hospital surrounding him. A pressure within me was pulsating. My breathing deepened to handle this increasing energy.

We took the elevator upstairs. We walked past rooms filled with machines, past nurses and orderlies with their carts. They wheeled someone by us on his or her way to surgery. There were people sitting in the halls in wheelchairs. Step by step the intensity grew.

Suddenly my mother pointed me toward one of the doorways. "Here," she said. I stepped into the room. My brother Bil was lying on the bed. Even in the comatose state there was movement in the right side of his body; the left side had been paralyzed. His head moved about as if he were dreaming. There were low, unintelligible growling sounds coming from him. The pounding pulse inside me intensified. I thought even the nurses could hear it. Consciously I had no idea why I was there or what I had come to do.

I watched the nurses move him like a big doll. They put a tube through his nose to his stomach. There was a needle in his arm and an oxygen mask on his face. His right arm was tied down to prevent him from pulling the tubes out. They cleaned and dressed him; all the time they worked they talked to him but there was no response.

I sat by him; I stared at him and tuned in. All the medical personnel left the room except one nurse. My mother was still there and my brother's friend Christine had come into the room. They were both standing by the end of the bed. I gradually moved closer to him. I put my hands on him, one hand on his neck and one hand on his face. I talked to him. I called to him. My voice echoed in my ears. I got no response.

In my study of Aikido I've given extensive attention to the aspect of *ki* healing, i.e., *ki* or life energy as it relates to the healing process. Through a series of practices starting with centering, relaxing and grounding I had trained to conduct conscious *ki* into the center of an injury. I remember experiencing *ki* in its flowing as a golden, honey-like substance, and I was impressed with how tangible it was. I had used *ki* healing a number of times but never in a situation like this. I began. From a realm of awareness I would describe as intuitive I found myself taking Bil's hand and moving its position into the form of an Aikido technique called *nikkyo*.

Nikkyo is a joint lock which when properly applied can bring a larger attacker to his knees with very little force. When applied with sudden or severe force it can easily dislocate or break a wrist. Through training, one can develop the precise control to neutralize an opponent's motion and intent without inflicting physical damage. I had been trained to emphasize the flow of energy through the technique into the center of my partner. From this training, merged with the application of *ki* healing, my attention was focused on the energy flowing through rather than on the pain produced as I applied the *nikkyo* to Bil. It seemed as though his eyes were moving and I called to him loudly.

"Bil, Bil, can you hear me?"

Though the sound was not really clear, I thought he said, "Yeah." Admittedly, I wanted to hear it very bad. I was afraid I was making it up. I put the *nikkyo* on stronger; I conducted more energy through him. I was sure his eyes were responding. I said, "Bil, who am I?"

In very garbled tones, from very deep in his throat, I thought

I heard him say, "Richard." I looked around the room. The nurse's eyes were wide open. My mother and Christine were standing at the end of the bed, holding each other. They were both nodding. Christine said, "I'm sure he said your name. I'm sure he said Richard."

I turned back to Bil. I put the *nikkyo* on again. I said, "Bil, can you feel this?"

He said, "Yeah." Each time he spoke the words seemed to get a little clearer. I said,

"Bil, say my name." When he said Richard this time we all heard it. We looked at each other. No one dared believe it; yet we all knew we had heard him speak. I increased the pressure, intentionally increasing the pain as well as the stimulation.

"Bil, if this hurts, say uncle." He almost yelled "Uncle;" and it was so loud and so clear that none of us in the room had any question. We looked at each other through tears, laughter, and smiles. The nurse stopped dead, looked at me, and asked,

"What are you doing?"

I told her I was involved in the study of life energy through an art called Aikido and that it was used for healing as well as for self-defense. I told her that I was flowing *ki* or healing life energy into my brother and that I was using this process to make contact with his awareness. She looked at me politely, but I could almost hear her thinking that one of the two of us must be crazy.

It was probably less than five minutes before a battery of doctors walked into the room. They'd been with Bil for four weeks and had seen no conscious response. As they walked around Bil, they poked and prodded him. They talked to him, trying to get a response.

Bil had meanwhile drifted back into his unconscious state and made no clear response. They saw nothing. They looked at me again and left the room. Just as they were leaving my father walked into the room. He started to say something; my mother interrupted him,

"Jay, Bil just said Richard's name."

I took Bil's hand and repeated my process of centering and

grounding until I could feel the energy flowing. I applied the *nik-kyo*. His eyes started to roll. His eyelids started to flutter and then open. He seemed to be looking around the room. I said,

"Bil, do you know who's in the room now?" He didn't respond immediately so I asked again, "Bil, who's in the room now?"

He struggled to speak and finally said, "Dad."

Joy streamed from my father. "I can't beleive it," he said. "It's incredible, just incredible." He kept repeating his response. It was rare to see my father so happy.

For years now there'd been an unspoken strain between my father and me. My younger brother at least had taken up an intelligent profession as a doctor. I had been out on the coast, goofing off, studying this weird martial art which my father had always thought was worthless. Suddenly Aikido had tangible value to my whole family. No one really knew what I had done or even if I had done anything. But the fact that Bil had responded and spoken was enough for us at the moment. I asked him one more time to say my name and he did. The thrill and excitement in the room were so intense I can still feel it. I let him drift back to sleep. My father sat by the bed. My mother and I went out to breakfast.

By the time we got back Gene was there. I went to Bil's side, took his hand and again started the process of centering, grounding and *ki* flow to bring him up to consciousness. Gradually he began to wake up more and more. I asked,

"Bil, do you know that we're here?"

His voice was deep and the formation of his words barely intelligible but he said, "Know you're here," or did he say, "Know we're here." It is possible for someone in light coma to simply repeat the words they hear. Was he thinking or just parroting? I rephrased the question and asked,

"Bil, do you know who I am?"

He said, "Know who you are." Gene and I looked at each other and at that moment we knew that Bil was with us, that he was hearing us, he was understanding us and that he could make an intelligent response.

The left leg was paralyzed and did not register pain. I used movements similar to the wrist locks and applied these to the leg and foot. Once I had a pain response I used it in measured amounts to draw attention into the paralyzed leg, thus, stimulating *ki* flow. Once again, I used centering as the doorway to the flow of energy. I concentrated it first into his physical body and then into his energy field. *Ki* flow follows the attention into the stimulated area. The *ki* actually does the work, but Aikido training develops the ability to direct it to where it's needed. The leg became increasingly sensitive and eventually ticklish. By the time I left he could move his leg in response to the lightest touch. I did similar work on his left arm.

It was late afternoon when Gene and I headed back to the hospital. Word must have spread like wildfire because when we walked back into Bil's room there were six of his friends there. They had been trying to talk to him with no response. I knew they were wondering whether or not anything had really changed.

Gene and I looked at each other; we moved to opposite sides of the bed. He took one hand and I took the other. We started the process of stimulating energy flow through Aikido techniques. I could sense everyone in the room squirm. Temporarily I ignored them and concentrated my attention on flowing energy into Bil's body, into his mind and being. His eyes began to move and gradually to open. They seemed to roll about the room. Once again, I asked,

"Bil, who's in the room with us?"

His eyes rolled around the room once more. There were some growling noises and then he said faintly but clearly, "Kaplan," the name of one of his friends who was present. The excitement in the room was so thick you could cut it with a knife. Tears started to flow. No one could believe it.

It was an overwhelming experience because something happened but none of us could be sure what it was. Was my timing just coincidental? Was there really something in this Aiki *ki* flow, healing nonsense? There is a similar feeling on a good Aikido throw when *uke*, the person falling, is surprised to find himself on the mat. I've experienced this specific element of surprise and not knowing what really happened or how Aikido really works from both sides of the training, throwing and falling. Often, if not always, I wonder if it's real.

But he had responded. That was clear. And he had responded repeatedly. My feeling was that enough internal healing had taken place that he was ready to be woken up. But the Aikido, the pressure or the power of *ki* itself, had been able to ground his consciousness in contact with the moment, with my voice, and with the rest of us in the room until gradually he was able to trace his way back into consciousness on his own.

I went home in a dream. Both afraid to fail and afraid to succeed, I had gone on an intuitive impulse. I felt I had been moved by some knowledge which I did not possess but which possessed me. It was as if I never had a choice about whether or not I was going. I went without knowing what I was going to do there. I had acted purely and spontaneously out of the core of being.

A friend came to see me off before I left for the airport. He approached, his eyes soft. He hugged me and said something that hadn't occurred to me the whole time. He said, "This is the best martial arts story I've ever heard."

O. Fred Donaldson

On Aikido, Wolves and Other Wildlife

A real experience of wildlife requires the participation of all our senses and an empirical knowledge more holistic than analytic. Most of us experience nature as scenery and wildlife as prey. We have lost the full range of knowledge or wisdom that is our legacy as humans. Our modern way of life has atrophied the expression of certain human potentialities that remain dormant in us and are only expressed under certain conditions.

It seems, for example, as if we have found no other way of participating so directly with wild creatures as engaging them in a contest in which the animals themselves are the "game." Such contests are "played for keeps," endangering and exterminating more and more of the animal contestants. What matters in these contests is not so much the animal as its usefulness, usually measured as trophies. In such contests the relationship between human and animal is one of winner and loser. Roger Caras put this well when he wrote, "A killer is never so much a killer as when a game is involved." The importance of killing the animal lies in the fact that only with the dead trophy does the human fully enjoy the success of winning the contest. If the animal lives, the human loses; it is only by dying that the animal can acknowledge the human's victory.

Contests, however, are not the only way for us to participate with wildlife. Black Elk, Tom Brown, Fools Crow, and Morihei Uyeshiba have shown that to perceive with the entire body, to know instinctively the habits of wildlife and to establish kinship based on trust need not be relics of our ancestors. The aforementioned teachers portray a quality of blessedness, of love, that emerges with intimate association with other living beings and has become an essential part of my experience of Aikido, wolves and wildlife. To walk with wolves and other animals with Aikido as a companion allows me to perceive sights, sounds and relationships that I had not, probably could not, have perviously perceived.

We can substitute the dead trophies of contest with the enlivening relationships of Aikido. Suppose that instead of hunting animals to kill, we sought them out to engage in *randori* (multiple person attack). Suppose that instead of heads and skins for our walls, we learned mutual trust. Suppose that instead of engaging animals with a 30/30 we learned to touch them with our hands. Surely if it is skill and stamina we wish to test, Aikido can provide excellent encounters well beyond contests in difficulty and excitement.

The ideas expressed in the following pages have been derived from three sources: my practice of Aikido, my play with wolves at Wolf Haven, a wolf sanctuary in Washington state, and my numerous wildlife encounters. Based on this experience, I will suggest that Aikido is both an effective way of developing a deep intuitive understanding and a practical means of interacting with wildlife. I find the use of Aikido in my play with wolves and other animals to be an enjoyable and effective alternative to contest. It's not only because I practice Aikido that I view animals differently. I experience through Aikido a different reality. I am not engaged in a contest. Rather my aim "is to harmonize . . . with the movement of the universe and bring [myself] into accord with the universe itself" (Uyeshiba, 1963, p.178). O'Sensei was correct: "This is not mere theory. You practice it. Then you will accept the great power of Oneness with Nature" (Uyeshiba, 1963, p.178). My Aikido and play with wildlife are like snowflakes falling into boiling water—the one dissolves, becomes and changes the other.

Aikido has become a bridge between my culture and wildlife. The viability of the bridge depends upon participation, the essence of which rises in my heart. Not in my heart alone, to be sure, for it is transmitted to my sinews and muscles by a subtle osmosis; but the heart is where Aikido and nature meet. There is wisdom in this feeling that I can only guess at. I cannot memorize it; I can only learn it by heart. This essence is the harmony that distinguishes the Aikidoist from the contestant and allows me to play with wolves. Wolf and I merge as *nage* (defender) and *uke* (attacker); criticisms, judgements, comparisons, and contests are suspended in a fusion of mind and body, of sincerity and playfulness. In such an encounter no one is treated as an object-in-general.

My introduction to play with wolves was like being in the middle of an Aikido *randori* exercise. Apparently there is a kind of wolf etiquette that forbids keeping one in doubt of his/her welcome. They enjoy greeting me each morning as I enter their enclosure by jumping on me, nipping at any loose piece of clothing and giving me "wolf kisses." What a startling and delightful surprise "wolf kisses" were initially to me. The wolf opens its jaws and shuts it with a very loud snap close enough to my face that its lips just barely touch or "kiss" my skin.

The wolves all converge on me at once. I retreat downward into a ball covered by seven cavorting wolves. Like skilled *ukes*, their sensitivity and ability to self-handicap more than make up for my aprehension. As we play we increase our ability to blend with one another.

As *ukes*, wolves are too fast, too full of surprise for me to depend on thought to control my responses. I use intuition and heart to blend with their movements. Some are very gentle, some quite forceful, and one is sneaky, always seeming to go around and jump me from behind. It became clear to me that they expected and required me to treat them as individuals, blending my movements to their individual reponses. I do not allow all of the wolves to jump on me nor do I push them away with equal force. Sybil, for example, jumps on me with such gentleness that I can hardly feel her touch. She is careful not to land on me with her claws. When she jumps up, she rests her paws on my arm while I rub and jostle her neck and face. One of her sisters, however, is always testing my response to surprise as she jumps me from behind or runs at me from the side, takes a quick nip and darts away. I use my arms in the characteristically circular motions of Aikido to deflect her rather forceful lunges. At first I was not sure that her quickness could be accompanied by care. But in time we learned to blend with one another. Although she is amazingly fast and forceful, she is also careful not to hurt me. She often caught my arm in her jaws as I deflected her lunge, but she never closed her teeth.

Such harmonious touch is based on a mutual trust and kinesthetic awareness. We both "know by heart" the correct firmness of contact and sensitivity of touch. When a wolf puts her/his jaws around my arm, they know exactly how much force to use. Likewise I know just how much and where I can touch each wolf. Two wolves, Sybil and Hambone, allow me to lift them up off their feet, which is unusual. Relying as they do on their feet for control and agility, wolves normally don't like to be picked up.

The blending and trust of the *uke-nage* relationship is an inexplicable caring for one another. It comes by sharing many grand and minute, visible and invisible acts and messages. One very special wolf, Sybil, shows me such caring. Her touch with teeth and claws is so soft and gentle that I find it hard to believe that it comes from a wolf. Her glance grazes my eyes, as soft and fleeting as a snowflake melting on my cheek. She admits me into her presence and inexorable intelligence. She did it so imperceptibly and quickly that it was only later that I fully realized what she shared.

Sybil and I shared a *kaiten-nage* (rotary throw) type of movement. When it first happened it was a surprise and a delight to me. She also seemed to revel in what was an amazingly quick movement of trust. She began by closing her jaws around my forearm. Usually I allow her to decide when to let go, but this time as soon as she tightened her hold, I swung my arm in an outwardly extending circle. She left her feet, while maintaining her hold on my arm. I brought her down on her back with my arm still in her jaw. She momentarily released her hold, showed me a smile in her eyes, stood up and shook all over. She mouthed my arm, and we repeated the "rotary throw."

It was an awesome thing, this touch we shared. It made me feel one with her. It was grace without excess. This relationship is what the Chimmesyan Indians of British Columbia, Canada call walking "In the Shadow of a Rainbow." If I had any doubts about the possibility of mutual caring, about O'Sensei's goal for Aikido as the realization of love, I have none now. Nothing, henceforth, can deny this feeling; it is more certain for me than all I seem to know.

The *uke-nage* relationship is characterized by paradox; I have felt it in *randori* as well as in my play with wolves. What appears to be a contest of skills is rather a blending of energies. In *randori*, for example, a *nage* deals with an attack by four or more *ukes* by embracing and joining with it, not opposing it. Like play, *randori* is only able to proceed with the intuitive understanding and mutual sensitivity of all participants. The result is that the speed and force of the attack is minutely harmonized with the motions of evasion, centralization and extension used by the *nage*. *Randori* is not a contest that one wins or loses.

Experiencing the harmony of *randori* helps me in my play with wolves. I often find myself in the midst of seven wolves, all of whom are so anxious to play and so jealous of my attention that they all come jumping, licking and nipping at once. As in *randori*, if I become fearful and retreat and lose my center, I cannot blend with them. There is no feeling of harmony; I feel tense and resort to ineffective blocking techniques, trying to control rather than blend. This is ineffective because the wolves can sense my fear and their speed and agility is far superior to mine. The result is a contest in which, feeling utterly without control, I become frustrated, clap my hands and send the wolves scurrying. And I lose an opportunity to share with them.

There are times, before I get to such a point of defeat that the alpha, or dominant male wolf, will intercede on my behalf by body blocking other wolves out of my way or by grabbing them with his teeth by the scruff of the neck. This is the same care shown in the *dojo* by senior Aikido students.

Experiencing *randori* also helps me participate in a wolf chase game that on the surface appears to be a contest, but actually is play. In this game a wolf picks up a stick in its jaws and begins to run. I join in with the other wolves and give chase. After a brief time, the wolf drops the stick, which is then picked up by a pursuer. Roles are reversed and the chase continues. As a pursuer I notice that the wolf with the stick runs at less than maximum speed. Paradoxically the wolf invites pursuit, as if being chased is a reward. The wolf being chased not only doesn't try to get away, she glances back to see if she is being pursued. In addition, the pursuing wolves do not try to catch the wolf with the stick. When I pick up the stick the wolves treat me as another wolf.

It is important in both *randori* and in the wolf chase game that all participants trust one another and share an intuitive understanding of the messages. Without such trust, for example, the movements and holds of Aikido are potentially disabling. In the case of the wolf chase game, if I or a wolf were to grab the stick and run full speed, we would be inviting aggressive pursuit, which could end up in being pulled down. For wolves in the wild such a miscue could mean a crippling injury leading to probable death and the weakening of the pack. If I were to make such a mistake, I would likely be pulled down like a prey animal.

I am also reminded of the paradox of touch that I felt when a *sensei* first showed me *sankyo* (wrist lock hold) and when a wolf closed its jaws around my head. In both cases, even though there was the potential for extreme pain, my physical and emotional experience was not one of fear and grabbing, but one of closeness and contact. The *sensei* taught me a lesson that was to be reaffirmed by a wolf: resistance on my part is what would cause me pain. By relaxing I am able to not only avoid pain, but signal my release.

My Aikido training and my wolf play demand a kind of participation that prevents simultaneous analysis. If I try to analyze Sybil's gaze or a *shomenuchi* (strike to the head) I no longer share in the experience. This feedback occurs to me often in my Aikido practice. I recall once being thrown across a room by a teacher in a demonstration of *kokyu-ho,* "breath throw." I attacked this teacher full-speed, grabbing for his lapels; I never touched him and went flying across the dojo in an airborne spiral. Rolling to a stand, I turned, shared a bow and a smile, and understood without cognitive analysis what "stillness in the act of movement" means. Such is the relationship shared only when a teacher lets a student use their own experience to verify reality.

I have walked among wolves and felt their stares of dominance, furtive glances of submission and special look of friendship. I have lain and rested among them, joined their play, feeling the sudden surge of power in their upright leaps and mid-air twirls. Their powerful, yet gentle jaws have held my hands, arms and head. I have touched, tickled and stroked; I have been jumped on, walked over, licked and mouthed. Within me now there is a furriness, a confluence of strength and gentleheartedness, a whisper of wildness and a smell of wolf. The reality of a wolf lies within these many images. Often I feel that if I am wise I will not try to explain a wolf or Aikido to anyone, but rather entice one to discover for oneself. Somewhere inside of me it is clear that this is beyond the reach of my intellect. But it is so powerful that I cannot overlook it. Nature doesn't allow it and neither does Aikido.

Through the physical and mental discipline of Aikido I learn to develop my intuitive judgment and to adapt safely to outside stimuli. This trust is playing life by ear, being willing to follow the uncertain path. Such paths are habits of spirit, turns of mind and directions of heart. My interactions with wildlife are not competitions, but based in the *aiki* way of harmony. At such times, being in harmony means not approaching or not following them. During the last months of a hard winter, for example, I do not approach elk; running to escape, they would use up valuable energy reserves which might mean the difference between life and death.

Both Aikido and learning the ways of wolves and other wildlife are lifelong endeavors. Patience and training are as demanding in learning to touch a wild animal as they are in perfecting *iriminage*, the "twenty-year" technique. But even after all the time and technique, without the spiritual intent I am left with mere gestures. I have spent countless hours over many years in contact with wildlife and have been able to touch only a few.

One of the most memorable was a bull elk with whom I shared

some moments on a rainy morning. I went out wandering one day in one of my favorite "wildlife finding places." I knew where elk rested within the cover of the forest's edge. On this day the sky hung down touching the earth like a heavy grey velvet stage curtain, hiding all within its soft folds. I walked in and out of the forest's edge, not so much looking for anything as much as for the fun of going in and out.

I came upon an elk resting within a small cluster of lodgepole pines. I circled to let him know of my presence and not startle him. I moved very slowly and softly until I could sit with him beneath the trees. After sitting for a few moments, I reached out slowly and touched his foreleg, gradually moving my hand up his side to his neck. He allowed me to stay very close for a time. My senses were filled with the bull elk — the damp musky smell, the soft wet hair, the undulating ribs, the shades of brown, the shared glances. He rose, dripping rain from his velvety antlers, and walked calmly past me out into the mist. Such an encounter is a fusion of mind, body and spirit; it is so fleeting in time and simultaneously so enduring in memory. It is the essence of Aikido.

It is exciting to tell of my adventures with elk, grizzlies and wolves, to recall the excitement of *randori* and *kokyu-ho*. But behind such dramatic moments there is the hard routine practice of seemingly "simple" things as moving and falling and days in the mountains less well remembered because they seem so alike. I must live by the unforgiving tenet that my moments of drama are built upon thousands of less remembered incidents and even more time spent in seeming non-incidents. It is the countless *ukemi* (falls) and endless stalking practice that make *randori* and elk touching possible.

If I take the time and open myself to them, lessons are constantly being offered to me. I see harmony in a flight of Canada geese. Each bird flies in such a way so as to unite it with all the others in a rhythmic form. This is done so that the entire field of energy is enhanced by the movements of each bird. Like the blending of an *uke-nage* relationship, the geese take and give energy not only from each other but from the whole field of air. The separate birds are linked together by the surrounding air as though by some elastic threads.

I watch a hummingbird and know of no better guide in the art of "stillness in the act of motion." On a crisp February afternoon when all things seem brittle with the cold and the winds are as straight and piercing as arrows, I hold out my hand with some seeds and smile as a jaunty chickadee descends from a fir and alights on my glove. Her perky presence seems to provide a lesson in faith — a kind of kinship with the seasons based on a trust that winter passes and spring renews. This chickadee knows the harmony of which Master Uyeshiba taught. When he said, "True budo is to . . . cultivate all beings in nature," he was correct.

The spirit and forms of Aikido are my gestures of deeply interested kinship, companionship and trust with wildlife. Aikido gives the lie to all forms of contest. The idea that I and other animals are basically of one kind is at the core of my Aikido. It seems to me that Aikido reaches a summit of perfection and harmony when I share the gaze of a grizzly, the gentleheartedness of a wolf, the trust of an elk, or the friendliness of a chickadee.

I delight in my blending of Aikido and nature; mixtures of grandeur and nuance, of apprehension and calm, of spirit and form. Aikido nudges me closer and closer to nature, which in turn, if I am aware, will bestow just enough of itself upon me to enlarge my sense of Aikido.

> He's so tiny, a fluff of grey, white and black, a warm bundle of intense activity, a jaunty actor, a gregarious acrobat and a gay friend. He is more than the sum of his anatomical parts, movements and energy. I see a chickadee cavorting and imagine O'Sensei spiraling.

134

Richard Strozzi Heckler

Aikido and Children

> By my body's actions . . . teach my mind.
> — William Shakespeare

For the past few years I have had the opportunity of teaching Aikido to two different groups of children. Since both groups range in age from six to nineteen I will alternately refer to these people as children, kids, or youth.

One group includes the children who live in the nearby community and regularly attend classes at the dojo. They learn the Aikido approach to self-defense; the principles of center, ground, *ki* extension, relaxation, and blending; and the skills of rolling and falling. They are taught the value of discipline and respect and to take responsibility for their actions; they also develop new awareness of their environment. Even though it is a cliché, it is nevertheless true that martial arts "build self-confidence." I see this in the way these children carry themselves and in their interactions with others. They develop an ease and aliveness that is then expressed in their daily life.

The other group of children and youth are categorized by the establishment as "emotionally disturbed." They are diagnosed as having severe "learning disabilities;" or they have become "criminal offenders." These phrases carry a heavy charge without really saying anything and for this reason I don't especially like them as labels. Yet, there is still a disturbance in these children; it is in their inability to contact and communicate themselves effectively to the world. They have few or no skills for containing and expressing their own excitement in a satisfying way. In their efforts to avoid their deeper feelings they limit that excitement, its communications, and their contact with others to fixed and unsatisfying channels. Their expression of their needs, desires, or creativity always follows the same patterns: violence for some, withdrawal for others, constant unbounded monologue for still others. But regardless of the particular choice there is a common underlying current of aggression and frustration that prohibits the child in them to sing and dance or to develop meaningful relationships.

I am usually asked by a county, state, or federal agency to teach these children. This already distinguishes them from my other group. In the community the children come because they choose to and their parents approve. In the group we are discussing I am brought into their institution without the children's choice, and they have to deal with me. These children and young adults have already committed some crime or are considered too troublesome to be handled by regular schools. They have expressed their frustration and need by hurting themselves or somebody else. Besides their academic courses they are also necessarily involved in some sort of therapy or rehabilitative work.

What is central in these children's experience is their tendency to limit their excitement to safely prescribed areas of their bodies, while making other areas virtually dead. It is as if they must keep some part of themselves quarantined in order to put other parts into a constant state of anarchy. This gives their tremendous flow of energy a limited but rigidly controlled outlet. Some children, for example, are quietly but angrily contracting and flexing their energy, while others are continually blowing off steam. Some children can only shout when they speak; others reserve their excitement for their heads, and they live in a world of distant dreams. In all cases there is no sense of democracy among their parts. These children live in a totalitarian system where one part rules to the exclusion of other needs and desires. Their internal dictatorship maintains an unremitting emotional brushfire that is always threatening to ignite into a raging blaze; this state also becomes an effective front line resistance that keeps others at a safe distance. If someone else crosses an unnamed but internally perceived line the unperceived dictator declares war and then projects this inner conflict onto others or the environment.

Because these kids, like most kids, have experienced the popularization of martial arts and its superstars through the media, they are both open to and have fixed ideas about what Aikido will be. They are eager to learn how to fight and to perform the dramatic kicks and punches they see on T.V. and the movies, and they are overjoyed to be up and out of their desks. I like this eagerness because it provides an available energy with which to work.

What I teach this group, through the form of Aikido, is a language of the body and spirit. I teach them an Aikido way of standing where they experience what it is to have a center and to be grounded. So when I later say, "Stand in an Aikido way," they respond by finding in themselves a position that is balanced, solid, and relaxed. Then I teach them an Aikido way of breathing that is full, rhythmic, and relaxed; Aikido ways of walking, relating, sitting and so on. These ways become a language of their body and energy that they can call on whenever they choose because it is always there with them. When they learn this language they have access to a bodily notebook of concrete sensations, temperatures, images, feelings, and emotions that puts them back in touch with their physical world. Using Aikido in this way gives them an entrance way to a direct experience of their bodily life. They then come into levels of contact that are inevitably more satisfying then their customary modes of running or fighting.

I teach this Aikido language by creating a situation where these children can experience a workable and effective way of dealing with pressure. I do this by first having them experience their habitual and personalized ways of dealing with pressure or stress. When these conditioned reactions become apparent I then show them an alternative to becoming a vicious aggressor or a resigned and bitter victim. I accomplish this, for example, through an Aikido technique in which one student will firmly grasp the arm of another. This grab metaphorically represents, and literally is, a pressure situation. After they recognize their conditioned responses to pressure, which are usually to become aggressive or to be overwhelmed, I teach them how to organize a new response from a centered, relaxed, and yet alive place. This initiates them into the Aikido language, and they experience that one need not necessarily respond to pressure with counterpressure. Through blending with a confrontative situation one learns to resolve the confrontation without being a loser, on the one hand, or hurting someone, on the other. The principle reveals itself through countless Aikido techniques and enables these youth to replace their conditioned reflexes with a more responsible and appropriate response.

As they learn Aikido, the fundamental thing that begins to happen to these young people is that their ability to feel and sense is awakened. When they allow themselves to feel, they are often terrified by the rush of sensations, streamings, and emotions that come with feeling. But as they learn to be with feelings from a centered and grounded place, they find a new sense of power and ease. They embody power instead of imitating it. To feel and experience life rather than pretend or fantasize about it is a fundamental principle of Aikido. It is a first step in throwing off the dictator within. This path of self-discovery emphasizes the importance of executing each technique with the proper spirit or energy. The kids quickly learn that Aikido is not necessarily a collection of techniques to perform on someone, but a presence of being that can both be practiced in the Aikido classes and lived in daily life. This presence is an attitude that includes a priority of self-responsibility — perceiving conflict and pressure as actual opportunities in which to grow and discover oneself, blending with situations as an alternative to fighting or running, and trusting their own feeling and intuitive dimension.

As much as possible this approach is introduced into the classroom and familiar life situations. If, for example, an argument breaks out, we may implement the concept of blending by having the kids participate in each others' point of view; we also can demonstrate that this blend is essentially the same blend we do while on the mat. When they are drawing or doing math problems we may encourage them to allow the same level of relaxation and open channelling that is taught in the Aikido class. The way they sit in Aikido, we tell them, can be the same way they sit in the classroom. When they are working with clay or other materials we remind them that the energy they feel in their hands in the Aikido class can be used for sculpting, woodworking, drawing, or writing. In every possible situation we attempt to include this language of the body and spirit in the classroom.

Most of these children tend to live in a world of abstraction and fantasy. This is not necessarily bad, it's just out of balance. Aikido classes can bring them into balance. They have habitually seen people and situations as objects and symbols rather than living processes, flowing constellations in which they are involved. They have been deprived of so much basic fulfillment during their brief lives that they have become addicted to their private fantasy worlds. Instead of directly asking for affection, approval, and love, they invent sterile imitations. Sometimes the frustration of a life of unfulfillment and rejections will suddenly burst out of their fantasy world in an uncontrollable rage. Their thwarted love becomes a hell that begins spitting fire. I've seen these children come up behind a classmate who is quietly working and kick him as hard as they can, or stab him with a sharpened object. If they stay in their fantasy world too long, they erupt out of it only as demons. Aikido encourages these demons to come first into broad daylight, to be dealt with directly and openly within the community.

In Aikido, where there are numerous throws and takedown techniques, it is necessary to learn how to fall without injury, so early on I teach the art of rolling and falling. When everyone has the fundamentals of falling, we will start with a basic technique. Then we really toss each other around. Besides the joy they experience in being able to fall gracefully and instantly to get up without injury, they also have the relief of being able to work more openly with their aggression. Just imagine: we are in a class of six or seven or eight children, all brimming with anger, and they are told they can begin to attack their classmates and throw them down. There are guidelines, of course, which take them back to the language originally developed through Aikido. They are aggressive for profound reasons and in deep ways rather than shallowly and symptomatically. Through the Aikido exercises they are more likely to feel the sources of their aggression as they actually are than to commit unconscious mayhem. There is, in other words, an Aikido way of handling someone's attack — a way to handle aggression without hurting someone. There is an Aikido way of falling and so forth. This keeps the basic structure intact so we never completely get lost in chaos. When we work with throwing techniques everyone gets a chance to fall, and everyone gets a chance to throw. I'll throw the kids, and they will throw me. Sometimes I let them all attack me at once; they come at me with padded boppers swinging with all their might. In this way they have the opportunity to vent their aggression in an open and direct way. I find that they discover a great satisfaction in using the large muscles of their shoulders and arms to unlock the aggression that is chronically held there. They also know they must exercise some skill for it is my option to dodge a swing and then throw them down.

The chronic fighting, pushing, and crowding that these children do has kept them from any genuine contact. Their constant reacting has never allowed them to explore the boundaries of who they are, who somebody else is. By introducing them to their bodily life through Aikido, I give them a reference point — a working ground with boundaries — from which to make contact. They learn the possibility of accepting their excitement and, with it, a more direct and genuine range of self-expression. Without this sense of boundary a child may get sick if his mother is sick, or, if I am angry with one young man, another may feel the anger is directed at him. When they learn to contact and live by their own excitement they show more self-reliance and an ability to distinguish their own experience from others'. They emerge from their fantasy world of imagined powers and shadowy fears, and their body begins to tell them what is real. From there they begin to feel what they want and how they can ask for it.

As these children begin to live more of their bodily life, I have to remind myself that the expression of their emotions and feelings will take new and unexpected forms. An emerging frustration for example, is often good news, for it may be a signal that the behavior hasn't quite caught up with a new insight. They see the possibilities of being in a new way, but the old conditions that have been grafted into their nervous system, their so-called "learning disabilities," continue to interfere with how they can operate at greater potential.

Although I believe that the Aikido movements that form a language of the body positively affect these learning disabilities, my work does not necessarily focus on techniques to rehabilitate them. What I do focus on are the principles of contact, expression, and boundary-forming. So if a child becomes angry when his learning disability prevents him from completing a technique, I encourage him to experience and express the appropriate emotion, but in a way that is in line with the new found body language. In other words, I don't want these children to act out and throw fits, but I also don't want to interrupt their excitement to do a particular exercise because they are stuck at a learning disability. I try to create an environment that offers the child first a place to recognize his experience and then a way to express it through the language of his body. This means that he can work with his anger without damaging himself or someone else. The child learns how to *say* directly he is angry and he can also directly *be* angry by using his voice, arms, legs, and breath.

My experience with a man-child I will call Carl illustrates this process. Carl is lean and willowy with very fair complexion. Protruding out of his almost bleached white face are eyes that are bright but fixed in a rigid stare. There is an intelligence about Carl that is reflected in his academic studies and the way he can articulate certain concepts. But his chest is drawn back, his stomach a tight knot of anxiety, and his head pushed forward of his torso. He is shaped like a thin wiry bow. While his chest, stomach, and pelvis are bowed back, his head and feet are almost on a straight vertical line with each other. His torso and arms are in the background while his feet provide a distant ground for his head. Carl is extremely sensitive, and I can sense how his attention probes the room and other people. While part of him is drawn back, like a tautly strung wire, another part probes the environment for approval and respect. Carl is also stymied by a number of learning disabilities. He has a very low self-esteem, and he acts this out by jumping into the trash bin when his inadequacy comes to the foreground. When I first saw him do this I was shocked. I know that I sometimes negatively judge myself, but to watch a child literally act out being trash was a fascinating and horrifying mirror. We were in the classroom one day and after an agonizing time of trying to solve a problem he began to argue with another student. Then suddenly he exploded and ran screaming from the room. His legs were scurrying but his frozen pelvis slowed him down and I quickly caught up with him. He wrenched free of me and bolted out the door. He was in an enclosed area, so knowing that he wouldn't go far I let him get ahead of me. When I got outside however, I couldn't see him, and I was momentarily dumbfounded. "Where could he have gone?" I thought. Then I heard a rustling, and saw a movement in the large trash bin. I looked in and there was Carl burrowing himself deeper and deeper into the trash. I wanted to cry, and I wanted to laugh. Finally I took some papers off him and told him to get out and go back to the class. He refused and he was adamant about it. He was so strong and clear I somehow trusted him. I made him give me his word that he would eventually return and I left.

Carl returned soon after, and I could tell he was much relieved. As strange as his actions were there was something self-regulating about what he was doing. His act had momentarily brought him into more harmony with himself. This incident revealed to me that to work only on Carl's learning disabilities would not touch his deep emotional wound. It was also not enough simply to talk about it. Carl needed to embody his emotional energy in a way that would bring awareness to it and give him an alternative to "trashing" himself and others.

Soon after this "trash bin" incident, I was working with the group on the Aikido mat. We were playing a connecting game in which each person holds the arm of a partner with both hands in order to guide him skillfully and evenly to the mat. Though not exactly the same, it is related to *ikkyo*, or "number one technique" in Aikido. Carl perceived how I did this and he excitedly organized himself to do it with his partner. He was in a feeling state, his intention was clear, there was virtually no resistance on his part to what we were doing. As he began the movement the action became distorted from the original impulse. One of his arms pushed, the other pulled. He immobilized himself in his own double message. His partner did not go down. Carl tried harder, but this only created more confusion. He began to hold his breath and hunch his shoulders; his face grew red. His partner began to struggle against him because he felt he was being forced; I could see a confrontation was near.

On some level it is probably true that an incomplete wiring in Carl's nervous system prohibits him from satisfactorily performing such a movement. It is also likely that the work of an occupational therapist could help integrate Carl's movement. It may even be true that the circular, spiralling, and up-and-down movements of Aikido will integrate this part of Carl's nervous system. But what I saw before me at that moment was the same energy building in Carl that had sent him to the trash bin. I also saw that he struggled with this energy; instead of being friendly with it, he let it become his foe.

I went over to Carl and gently encouraged his emotion. I told him that I could see he was angry and I assured him there was room for that. He was on a thin edge, and I was not sure if he would make a dash for the trash can or not. "Yeah, I'm angry," he shouted, 'What do you think. Michael won't go down. I can't do this, I'll never be able to do it." He was standing very rigid. It was hard to tell whether he would topple over suddenly like a stiff, unfeeling two-by-four, or just explode. I told him that it was okay to express some of his anger and he began to shout and stamp his feet. He blamed Michael, Aikido, me, his mother, but most of all he was venting his emotion without trashing himself or physically striking out at someone else. He began to soften and some deeper breaths came into his body. He saw that I was on his side, and be began to let deeper feelings emerge. He had been hurt in the past and this angered him now. He talked about his mother and father fighting and then breaking up. He implied it may have been his fault. He said, "It's so messy. I made such a mess." He wants the love that is now missing. This gets acted out into, "I want to fight," when what he means is, "I want your love." In this instance I showed him love and acceptance and, at the same time, that there was room for his anger. We were together in a way that was honest, in a connection that was healing. After expressing his anger and hurt, Carl went back to the movement and, working with the Aiki principles of center, ground, and blending, he performed it correctly.

I don't think that Carl was "cured" of his neurotic tendency in that session, but I do think that an accumulation of these kinds of connections can begin to build an alternative way of behavior. Each time I would have some real contact with Carl, he would stand a bit straighter, breathe a little easier, and see a bit more with his eyes. The quality of our contact would then become more relaxed and more direct. When his frustration and rage would emerge he took more responsibility for it and spent less time blaming others. After a while Carl began to take the regular children's Aikido class at the Aikido dojo and, later, he also transfered to a public school. Working with the energy of Carl's emotion instead of stopping to rehabilitate a motor dysfunction, I was doing Aikido in the larger sense of blending with "what is," and guiding Carl into harmony with his own energy.

This is the kind of Aikido I do with these children. I ask them to experiment with new ways of being so they may regain a trust in their own excitement, and not necessarily to make them better citizens or to socialize their unruliness. My hope is that by coming in touch with their energy and their bodies, they will find a meaning and purpose in their lives. As Aikido helps them become responsible for their feelings, actions, and thoughts, they begin to discover something that interests them. And they learn to trust their own intuitions and talents. Bringing them into connection with their lost energetic identities, I give them the possibility of a change from the inside out. In this way they become who they are because they relate to their own experience and not to the exterior demands of the social norm.

I believe this work is as valuable, if not more valuable, than traditional talking therapy. Through the Aikido training these children deal with issues of competition, aggression, intimacy and contact while they learn to unify their minds and bodies. But it is not a shining and effortless pathway of transformation as soon as the children step on the mat. Working with them is more often rewarded with small victories and large frustrations. For one thing they are mirrors for my own levels of patience and tolerance. On days when the resistance is thick enough to choke on, then it becomes truly my own Aikido practice at stake. I need to be centered, to be grounded, to blend with the situation, to resolve the conflict by using its own force. A path like Aikido makes this possible.

I would like to relate one of my small victory stories that supports my inner desire to go on with this work. It concerns David, a man-child who learned that not hurting someone can stop a fight more than hurting them. David is big for his age and he can easily dominate other children, which he does. I'll often have to admonish him for pulling hair, pinching someone, putting extra pressure on a wrist-lock, or tripping someone from behind. He does nothing really major, but more often than not he will have some child crying under his tyranny. He comes from a family of huge people and is the youngest child. I know his swaggering tough act brings him attention. I used to retaliate with my own kicks and shoves until I realized that this merely instructed his own strong-arm techniques. So I gave him a position as senior student with some responsibility to the younger students. When he received this additional respect and attention he eased back a little on his dictator role, but he always had an edge and I kept my eye on him.

David periodically would tell me about this other kid that used to "bug" him, and how they would often have it out after school. David always said it was this other kid who started it, and though I didn't entirely believe this, I always encouraged him to try and deal with the situation in an Aikido way. His foe must have also been tough because David would sometimes have cuts and bruises after one of their tussles. But after a while his stories about "this other kid" became tedious, and I felt a sense of weariness in him about it. His war stories about fighting were more infrequent and once he confided that, "It seems so stupid that we keep doing this. One of us always gets hurt, and I don't care anymore if he thinks he's tougher than me or not. I always feel bad when I hurt him."

Then one day after showing a wrist technique, I asked if there were any questions, and David raised his hand. "Well, this isn't really a question, but I want to tell you what happened to me yesterday. This guy comes up to me, and grabs me, and without really thinking about it, I do this *kote gaeshi* technique." (This is a wrist technique and if done properly, could easily break an arm or wrist and the children all know this.) I immediately think, 'Oh, no. David probably broke this kid's wrist or threw him so hard he cracked his head.' I imagine teachers and parents and lawyers knocking on my door. David's face then brightens and he says, "And he fell down, and it was like I hardly did anything . . . . But the best part of it was that he wasn't even hurt!" David stood up straighter for a moment, looked at me straight in the eye, and let out a huge grin. "Yeah," he repeated, "it was so simple, and I didn't even have to hurt him. He just looked at me and then got up and walked away. I don't think we will have to fight anymore. It was great." David was beaming all over the room.

A small victory but somehow it felt big inside, and the way David grinned told me that I would keep doing this for a while.

Megan Reisel

A Turn To Balance

It was an odd place for a bruise.

I sat in the kitchen and looked at my wrist. It was bluish-red and would not be easy to hide. At that point, my roommate walked in. She asked me what happened. I told her that it occurred last night, in my Aikido class. "What were you doing?" she asked. I stood up and took hold of her wrist. I tried to imitate how my teacher had held mine. He seemed to have a special technique for holding wrists. Not only did his hand seem to wrap around my wrist more than once, but he pressed one of his knuckles deep into a nerve along the bone. He was massive in size, too. So, I tried to give her the impression that I was bigger and tougher than my 5'3" frame could command, and to squeeze her wrist with as much ferocity that my teacher had squeezed into mine. I held her intently, as he had done; glowered into her eyes and tried to intimidate her. I continued to squeeze until it seemed her hand was going limp, numb, blue. She was somewhere between giggling and crying and asking me to stop it, when she said that she could see now how I got bruised. I let go. Then I told her that all the while that he was holding on to my wrist, he was also pushing me back with the force of his strength. I was soon up against the *dojo* wall, on the verge of tears. He kept yelling, "Turn!! Turn!!", as I would stare back in bewilderment. My shoulder was shoved up to my ear and I was out of control of my own movement. I wondered what the hell I was doing here. I knew all along that he was trying to teach me something, but the intimidation made me freeze. Even as I tried to recall that kindness was his predominant characteristic, he was being the menace so effectively that

I felt caught. Caught and in pain. When he said, "Turn!", I would, but only into more pain. I started to plead with him to stop — that I gave up. Fortunately, his kindness came through.

He was trying to teach me to not lose control in the face of danger. That my wrist was not my mind, nor my feet, nor my shoulder. He said I got stuck in his eyes, in his intent and then, in the pain in my wrist. If I could have turned my whole body away from his grasp, not in front of him, but beside him, I would have dis-empowered his attack. But I held onto my pain. In effect, I was helping to maintain the hold as much as he by giving in to the pain. He was asking me to re-examine what fear is. He was asking me to consider what power is and where it might come from, who could have it, use it, release it. Was I necessarily a victim to physical violence because I was small? Could anyone grab onto my mind, or my spirit, the way that they could grab on to my wrist?

I asked my friend the same questions. I wondered if she felt the same way about fear and pain as I did. I knew I was on to something pretty exciting, that this Aikido would give a major jolt to my life. I trusted what my teacher told me about Aikido, but I didn't know if these training methods could ever teach me about fear and power, and my mind. So I asked her what was frightening to her, what she knew about power, if she thought she could defend herself against a physical attack. She said she knew she had fear, that everyone did. She looked down at her wrist and rubbed it where I had held it and said she wasn't too clear about any of those questions. She had ideas, but nothing definitive enough to give any thoughts to me. I asked her to come to class sometime. Maybe we could find some of those answers.

That event took place sometime during the winter of 74–75. Since that time, my Aikido study has taken me through the exploration of many more questions than those mentioned above. Those initital questions have come close to being answered, but they seem to have a life of their own. There are moments when an answer seems clear as day, and then the same question will pop up at some other time and be illusive and mysterious once again. When I reflect on what Aikido has taught me, I am amazed at how many levels of understanding about myself and about Aikido that day to day training has brought me through. In relation to the questions of fear, power and spirit, I seem to be pursuing a path made up of several tangential and intermediary questions of value in and of themselves.

In those first weeks of my Aikido study, I was faced with confrontation. Today, I continue to learn about confrontation on other levels. Aikido seems to challenge you almost instantly with a confrontation of some sort or another. At the beginning of my training, I thought I had jumped into a world seething with aggression. Not only did I have to get it, but I had to be it too. I didn't know which was worse. Aikido asks you to strike, punch, grab, hold on to another person. Then it turns you around and asks you to receive strikes, punches, and grabs. Techniques teach you how to be safe in both respects, but it's up to you to make it real.

At first, striking out or grabbing on seemed impossible. I didn't want to hurt anybody and, I surely didn't want to *be* hurt. But Aikido demands that we create a fighting situation so that we can learn to face our fears and face our foes, whether they be inside us or in the real world. If I held back, if I refused to strike sincerely, I denied my partner the opportunity to learn. I had to take the risk. Since I am a shy person, it felt like Public Speaking III all over again to me. I had to put out. And I had to put out from a source inside that would be pure.

Learning to be aggressive in Aikido felt as though it was damaging my feminine self-image. I didn't think of women as fighters, as warriors. I never said it to myself in those words, but I discovered that I believed it in some alcove of my mind. Being aggressive wasn't an attribute that I associated with being feminine. Aggression was masculine. Warriors were men. Was I training to be a warrior? How could I be masculine? After all, Aikido is a martial art and martial arts are masculine. I was a woman doing a masculine martial art. Simple enough. Now I was questioning what masculine and feminine had to do with male and female. Could I be aggressive and still be feminine? Or did I need to be masculine in order to be aggressive? I knew I couldn't *imitate* the men because then my attacks would not be sincere. I needed to discover, on my own, where aggression lay inside me. Then I stumbled over anger.

My anger seemed partly from not knowing what was feminine and what was masculine anymore. It also grew out of a reservoir of anger that I'd never expressed. It came from feeling out of place in a world of martial arts that is traditionally for the guys. My anger grew into hostility. I wanted to learn Aikido but I was way out of my element. I grew impatient. I found myself intolerant of many things. Studying Aikido was cultivating an angry fire and I wondered why I kept it up. I didn't like myself that way, and I didn't get much help in my training. Anger was burning me. It was alienating me from kindness. It wasn't doing me much good, all this anger. I had to find out where it started and how to distill it into something more positive. When I discovered that my anger was actually coming out of the experience of sensing my own limitations I began to feel more curiosity about whether those limitations were true or not, whether they were something that could be changed, or whether they just needed some re-evaluation. I needed to take a good long look at what confinements were created out of my own self-image, including my feminine and masculine definitions. I had to evaluate the difficulties of being a woman in a martial art. I began to see that the warrior was a way of life, not specific to men.

One thing became certain. If I was going to excel in Aikido, I needed to find my own masculine attributes without sacrificing my femininity. This meant that I had to overcome my male and female stereotypes. I had to stop labelling common associations of femininity to women such as: passive, fragile, graceful, soft, receptive but incapable of self-protection. I had to remove other associations from purely masculine definitions of men: aggressive, dominating, hard, strong, controlling. All that seemed like T.V. I wanted to shake them around and let them roll and settle where they may. I was seeking balance of character, but I didn't realize that until quite a while later. My task at the time was to stop feeling strangled by my limitations. I used my Aikido practice to give expression to new ways to be. I wanted to train as rigorously as the men and give them a challenge as well. I didn't want to be less skillful or powerful because I was a woman.

Now I was confronted with competition. Competition involves perennial ambivalence. On the one hand, it is regarded as one of the best practices to fulfill your potential, to meet your goals, to gain success. On the other hand, it can pit ego against ego, drive one's ambitions into obsession and thwart one's initial purpose to excel. Creative competition means to strive against one's own inner power. To find the resources to do what you think you can't, not merely to use others' excellence to define one's own ability.

When I started to train competitively to find my own proficiency in Aikido, I couldn't help comparing myself to others: Who could do the throws better, who could take better falls, who had a good attitude, who was advancing faster, and who was favored by the teacher. I was deeply immersed in competition.

That sort of battle quickly got boring. I had jumped into a me-against-them sort of training. I was so concerned with my own progress compared to others that I excluded to a certain degree my own natural inclinations of style. I wanted to fit in and be received by the male contingent — and to be important to the teacher too. So instead of using other students as my models, and male teachers as well, I decided to return to basics. I took the metaphorical turn that my first teacher had commanded me to do. I had to go into my own nature and find there a receptivity for all the things that were going on in my life as well as in Aikido practice. When I trained with both men or women, the rhythm and dynamics began to depend upon who I was training with and what we were capable of achieving together. I practiced receiving the strikes, punches, and grabs without needing to demonstrate skill. Just accurate execution of the technique. I began to take my training more playfully and to explore different emphases in techniques. I would train rigorously, then gently but firmly. Then patiently and steadily, then gracefully, then dynamically. The new questions I asked about Aikido, about myself, didn't concern what masculine or feminine is, or how to be aggressive, or who is doing it best. What I wanted to know was how to learn. I wanted to know how we help each other. I didn't know if I could help anyone. I looked to see how people help me. I needed to learn how to study, to probe, investigate, and explore. I later realized that I had passed through a threshold unknowingly. I came into the martial arts and was suddenly confronted with my life in what appeared to be a man's world. The distinction seemed to highlight my femininity and my limitations more than my ability to blend right in. I had to work within the rules of a masculine art. My feminine self-image became obvious to me. It soon became necessary to abandon many preconceptions. I still continue to uncover more preconceptions about men and women as different confrontations arise in my life. Aikido can be an arena in which to challenge your character in qualities of being. I've had to find a neutrality for those qualities in order to give them fair expression. They needed to be just "actions to do." Consequently, I felt neither masculine or feminine, but simply human. Where I had first entered the dojo specifically as a young *woman*, I now go to practice as simply another *person* who does Aikido.

Leaving behind the world of stereotypical roles for men and women opens our lives up to finding deeper balance. We lose the burden of trying to define ourselves only by our limitations. The more we find balance in our character, the more simply human we can feel about ourselves, and others. Then the natural differences between men and women and between individuals will provide us with true authenticity. I am careful not to erase what I know to be my feminine nature. The Oriental definitions for yin and yang are a good guide, but the best is intuition. It is important to me to know what is drawn from my intuitive feminine and what are the qualities that emerge from my masculine shadow. Aikido practice definitely demands both. By my conscious effort to draw upon my masculine qualities, I avoid imitation of men — even during moments in practice when I need to be assertive or extremely focused in a brief moment of time. It is in the techniques known as *irimi*, or entering, where such abilities are needed. I feel tall and strong and mountain-like when I do these techniques. The other side of practice, which allows my feminine side a turn, are those techniques which practice drawing in the attacker's force, into a spiral, and then into release. These techniques are called *tenkan,* or turning. They feel more like the movement of water, smooth and graceful; and at times, turbulent. *Irimi* and *tenkan* are the two basic moves in Aikido, and for me accurately define yin and yang. Within each *irimi* technique is a touch of *tenkan,* and in *tenkan* there is a touch of *irimi.* They demonstrate the balance of movement necessary for effective techniques. If we can embody the understanding that yin is not without its yang (and vice versa) then we can be feminine with some masculine and masculine with some feminine. The balance is to our advantage.

A particular technique in Aikido demonstrates the power of balance most profoundly. It is called *ten-chi nage,* which means heaven and earth throw. It is a marvelous lesson that O-Sensei has given us. The move is extremely difficult to enact and appears miraculous when done correctly. To do *ten-chi nage,* you have to separate the attacker's straightforward grab into two different spirals. As s/he takes hold of both of your wrists, you must simultaneously draw their force upwards and downwards, up to heaven and down to earth. If the separation is equal, then an attacker's body is lofted into the air horizontally, their feet being released from underneath and swung up in front of them. Something like slipping on a banana peel. If there is too much force in one direction only, then the technique is not *ten-chi nage.* It needs to be a delicate balance of energy. It requires a very subtle understanding about the power inherent in true balance. This was the founder's genius. He must have enjoyed that subtle understanding to give us such a technique. And that's only one example.

Ten-chi nage also says to me that I can only go in both directions at once if I already have both directions in me. From my center, I can reach out in any direction if I don't forget about my opposite. If I reach out with my left hand, my right one is not dormant. It is actively grounding the movement of the left hand. If I move both arms, then I send down grounding energy through my legs. So I am always polarizing my movements, thus my energy. This brings balance into my techniques.

When Aikido instructors instill a balance of yin/yang into their teaching, they provide men and women in Aikido a broad training in which to discover their abilities. I know for myself, that when a teacher has incorporated an understanding about the needs for all of us to be both masculine and feminine, then the class seems to cover all kinds of levels. S/he will be able to demand physical, mental and spiritual development. If teachers are lacking in some respect — say, all their techniques have a hard dynamic style — then my reaction is sort of rebellious in that I want to do blending and turning practice as well. If the emphasis of the class is on physical expertise only, then I yearn to bring out some attention to the more invisible aspects of practice. Balance is necessary to make up a good class. When we train with a sense of balance we feel a sense of completion. This carries over into our lives.

Master Ueshiba did not leave us a treatise on how to practice Aikido, all neatly spelled out in a book. He hid it in his art, in his techniques. As you practice, so shall you uncover his philosophy. (If I didn't know better, I'd risk saying he found a gentle way of brainwashing us all.) All his techniques are consistent. They all teach us about harmony, about the nature of movement in the universe, about balance and power. He is guiding us actively towards learning how to live together respectfully. If you practice open-heartedly, the lessons will begin to emerge. He was a clever man. He said his Aikido was to teach Human Beings to be one family. He never said how. He didn't have to. The art says it for him by talking to our bodies. It's up to us to let our bodies speak to our minds and hearts.

Jeff Haller

Aikido on the Basketball Court

Athletic performance comes from a subtle integration of skills and training; yet most contemporary coaching focuses only on rote teaching of techniques and neuromuscular skills. Athletic educators do not broach the real factors behind cohesive functioning, the exercises whereby our brains deepen and enlarge our capacity for complex activity.

In 1981–2 I spent six weeks of preseason training with the basketball team at St. Joseph's University; I taught Aikido principles of movement and self-awareness to the team. For thirty minutes each day before practice I had an opportunity to expand the players' perception of their habitual actions and to give them new sensory possibilities for blending with their game at greater efficiency, even under the pressure of playing at the NCAA Division I level.

For example, I spent some time with Bryan Warrick, now a guard for the Los Angeles Clippers NBA basketball team, then an All-American at St. Joseph's. On one occasion I asked him how many times he had played defense during the game against Syracuse (the previous night). Now he and I had come to the conclusion in our talks and lessons that the meaning of defense was quite different from that usually taught to university-level basketball players. In most instances defense has been regarded as a sequence of reacting to what the offense is presenting, but we practiced as though defense was mainly a means of beginning our own offense. Properly played, defense forces opponents out of their offensive patterns and routes of action; applied pressure increases their chances of making mistakes or hurrying into poor shot selection. Good defense prevents an opponent from developing its court rhythm, timing, proper execution, team cohesion, and, in that way, it ignites a powerful offense. A good defensive player moves and acts so that his offensive opponent is never allowed into the game. Now when I asked Bryan about his defense after the Syracuse game and how many times he actually played, he looked at me with some apprehension because he knew I had been watching him closely. As he fidgeted around, he finally said, "Twice." Then, to minimize the full implications of his really being in charge of his man only twice during the game, he added, "But the rest of the guys on the team weren't calling out the back picks for me to move through." I asked him whose responsibility that was. After all, only he could feel the screens as they came up behind him; only he could develop his own total court sense out of the limited vista of a flat linear court in front of him.

Now Bryan wasn't guilty of not hustling, or lack of effort; rather he was in a position of not knowing how to enact a skill he had never been tutored in by someone else or thought up himself. In all of his years of preparation to become a top-level basketball player no coach had trained him in enhanced proximal awareness or awakened him to his own force in space. Bryan was a fine athlete, but he had never been taught to feel his presence or position and move freely through a crowded space; he could not perceive collectively the opponents blocking his potential path of action. Again and again, because he didn't have the skill to apprehend the screens being set on him, he was caught and prevented from controlling the movements of his opponent.

It is hard for athletes to learn how to move with a greater sense of self-command during a game because no one coaches subtle awareness and differentiation. There is no way to be trained in how to feel what is taking place behind them. This is where the principles of Aikido come into the world of sports.

In this case I had developed a drill in which the team went through the sensory experience of generating a bubble around themselves. With a partner moving into the bubble and out, each player began to differentiate within himself the feeling of a person coming near him from any direction. Like a bumper on a bumper car, the players' bubbles allowed them to move in space without running into the bodies of their teammates. Eventually they found they could run easily on the court amongst each other without making contact, even while moving backwards. Our backs are sensory organs too if listened to in an appropriate way. Previously, the players had been so accustomed to moving in relation to the electromagnetic impluses their eyes had received they weren't able to use the other sensory data available to them.

Now if you were coaching, would you choose to have players on your team who were gifted physically, or would you rather have players who just happen to be in the right place at the right time and make the right play when it counts?

Clearly I believe that the intrapersonal skills athletes need to occupy their own bodies and expand their self-images can be taught. Athletes' repertoires of movements and postures can be expanded so they are able to meet the challenges of the court, but this special training does not come from learning rote basketball techniques and strategies. It comes only from involving themselves in a training that allows them to discover their own personal reactions under pressure, to become fluent in their communication with their own bodies, and to discover new and more functional means of handling the situations they face.

Tony Costner was a sophomore at St. Joseph's when I was working with the team. He was 6' 10", weighed 235 pounds, had a sweet shooting touch, and a thorough understanding of the game of basketball. He had led his Overbrook High School team to successive undefeated seasons in Philadelphia, but he had the tendency almost to hide behind himself and disappear on the court. It was hard to believe a man that large could take up less space and be a less imposing presence on the court than the team's point guard, six-foot Jeffrey Clark. Tony walked with his shoulders hunched, head bowed, and had serious problems in establishing offensive and defensive positions on the court, not to mention his difficulty moving his feet so he could come to the ball and catch it. My job was to develop an increased sense of body presence and size on the court. As soon as I was able to teach Tony to make a deeper connection with his own feet, body, and hands, he was able to move his whole self through the game with much greater ease. He became a more integral part of the offense because he was visible and the offensive patterns could flow easily with him participating fully. Virtually no one came into his key to score on him. Tony was "the man," the defensive backstop. The entire team's cohesion and confidence was intensified because they had a big man to go to when they needed it. This slumbering giant eventually became our dominant factor and led us to a 25 win, 5 loss season and a chance in the NCAA tournament.

What changed Tony was this. One day I walked on the court with a three-foot length of one-inch diameter lead pipe. I aked one of the players to swing the pipe directly at my head. I easily moved out of danger. Then I asked them to line up and told them I was going to swing the pipe at their heads, making a direct cutting motion downward. This threat, especially to a group of inner-city Philadelphia athletes, has the effect of enlivening a training session, and getting their attention. Without prior training in moving with this form of pressure each player was able to discover his own particular neuromuscular pattern of anxiety and move away when faced with the swinging pipe. The typical initial pattern of anxiety was to contract those muscle groups which prepare for fight or flight — the neck, pectoralis groups, abdominal erectors, and hamstrings. In other words, the head is pulled forwards, shoulders contracted, abdomen tightened, and pelvis tucked under. In this instance of pressure the players all looked like Tony. I was then able to teach them to move out of harm's way with the least amount of effort from an easy erect posture. After many repetitions of this process, the players found they could maintain their posture in moving and actually have a sense that they grew in sensory size and presence, adjusting themselves to the threat and the pressure it put on them. They also discovered they could translate this manuever to other pressure tasks they faced. Tony soon experienced that he could keep his head up and move. As he encountered the upper reaches of himself, a real internal transformation took place. Tony not only got big, he knew and felt himself to be big.

Have you ever noticed what happens to the crowd when your own team is playing in an opponent's arena and your player is on the line about to shoot a free throw? The crowd goes crazy in an attempt to distract the shooter. This, of course, brings up the question of who really is in charge and who has whom conditioned. If a player's free throw accuracy is affected by the crowd's antics, then the crowd is literally in the game and in control. The player, however, can determine how quickly the crowd sits down and becomes quiet. If he continues to make his shots, especially down the stretch of a high-intensity basketball game, he forces the crowd right back out. Think of it: it takes great personal power, self-esteem, and self-confidence to make 17,000 people sit down at will with the flick of a wrist. Yet this change of a player's internal capacity can be developed just as the ability to shoot a basketball can.

Prior to the Carrier Dome Basketball Classic in Syracuse, St. Josephs' had been shooting a miserable 59% at the free throw line, and they had been playing in small relatively quiet arenas. They now faced playing before anticipated crowds of 17,000 to 25,000. During the days prior to the tournament I gave the team specific Aikido exercises which would expand their sensory base of information and help them play on an opponent's court — not just play, but actually become more attuned to the court than even the home team usually is.

Each court and arena has its own atmosphere, crowd sense, timing, and vibration. A team which adjusts itself to an opponent's court and to an opponent's timing and rhythm will have a much improved chance of controlling environmental influences governing the game. Being able to make your free throws on an opponent's court is one of the major ways to settle a crowd. It was incredibly thrilling for me to watch a group of young men during the course of the tournament begin to find themselves in their environment and exhibit new internal skills. Down the stretch in the championship game beating Syracuse as a decided underdog, they made every free throw.

In my Aikido free-throw clinic, we began by learning what standing in a balanced, centered way means. Most athletes, especially in pressure, tend to have an upright head rather than a body orientation. This is especially true on defense when a player will follow the movement of the ball with his eyes while coming up slightly from his defensive body stance. The alternative is to learn to watch the ball with his body. To teach this I began with them standing in pairs. Each player would give his partner a slight push on the chest. This way they discovered just how difficult it was to just stand under pressure. I then taught them about *hara* — centering from a point just below the naval. After several repetitions the players found they were naturally more stable, less topheavy. We then moved onto exercises in which the players had to come to quick full stops and remain balanced in stopping. As I made the practices and routes more and more intricate they needed to discover how to orient themselves spatially with greater and greater clarity. Internalization was the goal here, not actual shooting at and defending hoops. Once they had learned to stand and move in a balanced centered way I had them try to extend their senses into all of the quadrants of the room and through limitless space itself, so their sense of size would shift with the room they were standing in. In this manner, I helped them acquaint themselves with each new arena in which they were playing. They became sensitive to details of the space. Some places might feel low and slow with little energy, while others were bright and very electric. They learned to play *with* rather than *against* the timing of each arena, so quite often they were more oriented and at home than the home team.

One evening our St. Joseph's team entered a cold damp arena at Lehigh, a school which is noted for its wrestling and football teams and fan participation but not generally as a basketball school. Although the arena was quite new, it was Christmas vacation, and clearly there would be no more than several hundred fans there. My immediate impression was "Oh Oh! We are in a little trouble here tonight." In the first place we were playing short-handed. Jeff Clark was recuperating from an injury to his large toe and Lonnie McFarlan was sitting out because he had missed practice during the week. Still the odds were hugely in our favor; the court definitely was not. We were a running race-horse team against a group of plodders. It was one of those nights on which, unless the players understood the circumstances and played within themselves and in tune with the arena, they were going to be upset. To play well they were going to have to slow their tempo, make crisp passes, and put up only good shots. In the first half my premonition was borne out as Lehigh moved easily into the lead. We were in a dog fight. Earlier I had taken the players around the arena and had pointed out to them that the timing was funny on this evening and that they were going to have to be on their toes. At half-time they came together and recognized the opponent for what he was. They won in a squeaker.

During the time I was working with the St. Joseph's players, I conducted a drill in which the players were asked to glue themselves to the movements of a player across from them leading their actions, not unlike what is learned in Aikido training. This process of mirroring begins with two players standing opposite each other. Moving slowly with his hands, and eventually his feet, one of the players provides a movement pattern for the other to follow. The partner must reflect the movement in a deeply connected way. Starting almost in time lapse, the players learn more and more to match completely the other's movements until the patterns seem as one, at which point the other player takes over the movements, and begins to lead. Almost imperceptibly the lead changes. The players become quite profound in this exercise and find they can attune themselves to their opponent so well and in such a deep bodily way that they no longer bite at fakes or other false moves but stay with their opponents easily and clearly. I must point out here that "easily and clearly" to me means that they are tuned in to their opponents and to themselves a higher percentage of the time. Obviously these players are not perfect and make mistakes, but the rapidity with which they recover and bring themselves back into the game is striking. Because they know what it is to be in their bodies and in the game they can feel when they are out. It is important to realize that Aikido does not so much bring an exotic method to basketball as it does awaken the players to the "Aikido" in basketball already.

Human beings have very individual means of accessing, encoding, and storing the information which is the basis of their actions. During the "mirror drills" one of my players who was naturally kinesthetic immediately began to move in a very gooey glued manner, while another player had to visualize about glue. The kinesthetic player became neuromuscularly involved in gluey actions; the other, in thinking about glue, actually decreased his ability to move, because his means of visualization didn't lead to movements which were actively congruent with glue. His actions became congruent only with visualizing about something. He wasn't kinesthetically in his body, so he couldn't feel a dynamic gluey set of possibilities for action. There was a communication breakdown between me and the players until I could explain the practice in such a way that all of them could bring their own personal body senses to what it was like to move in a gluey manner in relation to an opponent's movements. All of the players eventually learned how to differentiate between the submodalities of kinesthetic, visual, and auditory action. With this skill the entire group began to communicate with a greater rapport and understanding of how each discrete person among them primarily encoded the world.

Jeffrey Clark became so good at glue he literally took his opponent, not only out of the game but in effect out of the season, as St. Joseph's beat their arch rival Villanova by 20 points. Jeffrey so glued himself to his opponent that he seemed to undermine that player's confidence and self-assurance. His Villanova counterpart failed to play well the rest of the season.

I have worked with athletes from all sports: in football, interior linemen and defensive backs; among golfers, a woman who had been assaulted and had lost her ability to compete under pressure and a man who was once a touring PGA pro but had severely damaged his knees in a car wreck and lost his touch around the greens; with skiers, a 20-year-old man who with two years of training went on to win the US Olympic trials for the biathalon. I trained one world-class runner from Ireland to work against high winds in races, unfortunately to the point she ran against herself and injured herself.

By and large, the area we have failed to incorporate in teaching our athletes has been the process of sensory self-awareness. This is where Aikido comes into the picture. In effect, most of our training methods involve memorizing rote moter skills and techniques and then practicing them over and over again. The problem our athletes face then is one of adapting a set of rigid techniques to a constantly shifting set of circumstances. Our self-image determines all of our actions. An athlete with a limited self-image will only have a few possible ways he can adapt himself to any given situation. Being limited in self-image limits his or her actions. Yet the only way we can expand an athlete's self-image is to provide an environment for him to discover new and refined sensory/motor possibilities, to give him an extensive enough resource base with enough choices so he can act creatively and authentically in pressure situations.

Aikido trains body awareness: movement in pressure, balance, efficient action, spatial orientation, concentration, proximal sense, attunement, and energy states of action. As a martial art growing out of traditions several thousands of years old, Aikido encompasses elements which we have only begun to broach in our contemporary sports with histories of less than a century. In Aikido we learn that our movements and the degree of our actions are governed by our internal sensations. By expanding our sensory base of action our self-image expands, a sense of resources and efficiency develops, and we adapt quickly and skillfully to new environments and complex tasks at hand.

One day during the St. Joseph's season Bryan was having trouble with his jump shot. I could see he was steering the ball and trying to determine its flight. I asked him to pretend there was a huge magnet in the basket and the ball would without fail be drawn there. In other words, the ball would be pulled naturally to the basket. After a few efforts he found his release improving; he became more attuned to the basket than to trying to shoot the ball. "Ball to the basket" was the auditory mantra I instructed him to shoot with — not "Bryan shooting the ball to the basket." The latter would have brought his conscious mind back into trying to control the process. The next game against North Carolina/Charlotte Bryan had a perfect 12-for-12 night from the field and shot 8-for-8 at the foul line. His 30-point effort led us to a win.

Quite often prior to practice I would just have the players stand on one foot and then shift to their other foot, in order to gain a more deeply rooted sense of balance. After a few repetitions alone, they would do this with a partner pushing on their chest to make the practice more difficult. Without a sense of center, keeping balanced is impossible. The more deeply a player could connect with himself the easier it was to work with a partner. From there the coaches would take the players into a rebounding drill. With their initial feeling of center and connection it became easier for them to find their man, block out, and, from deep roots, keep their rebounding position.

Aikido practices are easily adapted to any athletic situation. Individuals who embark on learning the sensory awareness of a skilled martial artist will find they not only develop new motor neural pathways of action but become quite supple in those actions. At the outset Aikido movements may seem foreign to an athlete, but the fact that they can absolutely transform his or her performance in a competitive situation and can be adapted to any game or sport usually breaks down any resistance. The Aikido grace of action and flow of form, while enhancing the beauty of sports and the internalization of its activities, also performs another role by reducing the chance of injury. An athlete who is self-aware is not as likely to place himself in a dangerous position or move in a way that injury can result.

Athletes retrained in this way not only meet their goals but actually find they can express themselves in ways far beyond what they even thought possible. Instead of relying on rote gymnastic drills as a means of training they actually generate new possibilities for themselves. Given enough new and differentiated sensory data in each training session, they approach perfection of movement in finer and finer approximations of their inner beings. Gradually they come to realize that there is no real "making it," only an on-going sense of "becoming" themselves in new and renewed actions, finely attuned to each varied situation they face in their athletic initiations. Through Aikido athletes become human beings and athletics serves as an exquisite means of self expression for them.

Cheryl S. Reinhardt

Inner Power: The Integration of Aikido and the Feldenkrais Method

The Feldenkrais Method is a gentle approach to learning through movement: re-educating what has become stuck or habitual in one's daily life. As a Feldenkrais practitioner, I feel challenged to introduce students to their own center and inner power. Through movements and manipulations—based on an understanding of the working of the nervous system in relationship to the skeleto-muscular system and the emotions—their muscles gradually soften, their joints open slightly, and most important, they develop a new recognition that freedom from pure habit is possible. The whole person is taken into account, from physical complaints to family life. What a person does with his or her toes or how a person handles strong feeling has a direct relationship to the alignment of the hip and back, which, in turn, affects the emotions and behavior. Often, my work consists of helping adults to experience how much they are overprotecting/defending an old trauma. As they let go a bit, the trauma can heal. Openness and vulnerability are being reintroduced.

Dr. Moshe Feldenkrais, before founding this work, was primarily a doctor of physics and held a high-ranking black belt in judo. His background in the martial arts was an inherent part of his understanding of the human condition. When he worked, one couldn't help but notice his breathing, full and steady as a warrior in training. But my own martial training had other sources that ultimately transformed my Feldenkrais orientation.

I was originally drawn to Aikido by what I had heard about

a specific teacher. Robert Nadeau's approach to Aikido was expressly from a spiritual point of view. He had defined "spiritual" as meaning, "There is more to me than I was aware of." He had emphasized Takemusu, "aliveness of being." I was attracted by the promise of learning more about energy and the universal laws of creation. Yet, I was actually quite hesitant to walk up the stairs to what would become my home dojo because I had a sense that once I did, life would be different. The reluctance I felt is similar to what people experience as they face any breaking up of their habitual mode. Habit is familiar and one learns how to live comfortably with its limitations; in fact, it is preferable. To free up a habit, to learn something new, draws tremendous energy into the human system — an energy which initially may be perceived as intolerable. Before my training, I had a tendency to seize on situations and exaggerate them out of proportion. Through Aikido, I began to respect situations as they were and to assess their actual size.

During my training, the philosophy of Aikido was consistently introduced with its techniques. So while we were learning to fend off attacks, we were learning to be with ourselves under pressure, to recognize our habits of withdrawal and defense, and, ultimately to settle into a much deeper center within ourselves. Within this center, we could find harmony with the laws of creation, and a sense of our own origins.

Probably the major quality I carry with me from training in Aikido is an ability to recognize my propensities and then to move beyond them. For example, my propensity to dramatize has become internally discernible. Although my tendency towards drama is still there, I am no longer locked into it with no key. Awareness of the habit allows me to drop my attention from an hysterical manifestation of energy to a centered functioning flow. Years ago, I had a dream that I was in jail. The cell door was wide open and it seemed that I had access to walk out; yet I felt chained, unable to take my freedom without my jailer coming and setting me free. Outside my cell, there was an Aikido class with my teacher and my friends participating. It looked enticing and friendly, but I felt I had to remain confined and left out. What I have now, as a result of my Aikido training, is freedom to walk through an open door that I sense has always been open. We each have an open door but we are locked in by our habits. This is what I teach in my blend of the Feldenkrais Method and Aikido.

It took me a long time to accept the martial aspect of Aikido as seriously as it was intended. As a girl, I had never physically fought, so, in many ways, self-defense was foreign to me. At times, my Aikido teacher would push me past what I experienced as my breaking point because my self-image did not include the tremendous power that became available through Aikido. The seemingly intolerable pressure evoked a phenomenal mastery in me that matched it. Once I experienced this, I could no longer be satisfied with my own passivity or with allowing my students to learn passively. I had to bring them into interaction with each other.

Gingerly at first, I experimented with them standing and doing simple pressure techniques. I felt as though I were sneaking Aikido in on my innocent Feldenkrais students. They were coming to do a very gentle moving form and I was introducing them, unnamed, to a martial art. They found themselves punching and grabbing, attacking and defending.

The Feldenkrais work and Aikido have come to fit together like a hand in a glove. I use a combination of solo movement and partner work, calling on each individual to pay attention first to his or her own body and then to what changes in that body once interaction with another (the partner in Aikido) begins. In my classes I generally begin with the students in stillness, flat on their backs on the floor. I guide them through an exploration of their sense of self in that state. People come in late, the doors slam, the traffic roars by on the street — gradually, each focuses on what is going on in his or her body, asking himself (herself), "Where am I holding? Where am I making contact with the floor?" These are questions that have counterparts all through the waking day.

I then introduce gentle movements to give them a framework within which to find themsleves — to detect the motion and feel of their normal functioning. Contact with the floor is a step toward making contact outside of themselves, beyond their personal boundaries. The floor is a safe inanimate partner, an objective witness, readying each for the next phase, another human being. I now ask, "What is your breathing pattern like? Is it shallow? Halted? Deep and steady? Is your head tilted to the left or right? Is your jaw held more than may be necessary?" There is not a wrong or correct answer to these questions, though most of us may judge ourselves immediately and quite harshly, but this attitude only inhibits learning. I more want to establish a situation in which each recognizes his or her norm, the starting place. Within this recognition, awareness is increased and a fuller self-image is developed. One woman described the experience as being able to take the lampshade off a lightbulb and letting the light shine brightly, unfiltered.

The next challenge is to let expansion continue as we stand, as we move into partner interaction. Aikido techniques are the form we work through and upon here, much like a trellis giving shape to growing vines. These movements are not loose or arbitrary. They have evolved from an ancient and sophisticated understanding of human physiology, social conflict, and universal energy. Within our relationship to a partner we come upon a pressure different from one we dealt with lying alone on the mats. Feelings, sensations, threats, perceptions about the self and others become more difficult to deny. With Aikido's principles of merging and spiraling energy, the student has the opportunity to recognize his capacity for blending at the same time he recognizes all obstacles he has erected to thwart this natural sense.

I ask students to carry their openness from the mat to its next step and to think consciously how to integrate this flow of energy into daily life where basic habits are formed. The Aikido forms offer us a situation to trace this process physically letting the answer emerge within the action.

During these classes, it becomes obvious, not only to me but to the other students, when someone is holding back or working too hard. The defenses revealed there are the same ones people survive by in their daily lives. Everyone has habitual actions that prevent them from being fully present. One fairly common tendency is what I call "the over-involved mother syndrome." Often, while executing a throw, the student becomes involved with the partner's safety more than necessary and at the cost of his or her own stability. They twist themselves up with all their attention on the partner and practically fall too. With Inner Power training, they can explore a new way of caring. They learn to maintain their own center and to let go of the partner, to assume the partner has the presence to take care of himself. The partner then can draw confidence from the lack of over-indulgent concern. This is a different kind of gift from smothering attention.

Jane

Jane came in strong, full of convincing, dominating power. She looked solid and seemed to move with comfort and without fear. She confronted me in the first class with the concern that the class might be too gentle for her, not confrontative enough. She also complained of shoulder pain and tension. In watching me, she was always impressed at my willingness to move in close to others.

In one class, where we were doing a basic blend which led into a throw, Jane was required to move in close and occupy her partner's territory while staying centered and full within herself. She started out hating it, angry, wanting it over with. She tried to bully her partner, scare him or intimidate him so he would fall. Jane's partner resisted being dealt with this way. Jane saw that her present mode was ineffective. She recognized her habitual pattern, that upon feeling fear, she would race in to get the situation over with as soon as possible. She integrated this insight. As she readied to do another throw, she said to herself (and let her body experience the sensation), "I am angry, I want to get this over with and. . . . " She needed to acknowledge such feelings, inhabit them, face them squarely and then move from them. If she couldn't look directly at her own resistance and acknowledge her negative feelings, they would always propel her action. Only as she slowed

170

down and met them squarely she created in herself a chance for transformation and perhaps some pleasure.

Jane learned to recognize her shallow breathing and her shoulders held tight as a physical signal to wait an extra moment, to settle and take a breath. The quality of her action shifted from pushing her partner away to moving in closer to him. She completed the throw, maintaining the relationship throughout. The partner felt touched, satisfied, not bullied. Jane expressed herself fully and stayed in contact.

What changed? How can a major change be so simple? It is simple and it isn't. Fully acknowledging who we are with our bodies, in our nervous system, our bones, our muscles, brings us closer to our essential self. Jane learned a way to acknowledge the negative habit she had and then to change to a more positive form of contact. Taking periodic breaks from interaction by lying on the mat allowed Jane to integrate her new information. The breaks give a sense of freedom as opposed to the harassment of time pressures or the constraint to understand and integrate too fast. It was the excitement of the physical movement that enabled her to rearrange herself and do it differently.

This isn't just an idea. The body shows change. What is remembered and taken home is the memory of how the student did the exercise and what changed. There is kinesthetic memory of change.

This lesson was important in Jane's personal life. She had recently decided to move out of a long-term relationship. Soon after that decision, her partner was forced to make a career change. Jane wanted to support her partner through this change. So, her challenge was to live in the present, knowing she was about to leave and yet being there with the person she loved without trying to get it over with.

There are so many situations throughout life that we find unpleasant but can't hurry. There are times when a child is in a stage of development that simply has to be waited out. There are instances in a marriage that are difficult and my require patience. When an adult has a dying parent, an uncomfortable situation must be faced day to day. The exercises done in class, like the one described above with Jane, carry over into the tremendously varied life situations of the different students. In all situations mentioned, the discomfort must be felt, acknowledged, faced with full knowledge that one would rather get it over with. The student learns to take the time to recognize what is a good place to make decisions from and when it is best to wait before taking long-lasting action.

Meryl

Meryl's starting place seems to be looking at herself, asking continuously, "How am I doing? Is what I'm doing okay with you?" Meryl seems frail. She is very thin and scared-looking. Her shoulders are rather rounded, chest a bit concave; there appears to be an emptiness, a dark hole, in the torso. When she lies down on the mat her first effort is an attempt to take up very little space. At the mention of power, she is definitive that this is something that she does not want. She gets cold easily. She looks to me to tell her what to do, to authenticate her. Meryl is an artist and her paintings are shown and bought in galleries throughout the world. From the beginning of our work I suspected there was power there, but I could not see where and how to tap it. It first showed when she disagreed with me about some money she owed. She was very sure of herself, became surprisingly strong, and she suddenly did not look wispy at all. She overpowered me. So there it was. Our challenge was to integrate this strength, which shows itself sometimes but is so lacking at other times. At home, when she is working artistically, she feels strong. It is out in public that she identifies only with her wispy self. On her own, Meryl has found art as a medium for expression. Comfortable in this medium, she functions not from her defenses but from a more pure open self-image. She has not learned to allow that expression to come through her body or her movements. When she is with other people, she loses her sense of identity, and becomes dependent on others' approval. Frustrated by always having to seek approval, she withdraws and seems anti-social; hence the rounded shoulders, the caved-in torso. If asked about anger and power, she says, "Not me," and yet it is all there. I find it in her art, in her boldly seeking me out, and in her struggle with me over money. Meryl's style becomes clarified doing a basic blend. She puts out her hand for her partner to grab. But she looks at it from a distance, almost seeing it more from her partner's point of view than her own. Her focus is external. She is not experiencing her internal sensations. She is numbing herself to what is really happening.

There are so many reasons why people don't stay present as the partner grabs. Some people don't want to take action for fear of not doing it perfectly; others think they shouldn't allow themselves to feel pleasure. Some people fear that if they express themselves, their anger will be overwhelming; others don't want to feel a deep lingering memory of abandonment. The variations are limitless. "Self-importance is our greatest enemy. Think about it — what weakens us is feeling offended by the deeds and misdeeds of our fellow men. Our self-importance requires that we spend most of our lives offended by someone."[1]

I point out to Meryl that she is too often just watching. From observing others discovering how to make an internal shift and from her experience as an artist, combined with the past year in my class, she has gradually become familiar with her bones, her muscles, and herself as a person who can move. Now she recognizes spontaneously when she is watching, rather than doing. That simple awareness shifts her attention from outside herself to a full experience from within. In the recognition she is present to herself as well as her surroundings. She moves into the blend. In the midst of the blend she begins to look at it again, stopping feeling; she doesn't seem to have the power or strength to complete it. Her actions are saying, "See, I am really weak." I point out the tendency of her flitting attention, and again with recognition, her mind comes back to only the move we are doing. She is now centered. After much practice over time, as Meryl is moving into a blend she doesn't withdraw or go numb. She is able to stay in contact with her partner and be in the middle of the present situation. The movement takes place and is powerful. The partner feels really affected. Meryl is a bit amazed at first, unfamiliar with an ease of self that is so effective. At first, it seems as though her body wants to say, *I don't feel powerful, I don't feel pleasure and I can't do this,* but soon her self image is changing, growing to encompass a bigger self that is fine with movement in the world. Meryl can practice this with her husband. Too often, they have conversations in which she is so concerned with what he is thinking that she loses touch with her own viewpoint. This is followed by total frustration on her part because she then does not feel fully understood. Meryl's challenge has been to follow her attentions and notice where they have wandered. When she is focused on an Aikido move, her breathing is fuller and she has more body awareness. A satisfying communication ensues. Practicing with the daily situations, Meryl has begun to integrate her new self-image, her fullness into her work and her life.

Dr. Moshe Feldenkrais often remarked during the time I studied with him, "You can, at any time of your life, provided I can convince you that there is nothing permanent and compulsive in your system except your belief that it is so, relearn anything that you would like."

Jacob

Jacob was desperate for some new form of physical treatment when he came to see me after years of back pain, hospitalization, and chiropractors. I worked with him privately, helping him to discover what he was doing in his daily interactions as well as with his body that was leading to such severe pain. We found he was holding himself almost rigid from the waist up. He was not allowing himself to feel much in his pelvis or legs. This is one of those "what-came-first, the-chicken-or-the-egg?" situations. It is fairly common to defend oneself from pain by not allowing feeling sensation in the areas surrounding pain. It is also true that when there is not much feeling sensation in an area of the body, there also may not be much movement in that area, which leads to stiffness and physical difficulty. Often, the pattern will be disclosed only as it is changing. People sometimes make the discovery that they have not had movement in their upper back only *when* they realize their potential for movement in the upper area of the spine. Through the gentle movements I did with Jacob, his awareness increased and his back pain decreased rapidly and he was able to join the Inner Power class.

This class was appropriate for him because it gave him a situation among other people in which he could discover his reaction to pressure in his daily life. He tends to jump into things fast and totally. He tells lots of people about the wonderful things he does and they benefit as well. This pattern shows up in the basic blend. His partner grabs his wrist, Jacob breathes, doesn't react too quickly. As he begins the movement, the partner feels connected with and pleasurably affected. But mid-movement, Jacob fades. The partner is stunned. A minute ago, there was so much there. Now, the partner feels alone, rejected. Jacob does this in his relationships. He starts well but is unable to go the distance. Working with Jacob in class, I see that his starting place is happy and exuberant. Soon this fades into a scared sense of feeling empty, not enough. It is almost as though, if he is not involved with something large outside himself, he feels dark and cavernous. Most people like Jacob. He does a great deal for other people. He is often the first to take on volunteer jobs. He has many friends, most of whom he stays in close contact with. He does extra work in the office for which he is not paid: he spends hours a week, for example, editing an in-office newsletter. He goes to bed late and gets up early. The back pain had to scream very loud for him to pay attention to himself, and then he had no idea where to begin —what his own body was and needed, separate from others and external demands. As he really inhabits his own emptiness and lives with it, he is beginning to feel the sheer pleasure of his power surfacing. He practices this in the partner techniques, catching his own loss of attention when it is about to rush off with him. He takes a breath, inhabits his feet in contact with the mat, feels sensation in his belly and legs, and senses his power. He follows through from this and deals with the throw and the partner completely. At home and at work, he is doing a bit less for others and spending more time just with himself, finding what he wants to do with and by himself. When teaching, Feldenkrais often referred to his exercises as a tool *to teach the person, mind and body, what was there naturally, but has been lost by social acclimation.*

There are numerous individual variations on this theme of people and their habitual patterns. In my class, I find it is helpful to do the gentle movements both before and in-between the Aikido throws and holds. The smaller quieter movements allow the larger movements to be broken down into parts. For example, an Aikido blend may be composed of many parts, one of which contains a spiraling movement of the spine that we have worked with lying on the mats. When the students can recall kinesthetically the image of doing that movement on the floor, they can then execute the movement with the right impetus and energy; much more so than if they are intent on force, the manipulation of their partner, or the mechanics of which foot and arm goes where. The gentle movements allow the individual to discover and clarify a self-image which is so often lost and confused in dealing with other people.

"If we do not know what we are actually enacting then we cannot possibly do what we want. I believe that knowing oneself is the most important thing a human being can do for himself. How can one know oneself? By learning to act not as one should, but as one does. We have great difficulty in sorting out what we do as we should from what we want to do with ourselves."[2]

When we do standing Aikido techniques with a partner, our habits become much clearer. In the beginning, most people are uneasy at feeling themselves. They certainly find it embarrassing to describe their movement patterns out loud. In time, the interplay between physical activity and mental perception allows a new "take" on the self and our own habitual responses. The group also becomes a tremendously nurturing, empathic audience. One becomes comfortable sharing what one did with a partner because most of the foibles and "mistakes" are so common among the group. We all do most of them and we can only change once we become aware.

The Aikido basics are fundamental in this class. There have been students who used my teaching as an introduction to Aikido and then gone on and joined a dojo. There have also been advanced Aikido students who came to this class for an alternative mode of practicing. The emphasis is on inner work, the processing that contributes to human growth. The martial aspect weaves its way into the student's being. One student recently reported feeling unattackable as she now walks down the street.

Inside each person, I believe, is locked a larger being which begins to emerge as one fully acknowledges and experiences oneself in the present moment (not who I'd like to be or should be, but who I am right now, human frailties and all). This emergence is the take-off point for transcendence or the spiritual dimension within this work. In class, I demonstrate how Aikido can provide a form for exploring what scares us, what threatens us, even what is negative within ourselves. When someone proceeds with an Aikido move they didn't think they could do, and then accomplishes it, quickly, with hardly any force used, that is transcendence. A person has done something not seemingly possible, by blending body and mind — and has thus revealed a bigger and possibly truer self.

REFERENCES

1. Casteneda, Carlos, *The Fire from Within*, Simon and Schuster, New York, 1984, p.26.
2. Feldenkrais, Moshe, *The Elusive Obvious*, Meta Publications, 1981, p.xi.

Donald T. Saposnek, Ph.D.

Aikido: A Model for Brief Strategic Therapy

Softness is the mind of a willow,
  Which turns the force of the wind against itself.
Suppleness is the way to be strong,
  Learn, thus, its exquisite utility.

—Japanese odes

The difficulties inherent in developing a graphic conceptual model for brief strategic therapy, which is based upon nontraditional concepts, assumptions, and techniques, can be eased by drawing parallels to a comparable conceptual system. Such comparisons can provide different perspectives and help to achieve higher levels of conceptual clarity. In a side note to descriptions of their therapy techniques, Watzlawick, Weakland, and Fisch (11) and Watzlawick (9) note parallels between the approach of brief strategic therapy and the art of "judo," in that resistances are utilized rather than confronted. Such an observation is insightful and provides us with a useful concept upon which to build. However, a more recently developed and more sophisticated martial art, Aikido, appears to provide much greater depth and accuracy than judo as a conceptual model from which to draw parallels to brief strategic therapy. In this paper similarities between Aikido and brief strategic therapy are delineated with respect to their contexts, basic principles of practice, and philosophical and attitudinal positions. An integrative case example is presented at the end of the paper.

Donald T. Saposnek, Ph.D.

Aikido

The Word "Aikido" (actually three characters in Japanese) means the method or way (*do*) for the coordination or harmony (*ai*) of mental energy or spirit (*ki*). Aikido is a Japanese art of self-defense founded slightly over fifty years ago by Master Morehei Uyeshiba. It is derived from a blending and adaptation of many martial art systems and is based upon ethical considerations contained in Eastern religious and philosophical thought but differs from other self-defense methods in its essential motivations and intents. Whereas other self-defense approaches (e.g., karate, kung fu) involve linear attacks on others and may be utilized to inflict injury or death upon an attacker (as is also true of judo), Aikido, in its most masterful form, is utilized merely to neutralize and harmlessly redirect the aggression of the attacker.

Contextual Similarities

The context of Aikido is one in which a person, or persons, approaches the Aikidoist with an intended challenge (attack). By his actions, the challenger is stating: "I am challenging you to deal with me and to try to change me. . . . I'll prove that you cannot and that I am more powerful than you." The Aikidoist, however, perceives this challenge not as a competitive or conflictual one, but rather as an "opportunity" both to learn about and teach the challenger more constructive and harmless ways of asserting his energy. Hence, the Aikidoist functions as a "teacher," and when the challenger (student) approaches, the Aikidoist, using his special techniques, proceeds to teach the challenger that it is futile and unkind to challenge him aggressively, and he tries to "send the challenger away (as briefly and harmlessly as he can) . . . somewhat wiser." *

Similarly, a client approaches a therapist with a comparable, often unconscious, challenge, as if to say, "I am challenging you to deal with me and to try to change me. . . . I'll prove that you

---

* Greg Brodsky, 1976; personal communication.

cannot and that I am more powerful than you." This often inevitable strategic resistance to change in therapy has been well elaborated by Haley (2, 1), Watzlawick et al. (10, 11), Watzlawick (9), Palazzoli et al. (5), and others. It was aptly stated by Pittman when he said, "People come to therapy in order *not* to change. . . . If they wanted to change, they wouldn't come to therapy" (6). Moreover, the brief strategic therapist also views himself as a teacher whose function is to help the client, as briefly and harmlessly as he can, to find more constructive interactions in which to engage his energies.

Similarities in Basic Principles of Practice

Systems and Interactionist Approach

The Aikidoist always views challenges from a systems perspective within a multi-level interactional context. The challenger is perceived in direct relation to the Aikidoist, in relation to his immediate surroundings (especially to other challengers), in relation to spatial and temporal factors (timing), and, on the most abstract level, in relation to all natural hierarchical levels. Moreover, the Aikidoist's movements are circular, and the Aikidoist always places himself as the center point of a "dynamic sphere" of interactions occurring around the periphery.

In contrast to the more linear Judo axiom, "Push when pulled, and pull when pushed," the Aikido axiom is "Turn when pushed, and enter when pulled." It is this spherical motion that in most situations gives Aikido its more dynamic and effective variety. The Aikidoist spins, twirls, and rotates as he blends with and maintains control of the interactions of the challengers. His body becomes like a spinning top, exquisitely maintaining its balance and by this motion spinning off or drawing in everything it touches. This motion has been compared to the natural phenomena of powerful whirlwinds and whirlpools. By conceptualizing and utilizing forces in a circular, interactional fashion, the Aikidoist assures that a strategy that has begun no longer has an original cause or an original effect. In fact, it often is not even clear who is the attacker and who is being attacked. An Aikido maneuver in action appears like a ballet. It is graceful, smooth, subtle, and effective, both functionally and aesthetically. The quick blending of forces makes indistinguishable the cause-effect relationships and makes apparent only the circularity of forces blended together for mutual problem-solving (neutralization of aggression and redirection of energies). Such a systems approach is in accord with the humanistic ethic of Aikido, which attempts to eliminate the concepts of "enemies" and "bad persons."

Similarly, the brief strategic therapist always views his clients from a systems theory perspective, perceiving the client in relationship to other persons within a context. Problems are not viewed as residing within individuals, but in the interactions between people, in acausal, regularly patterned, systemic sequences of behavior. Once he accepts the challenge of helping a client to change, the therapist becomes a facilitator-contributor to the interactional sequence upon which he focuses his interventions (1). Using his unique "centered" position as leverage, he proceeds to direct the ongoing interactional sequences in a more constructive way. The therapist is best seen as a "verbal spinning top," maintaining his own conceptual balance while spinning off challenges, using reframing and distraction, and drawing on the client's motivation by speaking his conceptual language. After maneuvering the interactions of the clients to a successful resolution, he pulls out of the ongoing system of interactions, respecting the integrity of the system. Viewing people from such an interactionist position allows a therapist to function more comprehensively and humanistically. It compels him to be more aware of the consequences of his interventions on the lives of other significant persons in the client's life. It helps him to avoid viewing people as "pathological" (enemies) but instead to view interactions as potentially positive.

Hence, the circular view of causality in brief strategic therapy closely parallels the circular movements and circular orientation to conflict resolution in Aikido.

Knowledge of Attacks

The practice of Aikido is not based solely upon a thorough knowledge and mastery of the Aikido techniques of neutralization themselves but also upon an equally thorough familiarity with all types and forms of possible attack, in accordance with the ancient Japanese axiom that "the very first requisite for defense is to know the enemy." (12, p.45) The importance of having comprehensive knowledge of the attack by studying and analyzing the various parts, forms, and patterns of attacks is especially essential because the attack itself contains the very elements that an Aikido defensive strategy will utilize physically, functionally, and psychologically in neutralizing the attempted aggression.

An effective brief strategy therapist similarly must know strategies of human functioning well. He must be able to perceive the functional aspects of a variety of verbal and nonverbal behaviors. He must understand the paradoxical nature and functional use of emotions and ambivalence. He must be thoroughly familiar with and able to isolate and describe a wide range of interactional patterns and strategies that clients use in resisting change and in influencing family members, strangers, and therapists. Such knowledge is crucial because the therapist uses strategies similar in form to those of the client but extracts the functional aspects of these strategies and uses them therapeutically for problem resolution, rather than problem formulation. (11)

Blending Without Clashing

An Aikidoist never confronts or clashes with the challenger. Instead he accepts, joins, and moves with the challenger's energy flow in the direction in which it was going. Through such blending, resistance ceases to exist because the Aikidoist offers nothing for the challenger to resist. The Aikidoist does not use any external force or coercion but utilizes only that energy already within the challenger. Hence the Aikidoist can successfully convert the potential resistance of the challenger into free energy in order to guide him into more positive and constructive directions. And this follows

poetically with the humanistic and harmonious spirit of Aikido —
"Aiki is not a technique to fight with or defeat the enemy. It is
the way to reconcile the world and make human beings one family." (7, p.177)

The brief strategic therapist likewise blends with the approach
and style of the client and does not clash with or directly confront
him. The therapist accepts and flows with the energy and direction of the challenge, thereby minimizing or eliminating the client's
resistance. By offering little or no resistance back, the therapist
can utilize the client's potential resistance as free energy that he
can guide into more beneficial directions. Hence the therapist may
talk the same jargon as the client, temporarily express acceptance
of the same values as the client, or agree with the hopelessness
of the situation, or even with the futility of therapy.

Both the Aikidoist and brief strategic therapist practice blending and bending, not defending. Yielding to the energy of the
challenger gives both practitioners the strength of flexibility. As
the practitioner yields, the challenger is simultaneously given permission to complete his challenge sequence. However, when a
challenger is given permission to complete his challenge, the act
takes on a different meaning and no longer seems so inviting. The
challenger is left, at that moment, feeling empty, frustrated, and
perhaps a bit scared.

Extending

After the Aikidoist has blended with the challenger's movement, he allows the movement to reach its natural completion.
He then *extends* the end point of the movement slightly further
than it would go naturally, leaving the challenger off balance and
vulnerable to an easy shift in direction of his energy flow by the
Aikidoist. While the challenger is in such a vulnerable stance, the
Aikidoist has much power and control over the direction in which
the particular sequence will go, and he can effortlessly guide the
challenger to a successful resolution.

Similarly, after the brief strategic therapist has blended with
the approach of his client (e.g., "I can fully understand why you

are feeling so depressed, as you clearly have lots of reasons to be very depressed. . . . "), he then *extends* the end point of the movement slightly further than it would go naturally (e.g., " . . . but I would like you to practice letting yourself go even further and get even more depressed than you are now. . . . ").The psychological disorientation and confusion generated in the client by such a move is parallel to the physical disorientation produced in the Aikido challenger at such a point. The client at this point is off balance and vulnerable to a shift in direction of his (psychic) energy flow.

Paradox and the Unexpected

The stance of the Aikidoist has numerous aspects of paradox. The moment that the challenger begins to approach with an attack, the Aikidoist, with open arms and open palms, "welcomes" the challenger. He views the challenge as an opportunity to learn more about Aikido and to practice it rather than as a dangerous or frightening event to be avoided. The "attack" is viewed as a "gift of energy," and the transaction is viewed as a creative system of "joining" rather than one of conflict. The Aikidoist proceeds to demonstrate the element of surprise — doing the unexpected. He does not respond reflexively to a challenger in the more typical and predictable manner, as by running from the challenger, defensively blocking the attack, or attacking first. Instead, the Aikidoist approaches the challenger, joins the attack form, moves in close rather than pulls away, and redirects the challenger into a creative ballet-like encounter — and then off into vacant space. Needless to say, the challenger is puzzled and intrigued by such an odd, unexpected stance. The Aikidoist has, paradoxically, "reframed" the challenger's energy from negative to positive. Thus the challenger will leave the encounter unable to explain what happened to him, yet experiencing some resolution (change) of what brought him there in the first place.

Similarly, the brief strategic therapist manifests many aspects of paradox. He welcomes, blends with, and extends symptoms, and he may even create new symptoms as he begins to deal with the client's challenge. He gives directives that appear illogical and intended to make the situation worse for the client. Then, when the situation actually improves as a result of the directive given, the therapist may act puzzled or even disheartened by the client for making improvements "too quickly." The therapist, strategically, may act irrationally and unpredictably. He may show more pessimism than the pessimist, more neurotic behavior than the neurotic, and more psychotic behavior than the psychotic. Utilizing the power of the unexpected, the therapist may express pessimism to a client about the possibility for change as he expertly induces change to happen. Then, as the client begins to change, rather than praise him, the therapist, paradoxically, urges him to "go slow" with any changes. Finally, after the client's problems have been resolved, the therapist may bewilder the client further by requesting a "relapse" of symptoms. As is true for the Aikido challenger, the brief therapy client also leaves the encounter puzzled and intrigued, unable to explain what happened, yet feeling changed and experiencing a resolution of his problems. Through the use of paradox and unexpected strategies, both practitioners are able to effect maximum change with minimum awareness, and hence minimum cognitive resistance.

"One-Down" Stance

When challenged, the Aikidoist assumes a humble, innocent, posture. He appears neither menacing nor threatening but rather relaxed, flexible, and harmless. Such a stance invites in and immediately disarms the challenger because of its unexpected lack of resistance. After the quick, effective, and harmless resolution of the challenge, the Aikidoist stands innocently in front of the challenger, displaying an unexpected humility before the great demonstration of power just made and, consequently, achieving a magnified degree of respect. Paradoxically, his power is born out of a no-power stance.

Similarly, the brief strategic therapist may assume a one-down stance. Being careful, strategically, to avoid getting stuck in the expected one-up "professional" stance, he may show pessimism at his ability to help the client. As he proceeds to develop his strategies, he may periodically apologize for his incompetence, inadequacies, and denseness. He may ask a father who is skeptical of doctors, "Do you mind if we proceed on a first name basis?" He might add, "I've never dealt with a problem quite like yours, and I'm not sure I'll even know how to help you. . . . " Then, at the resolution of a problem, the therapist may act innocent, humble, and naive as to the reasons for the change. Finally, he gives credit to the client for making the changes and sends the client on his way.

Pre-Empting

A basic technique in Aikido is to move before an attack begins — as soon as the challenger mentally gets set to attack. When a challenger is intent on performing a certain action, he develops a one-track mind and since his mind then is already committed to a specific challenging movement, he is unable to react to the Aikido technique until it is too late. Hence, the Aikidoist begins to apply the technique when the challenger is raising his hand or pulling back his fist. At this point the challenger is highly vulnerable, his energy is drawn backward in preparation for the attack. His desire to challenge has thrown him off balance and out of harmony on both a psychological and physical level.

Watzlawick (9) has coined the term "pre-empting" to describe a technique of brief strategic therapy that seems closely to parallel the Aikido technique. With this technique, the therapist anticipates resistance (a challenge) and makes a statement that pre-empts the resistance. For example, the therapist might say, "You are probably going to think that I'm being stupid, but. . . . " Pre-empting, thus, leaves the client off balance, disarmed, and vulnerable to accepting the therapist's directive, because not to accept it would be a sign of limited compassion, understanding, or courteousness.

Multiple Challengers

Aikido can effectively be used with one challenger, but it can just as easily deal with multiple challengers. If approached by six challengers at the same time, the Aikidoist does not try to neutralize all at once. He begins by working on two at a time, subsystems of negative energy. He may turn and shift the direction of the first person's approach into the second person, who, in turn, makes it impossible for the third person to get near him, at which point he gently squats down and flips the fourth person over his shoulder, who then rolls into the fifth person, blocking the sixth person from getting near him. While spinning in circular, fluid movements, the Aikidoist effortlessly utilizes the challengers' own energy and actions to generate the particular strategies used.

Similarly, a brief strategic therapist would make just such an intervention in a family system. He would pit and pair one or two family members against each other until each subsystem of the larger family system has been dealt with sufficiently to effect a major change in the family system that maintains the symptomatic behavior (an example follows later).

Having a systems view of challenges allows one to deal as effectively with one person as with a group of persons because the level of conceptualization and resulting types of techniques used do not change when performing either Aikido or brief strategic therapy.

Similarities in Philosophical and Attitudinal Positions

The Illusion of Simplicity

Although the fundamental effective techniques of Aikido are simple to learn and use for basic self-defense, Aikido is much more than simply a set of techniques. It is a disciplined, philosophical stance on life grounded in a solid set of optimistic, respectful, humanistic values. Individuals are viewed in harmonious relationships with one another, and a deep appreciation exists for the coexistence of opposites in balanced relationships as the natural order of the universe. Mastery of the attitude and "stance" of Aikido requires many years of disciplined, committed practice. And, mastery of Aikido is never actually achieved, only approximated. For example, there is a seemingly simple technique of Aikido

("Kokyu nage") called "the 20-year technique." Although beginning students of Aikido can demonstrate the technique in a mechanical way, only a student of 20 years can demonstrate it in its exquisitely aesthetic intended form. Finally, even Master Morihei Uyeshiba, the founder of Aikido, claimed before his death that he was "just a beginning student of Aikido."

Casual observers of brief strategic therapy similarly may believe it to be merely a set of gimmicks or simple tricks for changing behavior. It, too, appears to be deceptively simple. However, even though the theory of brief strategic therapy is in its infancy, there already exists a solid ground-work of philosophical and attitudinal assumptions that are strikingly similar to those of Aikido. The attitudinal stance includes deep mutual respect for the basic goodness of all people and for their differences, a solid conceptual grasp of systems theory, and a deep appreciation of the roots and solutions for individual problems within their interactional contexts. Moreover, there is a deep respect for and appreciation of paradox as an essential element of human functioning. (2, 4, 8, 9, 10, 11). Although beginning students of brief strategic therapy can demonstrate skill in temporary behavior change, disciplined, lengthy training and practice are required in order to approximate mastery of the approach and yield long-lasting problem resolution and systems change.

Eclectic Flexibility

Aikido is the synthesis of a great many martial arts (including judo, ju-jitsu, sword, spear, and staff arts, etc.) and of the tenets of a number of Eastern spiritual disciplines (including Buddhist and Shinto traditions). Being a completely defensive and responsive art, it flexibly and pragmatically utilizes elements from many other martial arts in order to achieve its central goals — the harmless neutralization of aggression and the establishment of harmony.

Any theoretical or technical rigidity would hamper the flexibility necessary to receive a challenge of any sort from *any* direction. Based upon a rapid assesssment of the particular positions, movements, timing, sequence, systemic interactions, and styles of the challengers, the Aikidoist selects the particular strategies to use for achieving constructive neutralization. In its ideal form, the nature of the challenge determines the nature of the Aikido strategy used.

Similarly, brief strategic therapy is flexibly eclectic. Its goal also is to achieve harmonious problem resolution among clients. In order to allow for maximum receptivity to the client's style (behavioral, cognitive, and emotional), and maximum effectiveness of interventions, an eclectic, flexible stance is necessary. Excessive technical rigidity limits receptivity to the client's style of problem-solving. It requires the client, implicitly and explicitly, to consent to deal with his problems conceptually, linguistically, and technically, within the therapist's framework only. A client who does not give such consent and who persistently resists change would, by traditional therapists, be labeled "untreatable." Such tautological labeling often reflects an inflexibility of the therapist to accommodate his therapeutic style and language to that of the client, rather than vice versa. This would be equivalent to a martial artist who required his challenger to attack only with punches to the left side of his body because he only defended himself against such attacks and refused to deal with right or center attacks, claiming "the attacker isn't attacking correctly."

In both brief strategic therapy and Aikido, it is ideal if the practitioner is willing to accept *any* attack or challenge coming from *any* direction, in *any* form and be able to neutralize the negative energy or redirect it as positive energy into more constructive, humanistic directions.

Potential Harm

Because Aikido is so flexible, eclectic, responsive, and therefore so powerful, it has the potential for harm. By using the basic form of Aikido and including strategies from other more offensive approaches, a practitioner could easily injure or kill a challenger. There exist levels of applying the techniques, from very heavy, lethal levels to very light, harmless levels. The determinants of the particular level used are basically (a) the skill and control of

189

the practitioner, and (b) the ethical intention of the practitioner. The highest levels of ethics in Aikido require that no harm result. As pointed out by Westbrook and Ratti (12, p.34), "A man must sincerely desire to defend himself without hurting others." This is safeguarded by one of the "Rules During Practice" that are posted at the Aikido Headquarter's Gymnasium in Tokyo. The rule states: "All Aikido arts are secret in nature and are not to be revealed publicly, nor taught to rogues who will use them for evil purposes." (7, p.174)

Moreover, because of the unusual and paradoxical nature of many of the moves in Aikido, it is important for a practitioner to be unequivocally committed to the form of Aikido once he starts a particular strategy. For, if he begins a move (for example, moving *in* toward a descending weapon) and, in the middle of the move, loses his commitment to paradoxical Aikido strategies and changes to a more traditional linear tactic, he or the challenger could be seriously injured or killed. Trusting the form is very important for a harmless outcome.

Aspects of brief strategic therapy similarly have the power to harm an individual or family. For example, in developing a paradoxical strategy, a therapist sets up a potential crisis situation. If the therapist does not have sufficient experience, skill, control over and unequivocal commitment to the strategy, plus a sincere positive ethical intention, the outcome could be seriously destructive to the client. To begin a paradoxical strategy and, as the created crisis escalates, to change to a linear approach, could cause harm to the client and to the future helpfulness and credibility of the therapist. Perhaps a rule similar to that in Aikido should be enacted to ensure that these therapy techniques are not to be taught to 'therapist rogues" who would use them for evil purposes.

Respectful Interventions

Aikido is intended to "neutralize the enemy's power thus stopping his weapon. However, if the enemy does not attack, there is no problem. Nothing occurs. The world would be peaceful. In such a peaceful world, martial arts would not be needed. . . . " (3) Hence, the Aikidoist neither offensively looks for problems (enemies) nor deals with a given challenger any more than is absolutely necessary to resolve harmlessly the immediate conflict situation. He accepts and respects all people the way they are. He views the challenger not as an enemy, but as a fellow human and teacher. The more angrily and aggressively he attacks the Aikidoist, the more grateful is the Aikidoist for the opportunity to practice the art well, using the challenger's "gift of energy." Each new challenger offers something new and valuable to learn — a new attack strategy, new timing, new perspectives, new ways to help people resolve their aggression. The infinite number of strategies available makes each new encounter an exciting and interesting experience.

Similarly, the brief strategic therapist has the goal of simply resolving the immediate conflict situation in as harmless and efficient a way as possible. There is a respect and appreciation for the various ways people change themselves daily and an excitement about continually learning these daily strategies. Clients are viewed in positive, healthy ways, that more easily point the way to positive outcomes. Because the strategies used by the therapist are the very ones used by the clients, albeit for constructive rather than destructive purposes, the therapist maintains a further respect for the client, in viewing him as a teacher who has the solutions to his own dilemmas. The ultimate respect for clients is perhaps most clearly manifested by the efficient and brief nature of the therapist's contact with the clients. In contrast to the more traditional long-term, regressive, insight-oriented approaches, the brief strategic therapist respects the client by sparing him such prolonged, painful experiences.

Hence, both Aikido and brief strategic therapy have "immediate problem resolution" as their goals. The wish for a permanent cessation of problems or "challenges" is recognized as an unrealistic goal, rarely if ever achieved. This concept, termed the "Utopia Syndrome," is tellingly discussed by Watzlawick et al. (11)

Lightness and Sense of Humor

An Aikidoist practicing the art manifests an easy and relaxed demeanor. There is a sense of lightness about him: he often appears to be having fun. Many of the strategies are so paradoxical, subtle, and confusing that an observer may chuckle at the novelty of the sequence. Moreover, during a particular maneuver, an Aikidoist might well tickle his challenger as he is guiding him through the multiple circular motions. Occasionally, even a challenger comes to laugh after being harmlessly maneuvered through a confusing sequence of disorienting motions.

Similarly, there is a real sense of humor and lightness in brief strategic therapy practice. In maneuvering a client through a sequence of paradoxical strategies, the therapist stimulates curiosity, novelty, and a sense of paradox, propelling a fascinating juxtaposition of thoughts, feelings, and events into creative relationship with each other. A client may experience a bewildering sense of fun and may laugh as he contemplates carrying out a particular paradoxical directive. Instead of the more usual "deadly serious" quality of traditional therapy sessions, brief strategic therapy often even elicits laughter from very depressed clients. Moreover, therapists who comfortably use this approach often report a refreshing sense of excitement, intrigue, and joy in going to work each day.

Maneuvering, not Manipulating

With the power inherent in the Aikido approach, it sometimes appears that the Aikidoist is manipulating or "playing with" a challenger. The paradoxical stance, with the invitation to a confrontation, followed by the absence of resistance, the illusion of weakness in the one-down stance, the confusion and disorientation of the circular and often complex movements, and the surprisingly harmless resolution of aggression through indirect, subtle strategies, can seem manipulative and deceptive. We can perhaps best address such concerns by distinguishing between the two terms, "manipulating" and "maneuvering"; they have different connotations. The essential difference between them may be viewed as the initiator's *intent*. Although "manipulating" has a pejorative, exploitative connotation, "maneuvering" has a more positive connotation. "Manipulating" is intended primarily to benefit the manipulator, at the expense of the person being manipulated. "Maneuvering," however, is intended primarily to benefit the person being maneuvered — for his own best interest. Using the gentle arts of distraction, illusion, and subtle persuasion, the Aikidoist, at his highest ethical levels, maneuvers and guides the challenger through a series of strategies to achieve the well-intentioned goal of harmless resolution of the challenge. Clearly these maneuvers are in the best interest of the challenger.

Similarly, the strategies of brief strategic therapy can be viewed as maneuvers intended to achieve what is believed to be the best interest of the client. When strategies are ethically conceived, carefully planned, and skillfully implemented, the therapist maneuvers the client to achieve the well-intentioned goal of constructive change and harmless resolution of problem behavior patterns. When the therapist is either careless or exploitative in his own interests, his strategies may be viewed as manipulative. It may be, for instance, that in the absence of any positive signs of change over a reasonable length of time, keeping a client in "therapy" is manipulative, because only the therapist may be receiving benefit — of a monetary nature. That can, perhaps, be equated to a martial artist who manipulates by using excessive and unnecessary roughness on a challenger when milder techniques would have been sufficient.

Stop Trying and Succeed

A central problem of beginning Aikidoists is that they try too hard. Their moves tend to be linear, their thinking logical, their aim to be muscularly strong and forceful. For effective Aikido moves, the Aikido student must unlearn linear, logical, and forceful thinking. He must essentially stop trying so hard and relax. He must let go of his reflexive ways of operating and be willing to go with the flow, trusting a positive outcome. Accepting the natural way that people's bodies move and energies flow results in successful Aikido.

Similarly, the beginning brief strategic therapist must stop trying to change his clients by doing "more of the same." (11) He must be willing to flow with the symptoms, think illogically, and trust that a positive outcome will result if he accepts the natural way that people move psychologically. When he properly gets the feel of strategic thinking, he realizes that the strategies follow naturally from the direction and force of the client's energy.

It has been observed by both Aikido instructors and brief strategic therapy instructors that even effective practitioners periodically revert back to more traditional, logical, linear ways. This appears to be a function of the many years these practitioners have had of life training in Western thinking. Clearly, more Eastern ways of thinking are required for both of these disciplines. With experience, however, practioners of both disciplines revert less often to traditional ways.

A "Brief" Example

In order to elucidate the usefulness of the conceptual parallels drawn in this paper between Aikido and brief strategic therapy, the following case example of brief strategic therapy is presented. The comments in parentheses refer to concepts elaborated upon in the paper.

Mrs. A phones a therapist to request an appointment for her 10-year-old son, Billy, who has been overly aggressive, fighting with peers, destructive of property, and recently suspended from school for slashing another student's notebook with a knife. Moreover, he constantly beats up his 8-year-old brother, Jimmy and causes constant aggravation at home. Mother adds, "He's had a year of play therapy with each of two other doctors, but there was no change in him. I decided to try again, although my husband isn't too hopeful" (the challenge). The therapist says, "It doesn't sound too promising, but I'm willing to try, so let's set an appointment for me to meet the whole family" (blending — initiation of systems view).

Donald T. Saposnek, Ph.D.

The family arrives. The therapist introduces himself to the family and suggests to the father that they proceed on a first-name basis (one-down stance). After some discussion, the following pattern emerges. Jimmy teases Billy; Billy hits Jimmy and breaks things; Jimmy runs to tell mother that Billy is breaking things again; Mother calls father, who severely punishes Billy, after which father catches mother's wrath for punishing Billy too severely, which adds additional strain to the marital relationship. Mother then comforts Billy, which piques the jealousy of Jimmy, who then teases Billy—and so forth (multiple challengers; interactionist view). The therapist (who centers himself in this dynamic sphere of interactions) begins to develop strategies to resolve these problems. First (by working on the sibling subsystem), he requests that Jimmy "help" his brother practice self-control by using his best techniques to tease Billy three mornings the following week, without telling his parents which days they are (blending, extending—therapist gets Jimmy and the rest of the family off balance momentarily by an unexpected move). The therapist then asks Billy if he has enough courage and guts to make a sacrifice in order to demonstrate that he is willing to try to make things better for himself and his family (pre-empting—therapist anticipates resistance and actively disarms it by inviting him in). Billy answers affirmatively, but the therapist then cautions him to listen first to the full request and give it more lengthy and serious thought (therapist retains control and keeps Billy off balance and receptive to the next maneuver). The therapist completes his request by asking Billy to make the sacrifice of allowing himself to get into big trouble the coming weekend, which unfortunately will probably mean missing out on his favorite camping trip the next week, because his parents will no doubt take that privilege away (use of paradoxical maneuver of encouraging and simultaneously immobilizing his negative energy). The therapist then requests mother and father to set up an alternate plan for the next week to take the family to the horse show, which Jimmy enjoys and Billy dislikes intensely, in order that they may help their son, Billy, practice making sacrifices (therapist uses parents to extend the maneuver, further immobilizing Billy). The therapist then further instructs mother to write detailed notes about each destructive incident reported to her and to allow father to review them daily upon his return home from work. Together, they are to decide upon Billy's fate for each transgression (therapist actively maneuvers parental subsytem into a unified constructive direction, strengthening the parents' postition as directors of the family system. Billy sees no desirable alternative but to control his trouble-making behavior). Billy controls his behavior and because he, thereby, demonstrates explicit knowledge of his strategies, he is no longer allowed to function that way in the family.

Although several more strategic steps were necessary to resolve this situation sufficiently, a total of three sessions produced major and long-lasting shifts in the family system's interactional styles.

This example highlights not only the parallel pragmatic techniques of Aikido, but the attitudinal ones as well. As the therapist centered himself in the systemic interactions and respectfully and efficiently maneuvered each family member against the others, he flexibly followed the flow of the family members' strategies and resistances and guided them to a satisfactory and harmless resolution of their problem — assuredly "somewhat wiser." Had he plugged away at "more of the same" (individual play therapy) and simply tried harder than the previous therapist to change Billy alone, he no doubt would have failed or even caused injury to the family system. Instead, he stopped trying (in traditional ways), and he succeeded.

Conclusions

This paper has presented a sample of the many similarities between the two conceptual systems, Aikido and brief strategic therapy. Conceptually grounding brief strategic therapy in a physical, but philosophically based, visual model elicits implications for future theory development, teaching, and training in this therapy approach. A further elaboration of these concepts is in progress and will be presented in a future publication.

REFERENCES

1. Haley, J., *Problem-Solving Therapy*, San Francisco, Jossey-Bass, 1976.
2. ———, *Strategies of Psychotherapy*, New York, Grune and Stratton, 1963.
3. Ikeda, K., "Kawaridane Nihonjin" (Exceptional Japanese), *Tokyo Shimbun*, 1963. As quoted in R. Frager, "Aikido — A Japanese Approach to Self-Development and Mind-Body Harmony," in C.A. Garfield (ed.), *Rediscovery of the Body: A Psychosomatic View of Life and Death*, New York, Dell, 1977.
4. Juhasz, J. B., "Psychology of Paradox and Vice Versa," *Psychological Reports* 39: 911-914, 1976.
5. Pittman, F., "Unconventional Intervention With Difficult Families," Paper presented at 55th Annual Meeting of American Orthopsychiatric Association, San Francisco, March 1978.
6. Selvini Palazzoli, M.; Cecchin, G.; Prata, G.; and Boscolo, L., *Paradox and Counterparadox*, New York, Jason Aronson, 1978.
7. Uyeshiba, K., *Aikido*, Tokyo, Hozansha Publishing Co., 1969.
8. Watzlawick, P., *How Real is Real?*, New York, Vintage Books, 1976.
9. Watzlawick, P., *The Language of Change: Elements of Therapeutic Communication*, New York, Basic Books, 1978.
10. Watzlawick, P.; Beavin, J.H.; and Jackson, D.D., *Pragmatics of Human Communication*, New York, Norton, 1967.
11. Watzlawick, P.; Weakland, J.; and Fisch, R., *Change: Principles of Problem Formation and Problem Resolution*, New York, Norton and Co., 1974
12. Westbrook, A. and Ratti, O., *Aikido and the Dynamic Sphere: An Illustrated Introduction*, Tokyo, Charles E. Tuttle Co., 1974

George Leonard

This Isn't Richard

(From *The Silent Pulse*)

There were four of us, three men and a woman, who shared an ordeal, a rite of passage. In a culture that has turned its eyes from challenge and chance and possible tragedy, this was a rare gift indeed. We were up for black belt in Aikido — Richard, Lawrence, Wendy, and I — and over a period of about a year each of us in our separate ways confronted injury, exhaustion, humiliation, and despair. Our list of injuries alone suggested the severity of the ordeal. In addition to numerous bumps, bruises, and abrasions, we suffered a broken foot (Lawrence), a sprained neck and torn ligaments of the elbow (Wendy), a fracture of the cheekbone and a multiple fracture of the arm (Richard), and a dislocated shoulder (me). These injuries might seem excessive in an art that so often has the effortless quality of a dance or a dream. But in Aikido no punches are pulled, and each attack proceeds to its logical conclusion, with the attacker pinned or thrown through the air. Thus, the Aikidoist must practice hard and long to transform the fear of falling into the joy of flying — an unforgiving if ecstatic practice.

But we should not linger over injuries, for that would only distract us from the true significance of what we faced. Our teacher, Robert Nadeau, is not your run-of-the-mill martial artist. Though skilled in Judo and Karate as well as Aikido (and, we all agree, a formidable man to meet in a dark alley), he views himself as primarily a teacher of meditation and alternative ways of handling life's pressures. For Nadeau, the mat is the world. Thus, he teaches us not to deny or avoid tensions and problems and pain in our practice but to welcome them as treasured gifts, as opportunities for transforming our lives. Far from working around our weaknesses, Nadeau zeros in on every divided motive, every pretense, every secret, well-guarded flaw. If the mat is the world, it is the world beneath a magnifying glass, where nothing can remain long hidden. In this setting, self-examination is not mandatory; it is unavoidable.

All of this comes to a painfully sharp focus during the three-month period leading up to the black-belt examination. Nadeau uses this period not only as an intensive cram course in advanced techniques, but also as a physical and psychological trial by fire. Anywhere from three and a half to ten years of practice might precede this ordeal. During this period, the candidate is expected to attend all of Nadeau's classes. For the first hour of training each night, which is devoted to basics, the candidate or candidates practice along with all the other students. When the second hour, devoted to advanced training, begins, Nadeau sends the candidates to the back mat. While the other advanced students go on with their regular training, the candidates practice the specific techniques that might be expected during the exam.

Fifteen minutes before the end of class, Nadeau seats the advanced students in the traditional Japanese meditation position around the edges of the main mat and calls the candidates front and center. He puts them through their paces, one by one, as the others watch. At the end, Nadeau arranges for a series of multiple attacks. First one, then two, then three, and even up to seven advanced students are directed to attack the candidate again and again. This goes on until the candidate is reduced to total exhaustion and either trapped or felled by the attackers.

Nadeau has a remarkable ability to know exactly in what technique each candidate is unprepared. On one occasion during my own ordeal, he told me to spend the entire advanced class practicing a technique called *irimi-nage* (entering throw). After forty-five minutes on the back mat, I was called front and center with the full expectation of demonstrating my well-practiced *irimi-nage*.

As I stood there waiting for the attack, however, I made the mistake of saying to myself, "I hope he doesn't ask me for *koshi-nage* [waist-throw]." As if in response to my unspoken words, Nadeau said, "Okay, George, let's see your *koshi-nage*," after which he let me flub one waist-throw after another until everyone present was painfully aware of my unpreparedness.

Over a period of nine months, Lawrence, then I, then Wendy faced our separate ordeals. Under physical and psychological attack, we discovered that a flaw is corrected only by being revealed, and that the true opponent is the one who resides within. Each of the three ordeals contained the tension and danger, the dark despair, the ironic twist, and the happy completion of which our most ancient and cherished tales are made. But it was Richard's experience that seemed to draw us into other worlds, joining us with the immense and the infinite.

In his early thirties, at the very prime and glow of life, Richard might have been a figure from the Elgin Marbles. With his finely muscled, perfectly balanced body and handsome face, he seemed a modern counterpart of the classic Greek ideal of physical beauty, and indeed he had been an Olympic athlete in his college days. Nor were Richard's gifts merely physical. He held a Ph.D. in psychology and was co-founder of a respected school of meditation, body work, diet, and interpersonal relations. He was a superb Aikidoist.

Dazzled by his gifts and grace, we might find it hard to discover any flaws in this man, and sometimes Richard did seem almost too good to be true. But eventually a certain quality of calculation emerged, summed up in a phrase from gestalt therapy often used by Richard himself: "Taking care of myself." The phrase was not meant to imply selfishness, but simply to clarify the healthy, openly expressed self-interest that can save you from dependency and the victim's role. Still, you couldn't help noticing that Richard wouldn't accept any invitation until he had carefully calculated what he would get out of it; then he would accept only if, on balance, he figured he would come out on the plus side. Richard rarely did anything on speculation. He took good care of himself.

There was, as well, the matter of name. Richard had contributed a great deal to the field of human growth. Yet a number of other people who had made lesser contributions had become better known. Richard was aware of this and, it seemed to me, had a burning if rarely expressed desire to make a name for himself.

I doubt very much if our teacher involved himself in this sort of analysis. He simply intuited, then acted: When he had told Wendy she would be going up for her test in three months, he had told Richard that he didn't know whether he would be going up or not. Richard could go through the three months of preparation if he wished. On the day of the exam, said Nadeau, he would let him know whether or not he would take it.

For Richard, this was like a slap in the face. He would have to endure a three-month-long ordeal with no assurance of any reward at the end. When fellow students would ask him if he was going up for black belt, he would have to say — though he would obviously be practicing hard for the event — that he didn't know. Not a very good plan for someone used to taking care of himself. Already, he had suffered the most serious injuries of anyone in the school. After breaking his arm (during a strenuous throw), he had continued practicing while wearing a cast. Later a break in his cheekbone (he had been kicked accidentally while down) had temporarily affected an eye muscle, and still he had continued practicing. Surely he had paid his dues in full.

Yet there he was on the back mat night after night, driving himself to exhaustion in the face of uncertain odds. As the weeks passed, Nadeau paid less and less attention to him. One night two weeks before the exam, I happened to be sitting next to Richard at the edge of the main mat at the end of class as Nadeau put the candidates through their paces.

"Is there anyone else?" Nadeau said, looking right past Richard.

Richard said nothing, and I heard myself answering for him. "There's Richard here. You forgot him."

"Oh yeah," Nadeau said dryly. "What's-his-name. Okay, let's see what he's got."

From this moment until after the exam, Nadeau never looked

at Richard or called him by name. Occasionally, he would summon "what's-his-name" to the center mat, and then make no comment about his performance. In the shower room three days before the exam, I asked Richard what he thought was going on.

"I don't know. I can't tell exactly. Something's happening to me. I'm beginning to feel some kind of transformation."

As is the custom, the exam was scheduled on a Sunday at one. It was a beautiful, cloudless June day. People began gathering early: Aikidoists from miles around, hundreds of spectators. An examining board of five ranking black belts would be convened to pass on the candidates' performances.

"Well, are you going up?" I asked Richard when he appeared on the mat.

"I don't know. Nadeau still won't speak to me."

The *dojo* had the feeling of a church before a wedding. Some people were meditating. Others were talking in hushed tones. Richard went into the office and came out with a strange look on his face.

"I guess I'm going to take it," he said. "I saw my name on the schedule. Nadeau still hasn't said anything."

To begin the ceremony, all the Aikidoists bowed to the portrait of a venerable Japanese warrior on the front wall. This was Morihei Uyeshiba, the legendary founder of Aikido, known to all as O Sensei, the greatest of all teachers, whose seemingly miraculous feats in his old age had been photographed, filmed, and confirmed by respected witnesses. Five candidates had already been examined when Richard was called to the center of the mat. With his *uke* (oo-kay, "attacker") he moved out in the graceful knee-walk common to the art. The two of them bowed first to O Sensei, then to the five examiners, then to each other. Nadeau called out the first series of techniques, and the exam began.

From the very beginning, it was apparent that something extraordinary was occurring. It was like one of those sporting events that are later memorialized, perhaps a World Series game or bullfight, during which every last spectator realizes at some level that what is happening out on the field is more than a game,

202

but rather someting achingly beautiful and inevitable, an enactment in space and time of how the universe works, how things are. As Richard and his *uke*, still on their knees, glided through a series of attacks and pins as precise and formal as a tea ceremony, the silence in the *dojo* became deeper and more vibrant. Nadeau called for the next series of techniques. The *uke* rose and attacked the still-kneeling Richard, who moved in sweeping circular motions to embrace the attack. So gentle and coherent were his movements that they seemed to capture time itself and slow it to a more stately pace. Sometimes when Richard pinned his attacker with one hand, he reached out with the other in a gesture of balance that I had never seen him use in practice. This supple, rather androgynous movement was obviously not needed for balancing the physical body. It was as if Richard's hand were reaching beyond the four walls of the *dojo* to a point of balance in the cosmos.

Nadeau called for the next series of techniques, which would have both attacker and defender standing. When Richard rose to his feet, there was a slight stir in the room; people here and there glanced up at the windows or the lights. What had happened, inexplicably, was that the room had suddenly become appreciably lighter.

From this point to the end of the story, I am relying, not just on my perceptions, but those of several other people, including Richard, all of whom I phoned the next morning. Without telling any of them what the others had said, I began to piece together a coherent account of the previous afternoon's events. My informants did not agree in every particular, but there was more agreement than disagreement, and a clear general picture emerged. I present it here simply as a consensus of subjective reports.

Everyone I contacted noticed the shift of illumination when Richard rose to a standing position. Some people also began seeing an aura—some described it as "golden," others as "clear plastic"—around his entire body. As the exam continued, the speed and intensity of the attacks increased, and yet there was still a general sense of time's moving slowly, at an unhurried, dreamlike pace. The spacious *dojo* began to seem smaller; an unfamiliar feeling of intimacy came over the Aikidoists and spectators around the mat, as if we were involved together in something usually reserved for our most private moments. During one swift attack, a hard strike to the belly, Richard slipped quickly to the side and made a bewildering gesture that none of us had previously seen. The *uke*, without having been touched, went down with a loud crash. This rather formal young man, a stickler for decorum, lay there for a moment looking up at Richard in astonishment, then laughed aloud. Later, Richard could not recall or reconstruct this remarkable technique. For his part, Richard was beginning to get the feeling that he was not "doing" anything at all, that the movements of his body were "just happening" without thought or effort.

The exam continued in this spirit, like a long, hypnotic phrase of music, through the body throws and defense against knife. Then, when Nadeau called for the *uke* to attack free-style, the illumination of the room seemed to go up another notch and the boundary of light surrounding Richard seemed to become denser, brighter, and unmistakably golden. The genius of Aikido is to transform the most violent attack, by embracing it, into a dance, and it was the essence of dance we saw there on the mat — neither powerful nor delicate, neither destructive nor creative, neither masculine nor feminine, but all such seeming opposites connected and drawn to a point of balance.

At a particularly radiant moment, Nadeau stopped the free-style attacks and gave Richard a minute to catch his breath before the climactic *randori*, the multiple attack. Richard turned away from the audience, in accordance with *dojo* etiquette, to straighten his *gi* uniform. As he did so, he glanced up at the portrait of O Sensei. A powerful arc of golden light seemed to be streaming from the eyebrows on the picture toward Richard's head, covering him, suffusing him with gold. At this moment, we in the *dojo* experienced a third brightening of the room. By the time the three-man attack was in full swing, the whole place was alight as if from within with the most delicious, joyful, almost palpable illumination.

To a first-time spectator, the rushing, swirling, tumbling,

crashing motion of a *randori* is simply overwhelming; the senses can't handle it. An expert Aikidoist observes techniques and moves, watches for breaks in the energy field that subsumes both defender and attackers. But on this day spectators and experts alike saw Richard's *randori* as harmony, the promise of reconciliation. No matter how hard or swift the blow, he was not there to receive it, but always at the moving center that holds all opposites in perfect tension. As for Richard, he experienced no effort or strain whatever; only a voice in his head, repeating, "*This isn't Richard. This isn't Richard.*" There, in the eye of the storm, stripped of the certainty he had always deemed necessary for survival, denied the support of his teacher, divested even of his name, Richard found the deliverance he had not known he was searching for. He had no question that he would be hit or trapped. If need be, he could go on forever, realizing all the while that "he" was not doing it. The voice in his head was clear: "*This isn't Richard. This isn't Richard.*"

"After the *randori*," one of the people I called the following day told me, "I just sat there stunned. I couldn't even move. It was only when the next exam started and the guy's technique was so crude compared to Richard's that I was shaken to the realization of what was going on—and that was *really* awesome. *O Sensei was in that room*. I *knew* it. I could feel the presence. Those crude techniques gave me the contrast I needed to sense it. O Sensei had been there all during Richard's exam."

Robert Nadeau

An Aikido Class

Introduction

Some of the guys in the area are doing an Aikido book, and tonight we are going to play with an interview *au naturel*. Why don't we warm up on something soft for a minute or two. [Pause]. Uh, what's soft? How about a little turn-blend. Let's try a right to right, turning blending. [Students practice turning and blending with their partners]. Let's try something like that, just to warm up on. Take it easy, but do give me what could appear to be control. Soft, but don't look sloppy. All right, that just to warm up, and then we'll see what we are going to do here tonight.

[Pause].

Fullness of Presentation

O.K., warmed up? It is important to have a sense, as you present yourself, of a *fullness* of presentation and in this case, Carol, the presentation feels to have a lot of ćir-cull [circle]. So try to start with that full circle feeling as opposed to waiting until you are in the middle of the situation and trying to turn on. It's feasible, but harder that way. Try to start already full. "Full" also, by the way, means down in the feet area. So, "full" is not a concept between the ears but a state. O.K.? And the state, in this case, is left and right, and *has depth*, which is under the feet. O.K. So a presentation. All right? Let's do it one more time and start more full.

Right to the right to the right. And left to the left to the left. Balance, Balance, Balance.

[Pause].

Don't (Verb) Be!

[To a student:] Don't crossover too much. Grab, but stay kind of straight. [To another student having trouble:] There must be a verb in there, "to do" which is different from "being." O.K.? So, pass on that verb. We're just going to dance on through it (demonstrating). It's more *be*-ing. Yeah, I like that. Verbs create friction. O.K.? One more time, a couple of minutes, the same technique. O.K.? Start with a good set-up like you're taking a promotion test.

Focus on Experience

[Training resumes and teacher visits pairs of practicing students].

[To a student:] You've got a little hollow spot in the back someplace. Yes, even just standing there. Which is not a negative; it's really the *beginning* of something—looks like a big column starting to happen. It's beginning right behind the back, probably equalized with the spine, so there's a faint energy column. As soon as possible let's see it. Not a verb, it's an experience. [To another student who is losing her balance:] What's coming up soon is something to your back and deep under as part of your basic framework; something to your back and under is starting to come into play. Part of your framework will begin to include a little more. So if it gets a little shaky back and deep, it's not wrong—it's the beginning of "next," and "next" has balance, like a kangaroo's tail, or a triangle, that third leg back there. Right before the next stage happens we sometimes begin to get a little shaky or feel a little bumped, O.K.? You've got to be smart and know you're getting close to the next stage. Otherwise you think that you're getting worse which is really impossible—but that is what it looks like for some moments as you progress along *the way*. Ta da (facetiously).

Presentation—A Framework for Energy Flow

[Pause].

207

O.K. Change technique. Everybody do forward roll? Let's do it lightly for a bit. Do it as falling practice.

[Pause].

Let's go on to a *tsuki* [straight punch]. You want to put the emphasis, still, on presentation. Presentation, today, let's say, is a *frame*work, a form. And if you present a pretty good *frame*work, then there is naturally — without you doing anything more — energy flowing, back and forth. So present your framework, and there is naturally energy flowing. I want to separate out the two [framework and energy flowing] because we're involved and confused about them. If I look at normal people, I can't tell energy from framework because the framework and the energy flow get kind of converged in there, and I really, in cases like this, don't know who's who. [Pause]. I can't find "you." "You" are so wrapped up in the two, energy and framework. For me it is a kind of a loss. I'm just trying to separate framework and energy flow so I can see who's in there. One way I want to do that tonight is using the words "framework" or "form." As you start to fully present framework or form (demonstrating with a partner), the energies flow through, and after a bit I can begin to see *you.* We're going to start to untangle. O.K.? So the name of the game for me is "Let's find you." Because right now we are all the same, we're entangled in here, and because of that entanglement some of the things you say are NOT REALLY YOU SAYING THEM. It's like you have an identity [real self] in a bowl of jello and you're talking about how you like to jiggle. And it's like — well, yeah, but that's jello talk, that's not really an identity. To make it worse some idiot over here is saying, "I'm green jello," and somebody else over there is saying, "I'm not hard enough yet." And on and on and on. But the jello is creation and there's an identity in it. You are so locked in creation that we are all confused, all of us. The name of the game is "who am I" — always has been.

Now to play the game, set up the technique with the form and a flow-through. Form has flow-through; in the very nature of doing form and flow-through I think we'll actually find you — in

the jello BUT *SEPARATE* FROM THE JELLO — CLEARLY SEP-
ARATE. I hope so or we're wasting a lot of time. Let's try it.

[Training resumes].

Framework/Flow-Through a Basic Pattern

O.K. Today we're using the words "framework," that is,
form, and "something flowing." The real names might be "an
awareness (framework)" and "the whole creation (something flowing)." But even so, the game is the same. It's the same game on
a larger scale, exactly the same game. That's why what we are
doing now is not a waste of time if you are interested in larger
levels of consciousness. The pattern/process is exactly the same.
Framework/flow and entanglement. The general practice is, we're
presenting a form — a *form* (demonstrating) — and in there is a
flow-through. Now, the form part of you will say, "Oh, I see she
spun around," (spinning partner around and throwing) and then
he thinks he is here to learn something and will start to try to control the situation. O.K.? But at that time you start the beginning
of entanglement again. You're going to go around again and a-
round again (demonstrating). [Pause]. Form is form; flow-through
is flow-through (demonstrating each one). Form should just keep
doing form. Maybe it gets deeper and wider and fancier, but it's
still form — and form has flow-through (demonstrating). I noticed
she went down a certain way — *downward*. But if the form suddenly says, "Aha, I've learned something and now I'm going to
bring her down that way again," you've just entangled again and
here we go again, repeating your same number. All of those are
possibilities. The entanglement is an on-going possibility, but a
simple way of clearing from that is — hah (demonstrating) — also
an on-going possibility. Recognize, through form or framework
as a daily reference point, your tendencies to do things that are
entanglement. And find something else, something else that allows
a certain possibility.

All right, this is based on an old number that we did. [Pause].
The beginnings of creation. [Pause]. You existed — "Wow, look at

creation!" And that was the beginning of getting involved, entangled, a certain way, to such a point now where it gets kind of scrunchy. When you're entangled you're weird, and you know it, and things are tight, and they shouldn't be that tight. I think that we can play the game a bit different. In this different game you can have an awareness, an awakener here and then creation. . . . I think that we can be involved without scrunching-in that way. I think we can retain — let's use the word — size. We can retain size — and be present and function in creation without scrunching-in. I think we can play with the jello without saying, "I'm jello." I think there can be jello without you locking in. What we are doing here is experiencing we are locked in — unweaving out of it so the true "you" will sort of stand up. As you first start doing that, you have of course the possibility of repeating your same old number; you know, verbing to get a result, trying to *look* good. We're fearful of not looking good for a moment, and trying to make up for it. [Pause]. Instead Framework. Just keep frameworking. Is that simple enough? O.K. let's try one more time. Still on the *tsuki* [straight punch]. Form form form, framework framework framework.

A Different Way of Learning

[Training resumes].

[To a student:] Framework, framework, framework. . . . naturally *allows*. . . . a flow-through. There you go. [Pause]. That one! See that. That was pretty to behold. O.K.? The system says, "Aha, I spun around a certain way;" now the framework will want to *repeat it*. So, one reason you enter into creation is — and it's true — to learn something. You say, "Wow, there's something I need to learn in there," and you step in. Your idea's right, but not that way. Because now you're all torqued-in and whatever you're going to learn is really going to be miniscule. But some of you keep doing that, so we have some forever students. [Pause]. There is a different way of learning — a sort of experiential allowing: Be as big as the jello dish/bowl? If you try to learn something,

210

the idea is right, but the way you've done it is . . . a bit strange. Normal, but strange. That's why we're all here . . . because we're torqued-in. [Pause]. I think that we can do it different. So (pointing to a student), that last one that she did here was more of the *allowing* that whole action to happen. Now if we can do it here, at this level, then we can do it on larger levels, because it's exactly the same game. So here, it's allowing a technique, but you can also allow the creation. That's the possibility.

[To a student:] Framework, framework. Nothing wrong; but stay with the framework. There you go.

[Pause].

Being a Do-Gooder and Entangling

So, you have to have the — guts, is it? When it doesn't quite catch, there will be a tendency to want to do it better. 'Cause a lot of us enter in the creation with: "I want to do good in God's creation." We're do-gooders. When we make a mistake, we want to make up for it. But that's also a way of entangling again, tighter and tighter. There's another way of doing good by experiencing more of the form and allowing. Allowing so you'll end up . . . doing good but a whole different way of doing it. The other way is entanglement again. Whose turn?

Preventing Entanglement

[To another student:] A little bit of reaching happens when the framework is starting to come out of its foundation. Do again. O.K.? Framework shouldn't have to come out of its *foun*dation, but that's a possibility. Framework.

[To a student practicing with a partner:] Do you understand what I'm saying? I'll exaggerate it a bit (demonstrating). Frame work leaving the foundation is already the beginnings of entanglement. I want to do something with creation. [Pause]. So we allow a bit more. Even that is an urge, but you've got to recognize your urge and pass on it for a change, 'cause that urge is what you have always done. You jumped right in: "Wow, look at creation!" And there was an urge and potential entanglement. And that's all you've been doing. Instead let's do something different, and see what happens. Because I think that in that there is the potential for untanglement. *Wakarimasu ka?* [Do you understand?] Should we stay on that for another couple of moments?

[Training resumes].

O.K. Looking pretty good. Let's take a little pause. Let's go back to a very simple basic. One-handed *kokyu*.

Basic Training for Not Entangling

Set up a basic *kokyu* again. Framework, form — and through that is flow. It might make it easier if you catch the flow as being ground-thigh-hip. [Pause]. O.K. Framework. If your framework's good it's already flowing. Recognize the framework, because someplace in there it's going to want to do the flow. It's going to say "Oh, I see." And it's going to want to (demonstrating) *do* him instead of doing just what it does, which is framework. If you have a good framework you can get good flow-through. All right. It's important to recognize re-entanglement because we're doing this to separate the framework and flow out.

(Stepping aside and looking around) If we don't separate the two I'm not sure who I am sometimes. Wait a minute (demonstrating again). In this situation, there are two things going on. Whatever the situation is, there are two things going on. The frame of it — (demonstrating) and, the flow of it. Although they occupy the same space they are very distinct. And every second they are potentially intertwined again because that's how it started back when — the beginnings of creation. The intertwining is going on all of the time, but I think if we don't bite for it, it also gives us a chance to *un*tangle. And every time there's an untangling, it's a little clearer who you are. But all along the way there's [another] potential, because you're going to see things, you're going to like things, you're going to be unsure, and all of those things are going to potentially *en*tangle you. But you don't have to bite for it. You *always* do that. Let's do something different for a change.

[Pause]. Framework, framework, framework (demonstrating) has a flow-through. All right. Basic, simple. Let's try like that for a while.

[Training resumes].

[To a student:] Framework, framework, framework has a floor-thigh-hip flow-through.

[To another student:] Framework, framework just for framework's sake. You're starting to torque too much.

[To another student:] Framework, framework. Framework allows flow-through. [Pause]. That one! [Pause]. Framework. Be distinct about framework. It's very simple, but sometimes we don't take the time to say, "This is this." Framework. [Pause]. Framework allows flow-through. [Pause]. Now the framework may get bigger in some way, or fancier, but the game doesn't change. [Pause]. Framework. [Pause]. Framework, flow-through (demonstrating). [Pause]. Framework—see, it's getting wider. But the game doesn't change. Framework has *flow-through*. I think some people think the name of the game is to get a bigger framework. There, I'm wider (demonstrating); I'll do it wider. Now they've locked in again. A bigger form than their norm, but they've locked in all the same. Then the game stops. [Pause]. Form, frame, flow-through (demonstrating). And on and on and on and on. But always with the possibility [risk] of torquing in. Framework has . . . (demonstrating) . . . the flow-through comes through the framework. [Pause]. There! That one was distinct. The simplicity of it is just being what you are at the moment. That's the simplicity, but we sometimes skip it.

[To another student:] Framework has . . . maybe . . . but another little torque. [Pause]. Framework has flow-through. You feel that little converging in there? There seems to be some kind of misunderstanding. Framework, and then we introduce the job, and then there's flow-through. And you say, "Oh, he went that way, O.K." And then you start going that way. This allows that (demonstrating). And I notice that he was uprooted, so I want to uproot him. Framework—and if it flows through and there's uprooting, that's just what's happening. And if I can't allow this little bit, how am I going to allow great universal beats? I won't be able to. I'm going to do exactly the same thing. I'm going to get excited about something, I'm going to lock into something, I'm going to try to repeat something. Wrong guy starts doing the right thing.

[Laughter].

Creation in Front of You

[To a student:] Still framework, flow-through. Framework, flow. Now it's getting more involved and I can feel myself wanting to converge in. O.K. Let's see. [Pause]. I'm supposed to remember a bunch of stuff. Ah (demonstrating). If you want to really remember, present that framework again. But you see, it's almost the opposite of trying to remember. So, at first I say, "Oh shit, am I screwing up? 'Cause I'm supposed to remember stuff." [Pause]. Framework, framework, framework, framework (demonstrating with partner) and you'll remember it in a different foremat. But at first I thought I had made a mistake, because I almost stopped remembering. O.K.? There are particulars that keep locking us back in based on truths. In the original movement (demonstrating) when there was a creation right in front of you, "Wow!" [Pause]. Really you probably came up in the middle of it, but this is easier to see. So, I like to talk linearly. Really everything is an overlay. O.K.? But, linearly is easier to talk about. [Pause]. "Wow!" Creation's important and it's important that I get involved somehow, but I'm supposed to remember (pointing to his own temple) that I am really an awareness, not jello. O.K. I'm going to remember. (Pointing and edging forward), I'm going to remem — . . . I've got to remember something. There's something important for me to remember (looking about)." You notice that people often tend to turn their heads this way (he turns his head up and back over his shoulder). You say meditate, and they go right (he turns his head that way again). They are trying to remember something. They are always trying to remember something. Like yeah, fine, but

214

you're going to go round and round on your wanting to remember something. You'll keep doing that (spinning). It goes on, God, almost forever . . . creation's big. If I say I want to remember — it's a three-part technique or something — I want to remember how to do it all — I've got this urge to try to remember it, and I almost don't want to . . . just framework (he demonstrates facing a partner) I think I'm screwing up. You're supposed to remember something, yes. And I really dearly want to remember something, but what if I just framework (carrying out move)? And what if I framework. O.K.? (move with partner completed). So, sometimes, you swear to God you're making the wrong move. But if you recognize your normal move, now and then you can say, "That's what I would normally do. Let me pass on that and do something else." Tonight we're calling it framework, or form and flow-through. So, you've all got some kind of urges in there. If you follow them out, and you're going to intertwine again. [Pause]. Aren't you bored with it? Intertwining again? Getting all tight again? If you aren't you're going to get bored with me real quick. O.K. Let's try it like that.

[Training resumes].

Recognizing the Beginnings of Framework/Flow Experience

O.K. Hold it right there, Cheryl; you're being pushed forward. Do you recognize that? Take a pause there for a moment.

[To everyone:] Take a look-see a second. She's being pushed forward here. You're also pushed forward the first time you're sort of wakened up — and there's creation. There's a push. Really the force beats back and forth — so that's why sometimes you're hesitant and afraid to move forward into something, because there's also a pullback. You've got two main forces there. And so you're pushed forward (demonstrating). You've got to recognize it and learn how to back off a certain way — or do something different. Just recognize it — you want to reach for him — I want to throw him, and normally I would. Or, I wouldn't. And, and — just frame it, just give us a frame, and just give us a form. And that's something different from what we would normally do, which is either go for it or back off from it. Then I think through this we can process and begin to get our size equal to handling the situation. But this and this are entanglements (demonstrating). [Pause]. One more time.

Form, form, framework. [To another student:] Framework, framework, framework . . . naturally allows flow. [Pause]. And framework, framework, flow. [To another student:] Let's do the *kokyu* one more time. Framework, flow-through is floor, thigh, hip. Recognize if there is an entanglement between the frame and the flow-through. [Pause]. Exaggeratedly (demonstrating). Framework frames; flow flows. O.K. First you're not clear on that; you say, "What does that mean?" [Pause]. You won't understand it that way. If you understand it that way you're already entangling again. There will be moments of real blank in there. Just keep setting up that same simple pattern. [Pause]. O.K. Framework/flow a couple of more minutes here.

Functioning Without Entangling

[Training resumes].

[To a student:] Framework. Be distinct. Flow-through. Go. [To another student:] Framework for framework's sake. If you feel yourself doing something else while framing we already have an entanglement. So, it's like Stop! [Pause]. Framework — you pick up a good framework through the arm (demonstrating with student) — as a flow-through. Yes. So, there is a certain feeling to framework that you begin to recognize after a bit. Framework has flow-through (demonstrating). There's a certain way the framework itself goes hummmm, and then the flow comes through. . . . When it really experiences itself, there's a certain flavor.

Questions

Blackbelts, any questions? (Working with blackbelt) O.K., it's already spiraling so I'm confused already as to who's frame and who's flow.   [Answer:]   Stop, and do frame again. Framework. We'll use this form because that clues me in. Frame. Flow-through. Yes. Be more distinct. It *is* instantaneous, but I can't tell, so let it develop. You see, he's starting fast, he's saying "Framework/flows." And, I can't tell who's who. Technically, he's correct, everything is instantaneous. But, right now, let's blow a moment. [Pause]. Framework is just framework (continues to work with blackbelt). And, flow-through is flow-through. [Pause]. That was neat, O.K.? And then again . . . framework, and double-check it — framework . . . to the fingertips . . . yes, is flow-through. Can you almost see it? It sort of sets a certain way. So, it's very simple, but. . . . do it, do it.

Any blackbelts? [Pause]. (Working with blackbelt) she has a question and the question's already converging. So, I know you have a question, but there's never an answer. Looking for an answer is converging and entanglement. You had a question on day one, at the beginning of creation: [Pause]. "Wow, what is *it*?" And you're STILL HERE. [Pause]. So, we all have a question, but . . . just give us framework for a moment. Framework, framework, framework (demonstrating). Floor-thigh-hip, flow-through. And again. Now you may have a question, but double-check. Ah! (demonstrating) the framework. And flow-through. Here we go. [Pause]. And you may still have a question, but give me framework, distinct from the question — framework, framework, framework — flow-through (demonstrating). After a bit, your question will be answered, not in the normal way of being answered, but as some kind of experience. It's like, *you* are the answer. But, looking for answers — gee, I've got this problem, maybe I'll find the answer in here someplace (looks down and about) — is entangling more and more. It started with that question; it's still going on here. Again, those are bad words, "here" and "there," or "now" and "then." Because it's "now." Entering creation is "now." It's a kind of replay all of the time. Is there an answer here? No, there's only framework and flow-through. Does that answer my question? Probably not. So give us framework and flow-through. There'll be an answer, but different from our normal form. Because your normal form keeps entangling you.

Let's do it different. O.K. Any questions on that? Do you want to bullshit on that for a minute?

Question: So, framework and the twisting-up, that's our personal style?

Yes, you each have your own style/styles . . . of entwining. And it's neat when you can recognize your own style. 'Cause then you can start passing on it. [Pause]. Here is what I would normally do. Call off pro and con, and I think I will frame instead. Another day we might say — reawaken. Framing will probably turn out to be what we would call an awakener, a very advanced-level awareness. Identity, identity, identity, levels of consciousness; a grand identity is an awakener. And, that's probably what the framing will turn out to be. And, the best back and forth will turn out to be creation. O.K. And, there is probably another level after that, so be ready. But, it should be the same pattern. If it's the right pattern, it should repeat.

Question: So, there's something neutral about it?

Yes, neutral, yet it experiences in a certain way. But when I say, I'm *supposed* to experience, there starts the entwinement. You're right, you *are* supposed to experience. But, not by saying you're jello. But, by totally being there, and jello goes on as a different kind of experience. That is a rarity. O'Sensei had it. He would say, "The universe is going through me. I'm not interfering with the harmony of the universe." [Pause]. That's big! That's neat! [Pause]. And I think we can all do it now in some form. Not necessarily Aikido, you know. You're going to allow your own experience. But I think we ought to have some kind of common language for a while. So, while we're all here doing this, we'll talk Aikido. But, we're really talking allowing a creation/beat within our system, or within our awareness, our awakener. O.K.? Which is different from the normal stepping-in and tighter and tighter entwinement. Does that sort of make sense? Anybody? Any dumb questions? Any intelligent questions? Any often-oft questions?

Question: Does it have anything to do with breathing?

Breathing is just based on the beat again. So, whatever. See, if there is an inhale/exhale, that's really (holds out arms) . . . framework, and right now I feel a *puls*ing back and forth. So right there I may inhale/exhale. But you've got to realize what inhale/exhale is, is really a lesser form of a universal breath. So, it's nice. [Pause]. Now it depends on what you're going to do with it. Does that entangle you? Then, the hell with it. Or, let's see it for what it really is. Within every framework, something is inhaling and exhaling. 'Cause within the framework of awakener, the whole creation is breathing back and forth — a million different aspects and colors and vibratory levels . . . and that's a breath. That's breathing. So, yeah, it's based on a principle. But, if you lock in as a breather, then you've got a truth but you've tangled in with it again — just like before. [Pause]. We all had a truth, and we tangled in a certain way. So, the real truth can't unfold or manifest, 'cause we're torqued in there, interfering with it. And yet, it's going on.

Aikido as Common Starting Point for Framework/Flow/Disentanglement

So, what the hell is Aikido? Aikido may be . . . a place where I can begin . . . begin to have this process go on — framing and flow. It exists in other than the Aikido world, but I've got to start someplace. So, I say, "I think I'll start here. I think I'll use Aikido for my parameters." Now, in the parameters of Aikido (demonstrating with partner), there's a frame and a flow-through. Once I catch that here, there's no reason why I can't take it out into a different set of parameters. But, at first I wasn't sure. So, I decided on parameters. I could have decided on any parameters; just the Aikido for me was easier. I think once you get the game, the parameters don't matter. But some people think, "Ah ha. I do Aikido. I do Aikido. I do Aikido. Wow, I must be spiritual, I must really be aware." And it's like, hell man, I used to do Judo the same way, what the hell's new, what's new? So, Aikido, per se doesn't give you any points. But, in Aikido, we can talk about level of consciousness, whereas in Judo, it was a rarity to talk that way. Maybe not for everybody, but for the guys I used to hang out with; we didn't talk that way really. But, in Aikido, it's allowed. So, I think I use the form as an *example* of a form.

Question: What's the importance of the frame?

If you're entangled, that means there's two things. As they start to disentangle, they're going to give themselves a name at different times. Frame is just one-half of the situation here. The other half is something beating back-and-forth through. It's half of the set-up. It's half of the thing. You can't catch onto anything with just half, you've got to have both halves, both parts. Probably there's a third part, by the way. I think the thing is a threesies.

Question: You said you remember before you had the frame, and then once you have the frame you don't remember anything.

Often you didn't really experience the frame when you first stepped off, and that's the problem. If you had, you wouldn't have stepped in that way. You just wouldn't have. But everyone said, "Wow!" or said "Wait a minute;" and because they weren't full, they got forced in. [Pause]. There's a push, there's power — the power that's allowed for a creation. It's pushing/pulling. And if you're not full, it pushes and pulls you. Same way as when you do a technique, and in the middle of the technique, you get pushed forward. Or watch on a group attack, sometimes, some guy will fall down about six times. He's being pulled downwards. So, there's always a push/pull going on. And if you don't experience your fullness you have no choice but to get involved. You see, so it's not negative to say we got scrunched-in here. It's not negative, it's just, I'm bored with it. And, I hang out with other people who are bored with it in a certain way. I think we can keep reawakening . . . reforming; then you start to get a different sense on things. And, I think we can make a quantum leap. Not just a little better form to do a little better Aikido, but using those parameters. [Pause]. Let's pick up the pace. Let's go back to *tsuki* [straight punch].

[Training resumes].

[To a student:] Framework, framework, framework, don't cut your framework short at the end. There will be a little tendency to catch the "flashy" of it, and, go for the flashy. Do you understand?

Allowing the Full Expression of Creation

As you practice being open, as you practice open-ness, or framing, or forming, a lot of stuff is going to go on, and it's going to catch your attention. Like maybe, framing, framing (demonstrating), "Gee that was soft, there was something that felt soft." So, the beat back-and-forth was soft. Now you may have a memory that part of the creation, or a main quality, is softness, and you'll want to say, yeah, softness. But now it starts to get confused again. O.K. [Pause]. You're going to pass through many different qualitites and kinds of movements, many colors. And you're going to have leanings towards some of them. And, I think you can appreciate them. [Pause]. I really enjoyed that softness, that was neat. And now, frame it again; frame it, and (demonstrating) allow. . . . whatever. [Pause]. And that one was kind of quiet, kind of still. Somebody might really like that one. "Gee, I really liked that one." And, frame again (continues demonstrating). [Pause]. So, there's going to be stuff that catches your attention at any moment, maybe *every* moment. And that's fine. But I don't want to see that. *You're* going to see it, and going to be aware of it and it's going to pique your interest. [Pause]. Pass on it, not in the negative. Just say, "O.K., I won't do that now." It's like, "Man I'd love to do that, I love that quality, but just for the practice, now — because I know I always go for that — just to do something different — as nice as *that* is — I think I'll just frame again and see what happens." Just to do something different — not that there is anything bad anyplace. Don't get uptight about passing: "O.K., I won't do that." That's just the opposite side of doing it and it also entwines. So, it's not that kind of — I want to do it so I won't. It's not — I want to, and if I don't I feel I've missed something but . . . and hahhh (demonstrating), frame it again, and let's see what happens. [Pause]. O.K. So, it's not a negative thing, we're not refuting. Don't hate aspects of God's creation; it won't work out well. But, let's not do our normal, for a change of pace. Our norm is to go for it, in some form. [Pause]. Within that system of allowing, there are some major things that happen a lot. For example, say after the first few minutes of basics . . . (demonstrates with a partner) . . . I think a circle . . . a circle center. Now, we could stay there. And circle center. And we could do every technique circle center. And just circle center, circle center. But now I've just glommed onto another level. It's nothing. It's another piece of the pie, but it's still a piece of the pie, or the jello. I'm not that interested in that because there's more. But, you're going to pass through it. And, all-by-its-own is a whole world of it. And you could package it and sell it. And write a book about it. And there's nothing wrong in that. But, can you also, at the same time, can you also, allow more? Can you frame it and allow more? Can you allow the whole damned universe to go on? Or, are you going to glom onto just a bit of it? And, can you use just a bit of it, just as a practice place, and use that as a place to get things going? Without glomming on? [Pause]. So, I see a lot of people *think*, just to upgrade their level. You may have upgraded your level, but you're still entwined. I think we have a chance of getting a full sweep going. I don't think O'Sensei was meant to be the only guy going on who could allow a full sweep. And I'm not just talking about Aikido. I don't expect you to do O'Sensei's Aikido. We've got to do what we've got to do. It's just an interesting way for us to get together and have a kind of common language.

Framework/Flow & Functioning in a Situation

In any situation, there's going to be framework. Even before I move, there's a spiral there, an aspect of my consciousness. All nature spirals. If my partner goes down, that has no bearing or anything. I don't care. What I do care about is that this next aspect of my consciousness, depicting itself as a spiral, was allowed to happen, and I, the lesser I, didn't interfere with that. I'm trying to set up techniques so that the natural happenings are brought to your attention. In some martial arts they may not be because someone's always talking about beating this guy: here's how you can kill him. When he comes in, get him here; get him here; get him there. They're so busy killing, they don't even realize there are other things happening to them that are other levels of consciousness. They don't catch onto it even though it makes them move faster and better. We're kind of lucky with Aikido because the founder made it spiritual. We wouldn't be able to get into some of these things in a football class. Maybe now. But not twenty years ago. Twenty years ago energy was electricity. There was no *ch'i* twenty years ago, no acupuncture. A hatha yoga teacher was a rare thing twenty years ago. Some arts have a spiritual connotation to them. Hatha yoga, prana. T'ai chi has a spiritual connotation. Boxing does not; football does not; although some people may trip into these truths, but the forms are not open to it, so they don't usually notice them. They're too busy with their technique to notice there's anything else going on. Flow is going on all the time, but not a damn one of these athletes is aware of it. The track stars are just beginning to catch onto it after they run eighteen miles. We continue doing our daily mundane things, at which time different levels of consciousness are going on, but no one has been aware, so we need an art to make you more aware Now I think any art can, but since this art already existed and had a spiritual connotation, why not use it? But I could teach you flow-music, flow-running, flow-golf, flow-anything. It's not that you're one identity and we're going to purify you. You're a multi-dimensional identity. Meditation means the same thing. You say, "Hey, I think something else is going on, and I'm going to sit quiet and watch it." But any movement can become a meditation. Levels of consciousness are daily things. What's neat about Aikido is that the founder used it, and he cleared a path, so that made it easier. Otherwise, you'd have to clear your own path. In Aikido it's already been done. The founder left us a lot of messages; he told us that it spirals, that it's harmonious. It may look disharmonious, but it fact it's so harmonious you can change the word to love. He tracked himself through the art back into a universal awareness, and said, "Oh, wow," and then began to present his techniques — from a physical dimension to a universal dimension back to a physical dimension; he said, "Hey, this is a Godlike movement!" because it holds in sync with the whole universal movement. I'm saying anything else can be brought to a universal and back, that you can have in anything a universal consciousness. Then you can bring it back into other careers besides martial arts.

Michelle, you were supposed to do a workshop a couple of weeks ago? O.K., "Oh shit, a workshop. I don't know what to say to these people." Already, because you have a situation, someplace in there is a framework. And I don't know what to say and I desperately want to know what to say. You're entangled already. And in this situation, there's always a framework, and suddenly I'm starting to feel that same thing we've been doing, but just in the context of doing a workshop. [Pause]. Framework [Pause]. I don't know what I'm going to say, but I sure feel a whole hell of a lot better. It's like, hey, it's going to be O.K. But, I still don't know what I'm going to say. And there's a framework here, in relationship to this workshop. And it's probably going to be something very feminine. Is it all nurses and stuff? Something about feminine, something about groundedness, power, and on and on. But, the answer itself is not important. You see, I'm not doing it for the answer, I'm doing it for the process of doing it. But, as I do that I start to get answers and insights. Don't glom on again. You'll just entangle. The process is first, the answer is second. The process is first, the technique is secondary. If it happens, that's nice. But, if you think the answer is it — Hell man, that's how you got here in the first place! And that brings you back to your insanity. There's an answer in there for you, only if you don't feel the fullness of yourself. Nothing wrong in that; it's just the way it happened. But, once you made your move, you're still making that same move. Some of you are looking for the answer, looking for the answer, looking for the answer, and there's sickness here. Or, just boredom, with the whole damn thing. Or, such a memory of more, that this ain't all there is, man. I can't believe this is the way it works. We have to do it a little different style. But, always in your style is: looking for an answer, because that's what you stepped off with. Or, wanting a technique. All right. There must be technique to understanding this. And you start to get technique-oriented. But, man, that's the way you stepped in; you're going to go round and round again. So let's do something different. I want an answer, and I'm afraid of screwing up if I don't go for the answer, and . . . let's frame it again. And again and again and again. 'Cause I didn't do that here; I stepped. O.K. And I'm tired of stepping, or stepping (stepping backwards). Whichever way. [Pause]. There's something else. And I think, after a bit, you'll catch your number. You'll catch how you entangle. That's half the battle, man. All right, enough for tonight?

Contributors' Notes

Bob Aubrey has a Ph.D. from the University of Paris and a 2nd Dan in Aikido. He is presently a management consultant for European companies on stress mastery, and is a private consultant in the United States and Europe.

Terry Dobson is a fifth-degree black belt in Aikido and author of *Giving In to Get Your Way* and *Safe and Alive.* He spent more than ten years in Asia where he was *uchi-deshi* (personal assistant) to Master Morihei Ueshiba. He works as a private consultant in the areas of security and conflict resolution.

O. Fred Donaldson has a Ph.D. in Geography from the University of Washington, where he taught Geography, Black Studies, and Native American Studies. He is currently involved in a long-term research project on play and Aikido as a form of communication between humans and wolves.

Jeff Haller has been studying the processes affecting human performance for the past fourteen years. He is a former university level basketball player at Oregon State University. He is a blackbelt in Aikido, and a Feldenkrais Practitioner, both of which he is teaching at INSIDE MOVES, his center in Seattle, Washington. Washington.

Richard Strozzi Heckler has a Ph.D. in psychology and a third-degree black belt in Aikido. He is co-founder of the Lomi School and author of *The Anatomy of Change.* He currently lives in the San Francisco Bay area where he is a practicing psychotherapist and consultant.

George Leonard, a contributing editor for *Esquire*, is author of numerous books, including *Education and Ecstasy, The Ultimate Athlete,* and *The Silent Pulse.* Leonard has served as a vice president of Esalen Institute and is a past president of the Association for Humanistic Psychology. He holds a *nidan* in Aikido and works as a partner of the editor of this book.

Richard Moon is a third-degree black belt in Aikido, a musician, and a student of yoga. He lives and works in the San Francisco Bay area.

Robert Nadeau began Aikido in 1960 and studied with the founder, Morihei Ueshiba in Tokyo, Japan. He is a fifth degree black belt and has an avid interest in the spiritual possibilities of Aikido. He teaches at Aikido of San Francisco.

Sadaharu Oh is often referred to as the Babe Ruth of Japan as he has hit more home runs (868) than any other professional baseball player. During his 22 years of professional baseball he also won the triple crown twice, the batting title five times, home run title fifteen times, R.B.I. title thirteen times, M.V.P. nine times, and the Gold Glove (for defensive play) nine times. Today he is the manager of the Tokyo Giants.

Cheryl S. Reinhardt has brought together her broad background in Aikido, Feldenkrais work, dance, and psychology to develop a working process that has come to be called "Inner Power". She is a certified Feldenkrais Practitioner who studied extensively with Dr. Moshe Feldenkrais and holds a Black Belt in Aikido.

Megan Reisel is a 3rd Dan in Aikido. She also has an extensive background in Modern Dance and training in Kabuki Dance. She presently lives in Los Angeles where she teaches Aikido and works in private practice as a movement therapist.

Donald T. Saposnek, Ph.D. is a clinical-child psychologist, lecturer in the psychology department at the University of California at Santa Cruz, co-founder and co-director of Family Mediation Service of Santa Cruz, and author of the book *Mediating Child Custody Disputes*. He has utilized the concepts of Aikido in all of his work and in his writings.

John Stevens, author of *Aikido: The Way of Harmony*, *Sacred Calligraphy of the East* and *The Sword of No-Sword*, is an Aikido instructor who lives in Sendai, Japan, one of the few Westerners teaching Aikido in that country. He is also a Buddhist scholar and priest.

Susan Stone is a free-lance editor and writer living in California. She has been an Aikido student for five years.

Kisshomaru Ueshiba, Aikido Doshu, was born in 1921, the third son of Morihei Ueshiba, the founder of Aikido. His formal appointment as successor to his father took place in 1969. He is a trustee of the Nippon Budokan, the hall of the martial arts in central Tokyo. His latest book is *The Spirit of Aikido*.

Further Reading

1. "Aiki News", c/o Stan Pranin, Demeure Saito #201, Daikyo-cho, 3-banchi, Shinjuku-ku, Tokyo. A bilingual magazine dealing with the martial art of Aikido. $25.00 for 12 issues, $15.00 for 6 issues.

2. Dobson, Terry and Victor Miller, *Giving in to Get Your Way*, Delacorte Press, 1978.

3. Heckler, Richard, *The Anatomy of Change*, Shambhala Publications, Boulder and London, 1984.

4. Leonard, George, *The Silent Pulse*, E.P. Dutton, New York, 1978.

5. Leonard, George, *The Ultimate Athlete*, Viking, New York, 1975.

6. Saito, Morihiro, *Traditional Aikido Volumes 1–5*, Minato Research Publishing, Tokyo, 1976.

7. Stevens, John, *Aikido The Way of Harmony*, Shambhala Publications, Boulder and London, 1984.

8. Tohei, Koichi, *Book of Ki: Co-ordinating Mind and Body in Daily Life*, Japan Publications, Tokyo, 1976.

9. Ueshiba, Kisshomaru, *The Spirit of Aikido*, Kodansha International, Tokyo, New York, and San Francisco, 1984.

10. Uyeshiba, Kisshomaru, *Aikido*, Hozansha Publishing, Tokyo, 1974.

11. Westbrook, A., and O. Ratti, *Aikido and the Dynamic Sphere*, Charles E. Tuttle Co., Rutland, Vermont and Tokyo, Japan, 1970.

12. *NEW* Klickstein, Bruce, *Living Aikido*, North Atlantic Books, Berkeley, California, 1987.

Major Aikido Centers

Aikikai World Headquarters
International Aikido Federation
17–18 Wakamatsu-cho
Shinjuku-ku, Tokyo 162

West Coast

Aikido Association of Northern California
5036 Telegraph Ave.
Oakland, California 94609

Kazuo Chiba
3945 4th Ave. Apt. #5
San Diego, California 92103

Midwest

Mitsugi Saotome
1103 W. Bryn Mawr
Chicago, Illinois 60660

East Coast

Yoshimitsu Yamada
New York Aikikai
142 West 18th St.
New York, New York 10011

New England

Mitsunari Kanai
257 Upland Rd.
Cambridge, Massachusetts 02140